KU-256-887

Green Parties and Politics in the European Union

Elizabeth Bomberg

London and New York

First published 1998
by Routledge
11 New Fetter Lane, London EC4P 4EE

Simultaneously published in the USA and Canada
by Routledge
29 West 35th Street, New York, NY 10001

© 1998 Elizabeth Bomberg

The right of Elizabeth Bomberg to be identified as the author
of this work has been asserted by her in accordance with the
copyright, Designs and Patents Act 1988.

Typeset in Baskerville by Ponting–Green Publishing Services,
Chesham, Buckinghamshire

Printed and bound in Great Britain by MPG Books, Bodmin

All rights reserved. No part of this book may be reprinted or
reproduced or utilised in any form or by any electronic,
mechanical, or other means, now known or hereafter invented,
including photocopying and recording, or in any information
storage or retrieval system, without permission in writing from
the publishers.

British Library Cataloguing in Publication Data
A catalogue record for this book is available from the
British Library

Library of Congress Cataloging in Publication Data
A catalogue record for this book has been requested

ISBN 0–415–10264–2 (hbk)
ISBN 0–415–10265–0 (pbk)

TO JOHN

Contents

Illustrations

Acknowledgements

An interesting variety of people and organisations have helped me complete this book. Early research for this project was financed by a grant from the Council of European Studies, the DAAD and the Center for German and European Studies (University of California, Berkeley). Later field work was supported by a grant from the University of Stirling. The Politics Department there deserves special thanks for their patience and support, not least during my periods of leave. The Centre for European Policy Studies in Brussels hosted me in 1995, a post facilitated by an ESRC grant on EU decision-making (R000235829).

For critical readings of draft text and editing advice, I wish to thank Steve Breyman (Rensselaer Polytechnic Institute); Stan Anderson, Michael Gordon and Peter Merkl (all three at the University of California, Santa Barbara); Neil Carter (University of York); Mary M. McKenzie (University of San Diego); Matt Paterson (University of Keele); Joachim Raschke (Universität Hamburg); and Michael Shackleton (European Parliament). Ralph Monö and the European Federation of Green Parties provided useful electoral data and knowledge. Ricardo Gomez (University of Glasgow) helped enormously with the compilation of data on national green parties (see Appendix I). For their Euro-hospitality and links in Brussels, I wish to thank Richard Doherty and Annette Schulte. Caroline Wintersgill (formerly of Routledge) offered editorial encouragement and understanding.

Given this study's heavy reliance on interviews, I am particularly grateful to all those who agreed to speak with me. All interviews were conducted on a non-attributable basis. My subjects included Commission officials (both in the services and *cabinets*), members and officials of the European Parliament, national green party members, environmental and industrial lobbyists, German, Belgium and British government officials based in Brussels and in national capitals. A complete list of interviewees and interview notes are on file in the Department of Politics, University of Stirling.

I am especially indebted to all members and staff of the Green Group in the European Parliament who took time out to be interviewed. Only two Green MEPs declined to be interviewed. Preoccupied with their quest for more openness in the EU, they were perhaps too busy to speak to this researcher. On the other hand, GGEP press attaché Diana Johnstone deserves a particular mention for her assistance. A special thanks to GGEP member Monica Frassoni for being a friend as well as a knowledgeable source.

Finally, I wish to thank my family (near and far) who offered unflagging moral support throughout the whole endeavour. My two sons, Miles and Calum, deserve credit for ensuring the book was not rushed or published prematurely. My deepest debt of gratitude is owed to John Peterson at the University of Glasgow. John edited the entire text without once losing his patience or humour. His advice, forbearance and support were far beyond that which I could reasonably expect, even from a husband. This book is dedicated to him.

Series editor's preface

The 'greening' of politics – electoral politics, public policy-making and even the internal politics of private organisations such as oil companies – is now an established phenomenon of Western European political systems. No Member State in the European Union (or, indeed, those 'aspirant' states in the newly democratised nations of Eastern Europe) has been untouched by the political advance of green parties, environmental pressure groups and more loosely organised green social movements. Green interests are easily the most successful of the new wave of non-producer organisations, including women's and consumer groups, that has impinged increasingly on the processes by which public policy is made – at all levels.

At least two important features characterise these new groups and movements. They are often run by quite entrepreneurial individuals who are adept at mobilising public opinion and constructing political agendas. Second, they face an array of opportunity structures – or different policy-making arenas and venues – that they can exploit to considerable policy advantage. However, just as there is no such thing as a free lunch, so there are costs as well as benefits to these new organisations. One of the costs results from the fact that their membership is often fickle. As 'credit card' organisations, they have to be very active in the political marketplace in order to retain old members and attract new ones. This may lead them into public marketing strategies that can be inconsistent with their main long-term public policy goals. A second disadvantage is that, in the long run, influencing public policy might well depend on the adoption of a more 'insider' based strategy, inconsistent with attracting new supporters in the competitive marketplace for political activism. In the end, they need to sit down with their opponents – especially as those opponents become more sophisticated in responding to the green challenge and as new policy fashions, such as deregulation, privatisation and competitiveness emerge. Thus, the political climate for green organisations is probably getting more difficult over time. To maintain their influence (which has undoubtedly been very considerable both at the nation state and European Union level), these organisations need to become more closely integrated into the detailed processes of policy-making, involving a wider range of stakeholders.

The analysis of this dilemma lies at the heart of Elizabeth Bomberg's challenging volume. As she puts it, the incentives for Greens to work with Europe are great, yet how can they work through institutions that, she argues, inherently violate green principles? This is, of course, the traditional paradox faced by all groups and parties who are, inherently, challenging the existing order and interests in society. To what extent do the benefits of participation outweigh the obvious (and not so obvious) costs of compromising one's 'purity' once one is on the 'inside'? As she argues, in many ways the EU is a singularly unfavourable political system for 'purist' organisations such as the Greens, because of its messy style of policy-making. This demands cooperation with sometimes strange bedfellows and last-minute compromises on fundamental principles. Yet, the EU is also an attractive opportunity structure – if only because it is a transnational decision-making system and is more suited, therefore, to solving environmental problems.

Thus, the central thesis of her volume is that this key strategic dilemma (purity or participation) informs all aspects of the Greens' European policy. Ignoring the EU is simply not an option – so much of environmental policy for Western Europe is now decided at this level. However, as her volume demonstrates so clearly, the Greens, although they have adapted their campaigning strategies quite considerably, are still a disparate grouping of actors and organisations who do not always cooperate with each other, let alone with their opponents. The shift from protest movement to professional electoral and parliamentary campaigning might have been achieved successfully, but, at the European level, national styles are still very apparent. Moreover, the basic conflict between the radical end of the movement and the more pragmatic advocates (similar to that in women's and civil rights groups) has not been resolved effectively. This, she argues, has reduced the overall effectiveness of the Greens as a political force at the European level. Her volume, therefore, makes an important contribution to our understanding of the actual impact of green organisations and green parties within the European Union. In doing so, it also makes a major contribution to our understanding of

European policy-making more generally and the important relationship between institutions, opportunity structures and political movements in the process of European integration.

Jeremy Richardson

Introduction

This book is about green politics[1] and parties within the European Union (EU).[2] It examines the *transnational* goals, strategies and impact of green actors in Europe.[3] Within this broad remit, the book's primary focus is on the role and impact of green parties working at the EU level, especially through the European Parliament (EP).

The Greens' activities at the EU level have been neglected by scholars of both green and EU politics. The literature on green parties and politics has focused primarily on the domestic fortunes of national green parties. Similarly, studies of the EU have taken little notice of green politics or actors.[4] This study seeks to fill a gap by analysing the transnational or 'Euro-level' activities of green actors, and their role in the politics and policies of the EU.

I GREEN POLITICS AND THE EU

The rise of green politics has been an important development in the post-war evolution of European politics. Whilst environmental concern is not new, green politics represent a broader and more recent phenomenon, embracing issues of environmental sustainability as well as decentralisation, global security and grassroots democracy. At their core, green approaches to politics offer a fundamental critique of modern industrial society by highlighting the environmental, social and human costs of economic growth and technological advancement.

Despite their radical core, green politics have made their mark on 'mainstream' political competition, especially in Europe. Public awareness of environmental issues has expanded dramatically in the last few decades. So too have green concerns of over-bureaucratisation, over-centralisation and lack of democracy. The political relevance of green issues is also reflected in the rising influence of green actors, including protest movements, pressure groups and political parties. In particular, green parties have gained representation in local, regional, national and supranational parliaments. Despite varying electoral fortunes, they are an accepted part of the political landscape in several Member States and within the EU.

Meanwhile, the impact of the EU on the lives of European citizens has increased dramatically over the last two decades. The acceleration of European integration – subject to setbacks – has forced analysts to redefine their understanding of sovereignty, accountability and governance. The expansion of the EU's competence has been particularly evident in the area of environmental protection. From an essentially economic community with no firm legal basis for dealing with environmental issues and a clear mandate to facilitate economic growth, the EU has taken on an increasingly central role in policy sectors related to the environment and quality of life.

In short, both 'EU politics' and 'green politics' are worthy of study in their own right. Yet a central contention of this book is that the 'greening' of European politics and the advancement of European integration are inextricably linked. On the one hand, the process of European integration has been advanced by a growing environmental awareness, as ecological problems by their nature demand transnational solutions. Yet on the other, the EU's development as a more important level of government has fuelled fears among Greens (and others) of increasing centralisation, bureaucratisation and damage to the environment caused by industrial growth. European integration has thus been a crucial factor in the rise of green activism across Europe. In short, the 'greening' of European politics and the acceleration of European integration have become intertwined: European integration has been a boon to green activism, whilst the EU's institutional development has been spurred by the rise of green concerns on Europe's political agenda.

II   THE ARGUMENT: GREENS' STRATEGIC DILEMMA

Greens offer an important critique of the EU's institutions, practices and policy outputs. Emphasising principles of ecological sustainability, decentralisation and grassroots democracy, their critique addresses wider public concerns. Yet their critique lacks both coherence and consistency. Greens' ability to conceptualise and act coherently is hampered by predictable national and ideological differences which impede most efforts to encourage transnational action in Europe. But Greens – especially green parties – face additional challenges related to identity and strategy.

Most Green actors emerged out of a social movement milieu; their roots are firmly in alternative, non-conformist soil. Yet in their attempts to enact policy change, many have adopted professional, parliamentary techniques and entered 'mainstream' political institutions. Campaigning for parliamentary seats in the 1980s, most Greens took on the identity of a 'movement-party' (Raschke 1985; Bomberg 1992). Half movement, half party, Greens felt they could form hybrid organisations that merged the best of both radical and reformist traditions.

Yet Greens underestimated the difficulty of the 'movement-party' balancing act. Most failed to recognise the dilemma faced by all radical political actors contemplating parliamentary participation.[5] On one hand, their radical movement roots implied an uncompromising adherence to non-conformist movement principles. On the other hand, their desire to succeed as mainstream political actors demanded compromise and dilution of these principles.

On the national level, many green parties have addressed – at least partially – the *identity* question by moving decisively down the parliamentary path. Their movement identity has been restrained by their participation in parliaments across Europe. Nonetheless, a core *strategic* dilemma has remained: on the one hand, any shift from radicalism undermines their distinctiveness and renders them part of the mainstream tradition they were formed to oppose. On the other hand, failure to adapt to changed circumstances means danger of electoral decline and marginalisation of green issues.[6] In short, how can Greens reconcile radical, alternative politics with mainstream, traditional institutions and practices?

This dilemma is even more pronounced on the EU level. The EU represents much that greens instinctively oppose: technocratic policy-making; closed, often murky decision-making procedures; distant institutions, and the dominance of inter-governmental bargaining. Moreover, the need for compromise is more acute in the EU than in most national policy-making systems because of the required size and breadth of most 'winning coalitions'. Policy influence in the EU depends on coalition-building, cooperation and compromise. Many Greens loathe such compromise because of the dilution of green principles it implies.

Yet for many green actors, participation in the EU is attractive if not imperative. The EU offers Greens a transnational forum in which to pursue reform of the European political structures, and work towards an alternative 'Europe of the Regions'. Membership in the European Parliament (EP) provides Greens with access to decision-making concerning EU environmental, energy, regional and single market policies. In some cases, EU legislation can prompt Member States to enact stricter environmental legislation than they otherwise would do (Sbragia 1996). Moreover, the EU's growing presence in global affairs, illustrated by its participation in international environmental agreements, fits with the Greens' desire for global action on issues such as global warming, deforestation and ozone depletion. Greens in Europe thus face a strategic paradox: the incentives to work through the EU are great, yet how can they work through institutions that inherently violate green principles?

These existing strategic dilemmas are exacerbated by additional conflicts and tensions caused by the tremendous variety of green parties working together on the European level. Whilst multi-national conflict is not unique to Greens, it is more important for them as they struggle, as a relatively new player, to become a cohesive political force in Europe.

The argument developed in this book is that this strategic dilemma matters: it still informs all aspects of the Greens' European policy, including their visions of an alternative Europe; their parliamentary and extra-parliamentary strategies; and their impact on European policies and politics.

III   STRUCTURE OF BOOK

This book is organised with a view to placing Greens' role in the EU within the context of both green political thought and EU policy-making. Chapter 1 places the Greens' European policy in its wider historical and political context. It outlines the key characteristics and relevance of 'green politics' and traces the emergence of European green movements and parties.

Chapter 2 introduces the EU as an increasingly more important forum for environmental and related policy-making. It analyses the pressures for transnational action on environmental protection which have led to increased competence for the EU in environmental matters. It introduces the actors involved in EU environmental and related policy-making, giving special attention to the growing role of the EP.

Chapter 3 explores the Greens' alternative conceptions of Europe and the European 'community' or 'union'. Invoking principles from ecological and regionalist movements, the Greens present a provocative critique of current EU structures, and offer an alternative construction of a 'Europe of the Regions' – a political system in which regional tiers of government become ascendant.

Chapter 4 analyses the electoral strategies and fortunes of green parties in four successive EP elections. It highlights the parties' shift from non-conventional, protest strategies to professional, parliamentary campaigns. It assesses the extent to which strategic debates have overshadowed more fundamental questions about the content of an alternative green European policy.

Chapter 5 examines the internal structure, organisation and politics of the Greens within the EP. It argues that whilst the internal coherence of the Green Group has improved significantly since green parties first entered the EP in 1984, the Greens' European activities have been hampered by two conflicts: a) between radical (movement) and pragmatic (parliamentary) imperatives; and b) between different types and styles of national green parties.

In Chapter 6, the Greens' attempts to influence EU policy-making are assessed. The chapter outlines the key features of EU policy-making and explores green actors' attempts to exert influence through lobbying and through the EP. It suggests that individual Greens occasionally have had a significant impact on the EU's environmental policy-making process. However, as a group working together the success of the Greens has been strictly limited.

Chapter 7 employs three case studies – on vehicle emissions, biotechnology and packaging waste – to study in more detail the Greens' role in policy-making on the European level. The case studies underline the fundamental dilemma faced by Green actors: policy influence within the EU depends on cooperation and conciliation, but Greens are under fierce pressure to hold out for 'greener' or 'purer' strategies and positions.

The concluding chapter provides an overall appraisal of green activity in the European Union. It reviews the central strategic dilemma facing green actors in the EU, and suggests possible directions of future green activity in Europe. Finally, it assesses the continuing relevance of green demands for European politics and policy.

1   Green politics in Europe

INTRODUCTION

This chapter places the Greens' European policy in its wider political
and historical context. It begins by outlining the key components and
characteristics of 'green politics'. Section II analyses the extent to
which green politics and issues have permeated the politics and
policies of the EU and EU Member States. Section III traces the
emergence and development of 'new social movements', the precursors of the green movement and parties. Section IV examines how
these movements developed into other political actors such as pressure
groups or political parties. Using the development of the German
Green party as an example, this section introduces the key ideological
and strategic characteristics shared by green parties in the EU.

I   INTRODUCING GREEN POLITICS

The terms 'green politics' and 'greening' have entered popular usage
but are open to a wide variety of interpretations. The meaning of
'green politics' may be clarified by providing a brief outline of its key
components.[1] Green politics encompasses more than a concern for
the environment. It includes both a unique set of values (content) and
practices (process). Works by both political theorists and green
activists suggest that the values, beliefs and practices of the green
movement differ significantly from conventional politics. At its roots,
green ideology encompasses a political, global, even spiritual critique
of advanced industrial societies.

Values

Whilst there are many different shades of green politics, a few shared
basic components provide its foundation and ideological base. First,

green ideology encompasses a wholesale *critique of advanced industrial✝ society*. Rudolf Bahro (1986: 11) summarises green ideology as a critique of the 'dominant ideology' which stresses economic growth and man's domination of nature. By contrast, Greens adopt a holistic 'ecocentric' approach that is based on a concern about non-human nature and the whole eco-system rather than purely 'human' concerns (Hayward 1995: 15).[2] Green thinking thus demands a reassessment of the relationship between the human race and its natural environment.

The green agenda is consequently ambitious. Greens want basic changes in the ways humans protect the natural environment, produce and consume goods, discard their waste, use and promote science and technology, and defend themselves against aggressors (Milbrath 1988: 4). The kind of society that would incorporate these ideological changes is often referred to as the '*sustainable society*' (Dobson 1995: ch. 3) or 'conserver society' (Richardson 1995: 9). Its key components are decentralisation and reduced consumption of resources and material goods, or what Greens call the 'economics of enough'. Greens see 'profligate' consumption and the materialist values underlying it as the main cause of resource depletion and pollution (see Martell 1994: 48). They argue that the finite productive limits of the globe make continued consumption at increasing levels impossible, and thus human aspirations to consume *must* be curtailed.

Green principles also have a *spiritual* dimension. For instance, Parkin argues (1989: 25) that the green celebration of the earth and the 'interconnectedness of all life' has strong echoes of ancient wisdoms and cultures which stressed a holistic spirituality as a positive and essential part of both society and politics. This 'eco-centred spirituality' could provide for wider and more profound forms of fulfilment than are provided by conventional society. Put another way, Dobson (1995: 115) suggests that green politics can fill the 'spiritual vacuum at the centre of late-industrial society, and the land itself is the cathedral at which we are urged to worship'.·

Related to the holistic nature of green thought is the uniquely *global* outlook and ethos of the green movement. Many green writers point to what they see as the global environmental crisis, reflected in increasing water and air pollution, shortage of natural resources, and exponential population growth (see Meadows *et al.* 1974; 1992). Green thinking stresses the importance of the finite condition of the planet. Greens suggest that by putting ecology at the centre of plans for personal and collective activities, individuals will discover that 'the needs of the planet are the needs of the person' (Parkin 1989: 26) and that there are inseparable links between 'ourselves and the planet on which we depend' (Porritt 1985: 19).

Equally inseparable are concerns for the well-being of the individual and *global peace*. Greens ask how security can be assured in a world of nuclear weapons designed to ensure mutual mass destruction. They fear that the major and constant risk of a nuclear holocaust persists, even after the end of the Cold War. For Greens, security through nuclear deterrence is by nature a system of global insecurity (see Hegedus 1987).

The Greens' emphasis on environmental disasters and the nuclear threat makes explicit the link between individual and global responsibility: 'We are part of nature, not above it; . . . all our massive structures of commerce – and life itself – ultimately depend on wise, respectful interaction with our biosphere (Spretnak and Capra 1986: 28).

Greens believe that it is possible and desirable to increase public awareness of how foreign policies affect local communities. Greens seek to mobilise local action in response to those policies: they urge individuals to 'think globally, act locally'. Belief in this mode of action helps explain the Greens' advocacy of participation in transnational institutions such as the United Nations Conference on the Environment and Development (UNCED), European Parliament (EP) and the European Federation of Green Parties (EFGP). For example, Greens embraced the 1992 UNCED Summit's global action plan for sustainable development, 'Agenda 21', which called on local authorities throughout the world to consult with communities to develop their own 'Local Agenda 21' (see Gordon 1993; Real World Coalition 1996).

These local activists challenge deeply rooted traditions that assume that action on foreign and international policy issues are chiefly matters to be dealt with by state authorities in national capitals. Green actors insist that the 'intrinsic character of global issues is such that they affect all human settlements' (Alger 1988: 332). The existence of a 'global consciousness' often seems overstated in their rhetoric, but Greens insist on the need to examine the transnational implications of human activity.

Thus, green ideology is based on a set of values and concerns considerably different from today's dominant ethos. The post-industrial 'good life', revolving around economic growth, sophisticated technology, expanding services and material goods is replaced by a simpler lifestyle offering a cleaner planet, less resource depletion, a nature-centred spirituality, and local action to solve global problems.

Practices

The green movement is characterised not only by its values and beliefs, but also by the way it expresses and pursues these beliefs. Green practices differ sharply from conventional policy methods. Grassroots democracy, holism, and a positive emphasis on diversity are defining elements of the 'green politics' process.

The importance of *grassroots democracy* is expressed in the German Greens' party platform: 'Grassroots-democratic politics means an increased realisation of decentralised, direct democracy. We start from the belief that the decisions at the grassroots level must, in principle, be given priority' (die Grünen 1980: 2). Green activists advocate a radically participatory society. In a 'green' decision-making process, 'discussion takes place and explicit consent is asked for and given across the widest possible range of political and social issues' (Dobson 1995: 26). More generally, Parkin argues (1989: 19) that perhaps the most relevant test of the 'greenness' of an organisation should be its approach to a decision, problem or issue.

'*Holistic*' thinking is a green strategy as well as a goal. Such thinking implies that all aspects and consequences of a policy choice be reviewed. Green thinkers argue that greater recognition of mutual dependence and influence will encourage a sensitivity in our dealing with the natural world. 'The best knowledge is ... acquired not by the isolated examination of the parts of a system but by examining the way in which the parts interact' (Dobson 1995: 39).

This holistic concern, however, is accompanied by an emphasis on individual *diversity*. A wide range of views and concerns are ensured by an emphasis on individual input and open, decentralised decision-making structures. Policy decisions are to be made at the lowest possible level and matched with local requirements. Thus, despite its 'macro-cosmic' emphasis on the 'interconnectedness of all life', the way in which green thinking may be taken up and adapted to suit local needs and customs is extremely varied. Greens argue that this is necessary to 'oppose and reverse present trends towards homogeneity, over-centralisation, the abuse of power, and an uncaring society' (Myers 1985: 254). Within the green movement, in other words, diversity is not only tolerated, but celebrated.

Coherency?

Green beliefs and practices represent a fundamental challenge to existing values and norms. However, green political thought does not yet represent a coherent or consistent ideology. Nor are Greens a coherent or monolithic set of thinkers or actors. In particular, several inherent contradictions, schisms and logical weaknesses plague green thought.

First, several of the green beliefs and practices outlined above are themselves contradictory. For instance, the practices of holism and diversity – both of which are central to green politics – lead to an inherent tension between individual diversity, on the one hand, and the need for holism and collective decisions, on the other. Greens ignore the question of how to attain desirable action whilst allowing for diverse forms of behaviour. Similarly, green politics reflect 'a considerable tension between advocating certain essential policy outcomes and valuing (direct) democratic procedures' (Saward 1995: 64).[3] For instance, green calls for grassroots, direct democracy do not always mesh with the need for a sustainable society and the imposition of regulations such a society may require.

These conflicts help explain the ideological and strategic splits found amongst green actors and thinkers. The Greens described in this book embrace in broad terms the key beliefs and practices outlined above. But they do so to varying extents and with varying levels of enthusiasm or consistency. Not all attach the same import-ance or priorities to these values and practices. Even when ends are agreed, means remain contested. The most noticeable ideological split is that between 'deep' and 'shallow' ecology (Naess 1973).[4] All Greens stress the importance of nature and the interconnectedness between humans and the environment. Proponents of deep ecology go further to argue that a new political *and* moral philosophy is needed that treats human beings as part of nature rather than superior to it. They call for the extension of intrinsic value, rights and moral standing to the non-human entities in the environment (Martell 1994: 6). 'Deeps' insist that only a fundamental, radical and immedi-ate shift in the nature of the economy and society will bring about necessary goals of ecological sustainability.

Advocates of a 'shallow' green approach adopt a reformist line, arguing that whilst far-reaching reforms may be necessary to achieve sustainability, these can be achieved incrementally, and by working within the present structures of society. Shallow environmentalists tend towards anthrocentrism. For them, according to Giddens (1994: 204), 'Nature is regarded as perhaps an object of beauty, separate from human beings, but not as intrinsic to the definition of an acceptable form of human life.' The focus is on the more modest aim of limiting the damage that humans impose on the physical world.

The two schools differ on strategies as well as beliefs. 'Shallows' would view schemes such as 'green consumerism' or the EU's 'Ecolabel' scheme (see Chapter 2) as valid, although incomplete, means towards environmental change. Such strategies are eschewed by 'deeps' as nothing more than a capitalist 'green con' (see Irvine 1989).

Yet the effect of these conflicts and splits should not be over-estimated. They do not diminish the force of the green challenge which advocates a transformation of modern industrial society. All Greens discussed here share a broadly similar ecological critique of modern society and its dominant values. Above all, Greens 'share the conviction that current political practices and beliefs must change fundamentally if the world is to have the chance of peaceful, equitable and lasting survival' (Lambert 1995: xi). However, the precise speed, nature and form of this change remain unclear and open to debate.

II THE RISE OF GREEN POLITICS IN EUROPE

The rise of green politics has been an important feature of the post-war evolution of European politics more generally. Moreover, to a significant extent, the development of the EU as a more important level of government in Europe has been advanced by growing environmental awareness, as ecological problems by their nature demand transnational solutions. Yet, European integration in itself has prompted concerns – across a wide political spectrum – about the centralisation and bureaucratisation of European political life, problems that have long been central to the green critique of the modern state. The 'greening' of European politics and the acceleration of European integration thus have become intertwined. This section explores how and why this process has occurred.

Environmental awareness

Environmentalism has a long history, in some countries dating back to naturalist movements or conservation movements of the nineteenth century (see Goodin 1992: ch.1; Dalton 1994: ch.2). But modern green politics have more recent origins. Their emergence needs to be understood in the context of a broader shift from industrial to 'post-industrial' politics. This shift is evident in both public and private behaviour on matters of key concern to green actors.

Beginning in the late 1960s, the political, economic and social landscapes of Western Europe began to change radically. Growth in

the size of the service sector and the decline of productive manufacturing, rising education levels, expanding bureaucracies and
rapid technological development marked the advent of a new era
in the political economy of industrial democracies. By the early
1970s, Western Europe appeared to be 'on the threshold of post-
industrialism, a coming society where economic growth and technological advance would reduce to a minimum the drudgery of labour
and satisfy the material needs and aspirations of the population'
(Urwin 1990: 116).

For younger, better educated citizens in particular, the prosperity
and rise in living standards enjoyed in the post-war era formed the
backdrop for a change from materialist to 'post-materialist' values, or
from 'old politics' to 'new politics' (see Inglehart 1977; 1981; Raschke
1985; Tarrow 1988; Poguntke 1993a).[5] Rising affluence meant that the
basic material needs (i.e. food, shelter, etc.) of a far higher share of
the population were being satisfied. Thus, many Europeans – particularly those entering political adulthood in the 1960s – shifted their
political attention from materialist concerns to 'quality of life' issues,
such as enhanced political participation, gender and racial equality
and, perhaps above all, environmental protection.

Growing environmental concern amongst the public was heightened by the continued degradation of the European environment.
Anxiety about the effects of air, water and land pollution increased in
the 1970s among the public at large. For instance, acid rain, caused
by burning of impurities (especially sulphur) in fossil fuels, has had
an enormous impact on the quality of life in Europe. By the late 1980s,
acid rain had caused serious damage to historic buildings and 77,000
square miles of European forests. It was also responsible for $1 billion
of damage to crops each year in the EU (Hagland 1991: 261).
Emissions of so-called 'greenhouse gases' such as nitrogen oxide and
carbon dioxide from freight and passenger vehicles rose by 50 per
cent between 1973 and 1993.[6] The scientific and economic uncertainty surrounding these issues increased public anxiety as the
ultimate effects of such degradation on environmental and human
health simply were not known.[7]

In addition to pollution worries, nuclear issues formed a core of
public concern in the 1970s and 1980s. In the aftermath of the 1973
energy crisis, several European governments embraced nuclear energy
as an alternative to oil in an attempt to lessen their dependence on a
commodity whose price had quadrupled overnight. The accelerated
construction of nuclear plants awakened or reinforced fears about the
safety of nuclear power and the problems of disposing of nuclear waste

(see Nelkin and Pollack 1981). The nuclear issue represented more than an environmental threat:

> Not only did it stand for a strategy of further unlimited economic growth with allegedly negative effects on the ecological balance . . . [it] also epitomised the departure into a 'nuclear state' where the immense potential dangers of handling large amounts of radio-active material would necessitate the perfection of state surveillance in order to prevent nuclear terrorism.
>
> (Poguntke 1993b: 382)

Major nuclear accidents, such as those which occurred at Three Mile Island (1979) and Chernobyl (1986), fuelled the anti-nuclear concerns. These were accompanied by non-nuclear environmental disasters, such as at Flixborough in the UK (1974), the Seveso chemical spill (1983) and the Sandoz chemical fire on the Rhine (1986).

Public opinion polls revealed that these disasters made an impact. By 1992, the protection of the environment and the fight against pollution had become an 'immediate and urgent problem' in the view of 85 per cent of EU citizens (CEC 1992a). Moreover, polls indicated growing awareness of the cross-national dimension of these issues and growing support for transnational (especially EU) action as opposed to strictly national measures. Eurobarometer surveys in 1989 and the early 1990s registered that up to 91 per cent of EU citizens expressed support for a common European policy for protecting the environment (CEC 1992c). At least eight out of 10 citizens in each Member State expressed their support for this policy. Questions on the environment evoked stronger and more positive support for unified EU action than did questions concerning any other area of policy (see Kivell 1989: 47). In short, the increased salience of environmental issues appeared a boon to European integration.

Public interest in environmental issues reached a peak in the early 1990s. In a climate of severe recession, especially in Western Europe, environmental concerns appeared to become less salient and the state of the economy became the most pressing issue for many voters. However, even as support for drastic environmental measures waned, opinion polls indicated that overall awareness of the environment was actually higher than in the 1980s.[8]

Whilst the end of the Cold War has decreased the saliency of peace and the anti-arms movement, other global concerns have risen in their place. The unification of Germany brought to the fore the urgency and scope of environmental threats facing Eastern Europe. Moreover, new threats or concerns, such as global warming and the protection of the ozone layer, have joined past fears of nuclear security and chemical spills. In short, whilst the intensity of environmental concern may wax and wane, the environment has become an ingrained fixture of European politics and public consciousness (Bennulf 1995: 128).

Growing public awareness of environmental issues has spilled over into private sector behaviour. By the 1980s, major industries within the corporate sector had realised that investment in environmental standards could yield commercial advantage by appealing to consumers who prefer 'environmentally friendly' products and services. In a comprehensive 1993 study surveying the reactions of European business to environmental pressure, Vaughan and Mickle (1993) reported that all companies surveyed stated environmental pressure to be 'very significant' already, and likely to intensify during the 1990s. Key European technology firms, especially those in Germany, Denmark and The Netherlands, have taken a clear global lead in environmental technologies (see CEC 1994). Self-interest has motivated other industries, such as the insurance firms, to push for tougher legislation to protect the environment. At the United Nations Environmental Programme (UNEP) in July 1996, a group of leading insurance firms pressed for legislation that would allow 'early and substantial' reductions in greenhouse gases. Their demand reflected mounting concerns in the industry that climatic change was causing an increasing number of severe weather incidents (such as hurricanes and flooding) that would lead to increased insurance policy claims.[9]

Environmental awareness may also bring additional potential commercial opportunities. They include cost-saving from reduced input and waste, new marketing opportunities, and the promotion of a 'clean and green' image to enhance stock market ratings (Vaughan and Mickle 1993). The draw of 'green consumerism' has become especially apparent as an increasing number of shoppers show preference for 'environmentally friendly' goods such as biodegradable products, aerosols without CFCs and organic produce. For consumers it means that their 'acquisitive lifestyles can be compatible with altruistic concern for the environment if consumption is adjusted in environmentally friendly directions' (Martell 1994: 65). Many Greens question whether such a strategy has any real impact (see Yearly 1992; Irvine 1989). However, 'green consumerism' provides the corporate sector with a rich resource of potential revenue and further incentives to incorporate environmental concerns into corporate strategies.

Partly in response to public and business pressure, governments of all political hues have competed to demonstrate their green credentials. In the United Kingdom (UK), Conservative Prime Minister

Margaret Thatcher surprised commentators in late 1988 by advocating urgent action to safeguard the ozone layer, curb acid rain and avoid global warming (McCormick 1995: 260). Her seeming 'conversion' was followed in 1990 by the UK's first comprehensive White Paper on the Environment, 'This Common Inheritance', which sought to incorporate environmental concerns into economic growth and integrate it into other policy areas.

More enduring was the Dutch government's 1989 National Environmental Policy Plan (NEPP) which also sought to achieve sustainable development by integrating environmental considerations into economic policies. The NEPP set specific targets for reduction of identified pollutants over a 20-year period, and included detailed costings (Weale 1992: 125). A follow-up plan (NEPP2) was published in 1993 and focused on the implementation of earlier principles and targets. In addition, various eco-taxes were established by national governments in Sweden, Belgium and The Netherlands.

The EU's role in environmental protection was strengthened and expanded throughout this period. The European Community's original Treaty of Rome did not contain any mention of the environment or environmental policy, but legislation in this sector, as well as energy and consumer protection, became an important element in the Union's *acquis communautaire*, or accumulated powers and competences. However, the EU's emergence as a powerful legislator on 'green' political issues prompted fresh anxieties – shared by Greens and 'non-Greens' alike – about the Union's distant, centralised and bureaucratic nature. One Green Member of the European Parliament explained:

> We Greens believe that decisions should be taken at the lowest effective level and there should be public participation in decision-making. . . . [But] the EU represents a centralisation of power and it's almost impossible for local people to have any say whatsoever.[10]

Decentralisation and de-bureaucratisation

Demands for decentralisation and de-bureaucratisation are less often directly equated with the 'greening' process. However, as outlined above, these concerns comprise a fundamental plank of green politics. This point has been reflected in the increasing political saliency of regionalism; the advocacy of small-scale (grassroots) democracy; suspicion of centralised leadership; and new forms of political action.

The rise of regionalism or 'meso-government' (Sharpe 1993) and concomitant calls for regional autonomy have swept across Europe. Regionalism has called into question the viability of the nation-state as the primary source of governmental power. Regionalist sentiment has not been unique to Greens; regionalist demands have been made by ethnic, populist and far right groups. The green influence has been seen in those regionalist demands that emphasise decentralisation as a means towards grassroots democracy. For the Greens, decentralisation is not just a pragmatic move towards more efficient governance. Greens insist that 'policy and policy implementation should be locally or regionally determined, with appropriate systems of elections and accountability at this level' (Newman 1996: 110).

Growing public mistrust with traditional parties and leaders suggest the wider resonance of green demands for 'de-bureaucratisation' and grassroots democracy. Public demands for less centralised bodies (including EU institutions) and more 'openness' or transparency in national and EU policy-making processes reflect this trend (see Peterson 1995c). On the national level, protest against 'politics as usual' was apparent in voter discontent towards ruling parties and governments in nearly every West European state in major elections in the early 1990s (see Butler 1995).

Most Member States responded with some sort of decentralisation or regional reform. Marks and McAdams (1996: 102) cite the transformation of Belgium from a unitary to a federal state. France, Italy and Spain created new regional governments in the 1980s. Even Greece and Portugal moved tentatively in the same direction.[11] On the EU level, regionalist demands resulted in the establishment of dozens of regional information or representation offices; a consultative Committee of Regions; and incorporation of 'subsidiarity', the principle under which policy decisions should be taken as closely as possible to the citizen (see Scott *et al.* 1994; Bomberg and Peterson 1998).

III   DEVELOPMENT OF GREEN ACTORS: THE NEW SOCIAL MOVEMENT MILIEU

Another indication of an incipient 'greening' process was the emergence and development of green actors, including social movements, professionalised pressure groups and green political parties. Beginning in the late 1960s, a proliferation of extra-parliamentary, non-partisan citizens' movements emerged that focused on specific local, regional and transnational environmental issues. Most active in these protests were Inglehart's 'post-materialist generation'.

Increased participation by post-materialists took shape in the rise of *new social movements* (NSMs) concerned with issues of peace, ecology and women's rights. The term social movement is loosely defined here as a collective actor seeking fundamental social change. It is made up of 'individuals who understand themselves to have common interests and, for at least some significant part of their social existence, a common identity' (Scott 1990: 6). Essentially, movements differ from parties in that they do not seek political office as their primary goal (Rucht 1987) and they have mass mobilisation, or the threat of mobilisation, as their prime source of power (Raschke 1985). They are further distinguished from other collectivities, such as voluntary associations or interest groups, in being primarily concerned with changing society, as opposed to influencing 'ordinary' political decision-making (Melucci 1989).

NSMs served as the antecedents to green parties and pressure groups. Five main characteristics distinguish these new[12] organisations from older social movements such as the socialist or miners' movements. The first defining element of new movements is the different *socio-economic background* of their members. Recruits of 'old' movements tended to be employed in blue collar jobs and were of varying age groups. By contrast, members of NSMs are found primarily among the young, well-educated, white collar class, especially those employed in the civil service sector (Rucht 1989).

Second, new movements are characterised by a widespread sympathy for *anti-modernism*. Members have broken with the traditional values of capitalistic society and thus do not accept the premises of a society based on economic growth (Offe 1985). Third, members commonly resort to *radical forms of action*. 'Conventional' political participation (voting, letter-writing, holding political office) are replaced by an extensive use of unconventional forms of action including protests, demonstrations and sit-ins (Dalton 1988).[13]

Fourth, the new movements represent a shift to *decentralised* organisational forms and avoidance of formal traditional left or right wing ideologies. Adherents of new movements prefer small-scale, anti-hierarchical, decentralised organisations that encourage direct democracy. Finally, *participation* in new movements is no longer just a means to an end, but rather is considered a goal in itself. The democratic, decentralised forms of movement decision-making operate as an example to the rest of society. 'Actors self-consciously practice in the present the future social changes they seek' (Melucci 1989: xi).

NSMs formed around issues of students' rights, peace, women's rights and ecology. Often overlapping in membership and ideals, these movements served as the antecedents for green politics and parties.

The student movement

Participation in the student movement arose from a desire for innovation and a change of the conditions inside European universities. Reaching its peak in the late 1960s, especially in France and West Germany, the movement was fundamentally anti-authoritarian and pressed for more power for students (Schoonmaker 1988). According to proponents of reform, the university structure had not kept pace with increased student numbers. Activists complained that irrelevant subjects were offered and that the university had become 'nothing more than a knowledge factory' (Klandermans *et al.* 1989). The student movement signalled a wider malaise. It demanded reforms not just at the university level, but in society at large. This concern was seen in the student outrage at the treatment meted out to demonstrators by the authorities, and student fears of the growth of what they viewed as an increasingly bureaucratised, repressive state (Hülsberg 1988). Nor were its concerns merely domestic. The movement helped bring global issues onto national political agendas, most notably through its opposition to the Vietnam war and its solidarity with the developing world (Kolinsky 1987).

The peace movement

The peace movement had many predecessors. But the movement that arose in the late 1970s and 1980s reflected increasing uneasiness and insecurity about life in the post-industrial, nuclear age (Papadakis 1986). 'Security' for most members of the movement meant something different from the conception held by their parents.

The peace movement was particularly strong in West Germany (see Breyman 1998). Situated literally on the front line of any superpower conflict, the Germans felt especially threatened with total annihilation in the event of a nuclear confrontation. The NATO decision to deploy Pershing II and cruise missiles on German soil considerably accelerated the growth of the peace movement in Germany and led to the massive demonstrations in the early 1980s. The peace movement transformed the problem of security into a post-materialist collective issue. These protests challenged as non-democratic the process surrounding the discussion of security, and questioned earlier traditional notions of 'security' and 'defence' (Kaldor 1990). Put another way, this was seen not just as a peace movement, but as a 'global movement for human security' (Parkin 1989: 116).

The women's movement

The women's movement emerged in most western states in the late 1960s. It took the oppression of women across the globe to be the root and symbol of all oppression. Shunning the male chauvinism and sexual discrimination they often found even in the student and peace movements, feminist activists broke away to found their own radical emancipatory movement. For example, feminist opposition to nuclear weapons in the UK took a highly visible form in the women's peace camp at Greenham Common (Carter 1995).

More generally, the women's movement advocated the formation of independent, local women's groups, seminars, workshops, coffee houses and bookshops. Men were excluded from many of these activities. The movement's members claimed that they did not want to fight against men, but felt that problems could be better solved without them (Schwarzer 1983). In both structure and content, the women's movement fit the post-materialist mould. It was autonomous, anti-hierarchical, highly decentralised, and worked primarily outside the system (Merkl 1986).

The environmental/ecology movement

The environmental/ecology movement began as a rather quaint preoccupation of nature lovers, but environmental protection soared to the top of priority listings in opinion polls across Europe in the 1980s (Kolinsky 1987: 327). Most notably among the 'post-materialist young', ecology became an issue of extra-parliamentary opposition in the early 1970s when it was perceived as an urgent problem neglected by parties. Citizen initiative groups (such as the *Bürgerinitiativen* in Germany) sprang up in several EU Member States. These local action groups were informal, sporadic organisations largely run by students and members of the educated, white collar class.

By the mid-1970s, the main thrust of citizen initiative movements was stopping the development of nuclear power. For instance, when the German government decided to accelerate its nuclear power programme in the wake of the 1973 energy crisis, the *Bundesverein Bürgerinitiativen Umweltschutz* (BBU) (Federal Association of Environmental Citizen Initiatives) was founded to facilitate communication between local action groups and campaigns against nuclear power plants. The BBU emphasised the need for cooperative action, first among local groups, and subsequently among national and international organisations such as the European Environmental Bureau.

By the late 1970s, other national umbrella organisations had formed to solidify and unify environmental movements within their own countries. In 1972, the Environmental Defence Union was formed in The Netherlands. The Danish Organisation of Information on Nuclear Power formed in 1974. Similar umbrella associations soon appeared in other countries (Müller-Rommel 1989: 6; Urwin 1990: 122). The consolidation of various local citizen initiatives into one national umbrella organisation facilitated the coordination of environmental protest both within and among different European countries.

European citizens joining these various movements were motivated by specific issues and a more general sense of dissatisfaction with the post-materialist age and structures. In particular, these citizens were responding to an apparent inability of traditional parties to address these issues (Lawson and Merkl 1988). Fundamental societal change led to the rise of fundamentally new types of concerns, politics and organisations.

Whilst all EU Member States showed some form of NSM activity, the extent and form varied dramatically. Inglehart's post-materialist thesis, a 'macro' explanation of the 'why' of social movement emergence, did little to explain the 'how'. It could not, for example, explain how there should emerge such different levels of green activity when the psychological and structural preconditions for social movement and political action appeared similar across Western Europe (Barnes and Kasse 1979; Müller-Rommel 1985b). Nor could it explain why some movements developed into green parties, and others did not. If the same general post-materialist preconditions existed in West Germany as in other countries – e.g. Sweden, France or the UK – other factors must explain national variations in new social movement/party development.

Scholars employ a variety of conceptual frameworks to explain how movements have developed, evolved or stagnated (see Klandermans *et al.* 1989). For instance, resource mobilisation theorists emphasise the importance of mobilising such personal individual resources as commitment, money and leisure, and institutional resources including access to organisations committed to change (McCarthy and Zald 1977). Other theorists seek a midway between 'macro' structural and 'micro' resource theories. Tarrow (1988) and Kitschelt (1986) apply the concept of 'political opportunity structures' to the study of movements and parties. Kitschelt (1986) argues that a movement's development and success will depend on 'opportunity structures', such as a nation's electoral system or the level of centralisation in the nation's policy-making apparatus. According to Kitschelt, 'closed' political systems – typified by, say, an autonomous judiciary, the lack of public resources to control private market forces, a weak legislature, and an inaccessible executive – constrain traditional forms of protest. By preventing conventional access for these protest concerns, closed systems such as Germany's 'unwittingly fueled the movement's mobilisation' and helped pave the way for the formation of the German Green party (Kitschelt 1986: 58; see also Koopmans 1996: 45).

By focusing on political resources and structures such as institutional 'openness' or electoral competition (see Richardson and Rootes 1995), these 'midway' and micro approaches taken together help explain the development of movements into green parties. They also help explain why some movements developed into parties whilst others remained loose movements or developed instead into pressure groups.

IV GREEN ACTORS TODAY: NON-GOVERNMENTAL ORGANISATIONS AND PARTIES

Whilst the media and much academic literature tend to refer to 'environmentalists' or the 'green lobby' as a single entity, it is helpful to divide green actors into three discernible groups: movements, pressure groups (or non-governmental organisations [NGOs]) and political parties. All three types of actor emerged from or were strengthened by the new social movement milieu, but each developed to play different roles in influencing politics and policy. A division can be made according to the primary *raison d'être* and basic operating strategies of each (see Table 1.1).[14] Despite differences amongst each set of actors, all Greens face a common green conundrum: how can they influence or infiltrate conventional political structures whilst maintaining their radical edge and grassroots ethos?

Movements that remain movements

Some NSMs with green objectives remain movements, in that they do not adapt themselves to participation in conventional politics. Contemporary examples include anti-road protesters or animal rights activists. Although they may offer temporary support to green pressure groups or parties, these movements remain independent of parlia-

Table 1.1 Green actors: goals and strategies

	Goals	Strategies
NSMs	social change; alternative society	non-parliamentary; non-partisan; non-conventional (spontaneous protest and demonstrations; direct action)
Pressure Groups	policy change often concentrated on single or limited issues	non-parliamentary; non-partisan; conventional and non-conventional (lobbying of media, public and government officials; direct action)
Green Parties	fundamental societal change across a wide array of interconnected issues	parliamentary and non-parliamentary; conventional and non-conventional; contest elections whilst maintaining grassroots links

mentary structures or professional organisations. They are amorphous, spontaneous, non-professional groups that emerge to campaign on or protest about a given issue. Kitschelt (1995: 138) notes that whilst such movements usually enter phases of dormancy and latency, what survive are 'networks of shops, cafés, educational projects and new media' which cultivate these movements' ideas. Whilst many 'one-off' protesters or activists may galvanise over a specific issue or for a limited time, the 'core' of the movement share a more profound critique of society's values and structure.

Pressure or interest groups

A second type of green actor is the green pressure or interest group. These include organisations such as Greenpeace, Friends of the Earth (FoE) and the World Wide Fund for Nature (WWF).[15] Unlike movements, these groups are established, (more or less) professionally organised groups with a core membership base and fund-raising operations. These groups vary widely in their level of radicalism, type of issue addressed and tactics employed. Yet they all seek to influence governments in policy choices, without themselves seeking to assume responsibility for governing. Rather than contest electoral campaigns, they are more likely to launch public opinion campaigns designed to influence the public, government agencies, parties and politicians.

One of the first such groups to establish themselves within Europe was the World Wide Fund for Nature[16] which established a national organisation in the UK in 1961. The WWF began as a conservation group concerned with the degradation of habitats and extinction of species. Whilst initially the WWF adopted fairly conventional means of pressure, it broadened its tactics by the 1980s to include more vigorous opposition and protests. Moreover, in 1990 it added to its mission statement the green goals of sustainable use of natural resources and the reduction of pollution and wasteful resource consumption. By the mid-1990s, the WWF had grown to 28 organisations across the globe, half of which were in Europe. It set up a Brussels office in 1989 to lobby specifically on EU issues.[17] Today its global membership is close to five million (Long 1995: 672–3).

Compared to the WWF's origins, Friends of the Earth began as a much more radical, politicised green organisation. It was created in 1969 in San Francisco by David Brower, a renowned environmentalist who had grown impatient with the more moderate views and tactics of the US conservation organisation, the Sierra Club. FoE was formed to take on issues 'that government officials and established conservation groups often ignored, such as nuclear power, industrial pollution and quality of life issues' (Dalton 1994: 39). The first European branch was the French Friends of the Earth (*Les Amis de la Terre*) which formed in 1970. British and Swedish offices also formed in that year. From its inception, FoE adopted 'blatantly active' campaign methods (e.g. street protests, dramatic boycotts) designed to attract public attention to key issues of pollution, alternative energy and transport (see McCormick 1995: 172). Its extra-parliamentary tactics attracted members from the looser student, ecology and citizen initiative movements, especially in France and The Netherlands (see Dalton 1994: 38). Established in 1971, FoE International today represents a loose coalition of over 50 national affiliates with no central source of authority.

One of the best known pressure groups in Europe is Greenpeace, which began as an anti-nuclear protest movement in North America. Their vigorous protest in 1973 against French testing of nuclear weapons above Moruroa Atoll in the South Pacific ocean elicited considerable public sympathy and media coverage. In the mid-1970s, Greenpeace began to widen its policy objectives to include protest campaigns against whaling and seal-culling. It soon became well known for its direct action campaigns (all carefully recorded on camera by volunteers) and high sea adventures. During the late 1970s, Greenpeace organisations were formed in several European countries, including France (1977), the UK (1977) and The Netherlands (1978). In 1975–6, a founding member of Greenpeace, David McTaggert, brought various European Greenpeace chapters together to form 'Greenpeace Europe' (Brown and May 1989: 51). An international confederative body, Greenpeace International, was set up in The Netherlands in 1979 to act as an international umbrella organisation. Greenpeace's profile in Europe was boosted markedly by the *Rainbow Warrior* incident in 1985, when the French intelligence service blew up a Greenpeace ship involved in protests against French nuclear tests in the Pacific, killing a Greenpeace volunteer.

In their early years, the activities of FoE and Greenpeace resembled those of a social movement. Their strategies were clearly protest oriented, non-governmental and, initially, loosely organised. Green pressure groups then became increasingly professionalised and pragmatic while softening their radical edge (see Koopmans 1996). But they have remained important green actors because of their continuing fundamental critique of current society and environmental practices.

Political parties

Finally, the development of green political parties is of primary concern for the purposes of this study. Essentially, parties differ from pressure groups and NGOs in that they seek to present a comprehensive view of a green society, and they operate in the electoral arena (Rüdig and Franklin 1992). Viritually all European green parties have some links with earlier NSMs from which they emerged. All seek to represent NSM interests to a certain extent, but the extent to which they do so varies tremendously (Doherty 1992). The relationship between green parties and NSMs varies widely in terms of ideology and strategic orientation, as is evidenced by the analysis below.

Ideological and strategic differences

The primary ideological distinction separating green parties is between 'purist' and 'rainbow/leftist' parties (Müller-Rommel 1985b; Poguntke 1989; Rüdig 1985). Some refer to this divide as 'green–green' versus 'red–green' parties (see figure 1.1).[18] Green–green parties, such as *De Groenen* in The Netherlands, adopt radical environmental policies, eschew leftist ideology, and seek to create a clear distance between their views and the views of mainstream parties, left or right. Red–green, or 'rainbow' parties, include the German Greens and the Dutch Green-Left. These parties adopt ecological issues as the fundamental part of their political strategy 'to radically change the contemporary "capitalist societies" in Western Europe' in line with leftist ideology (Buck 1989: 167).

Figure 1.1 Green party types

RED–GREEN (RAINBOW) PARTIES	GREEN–GREEN (PURIST) PARTIES
Grünen (FRG); Groen Links (NL)	Les Verts (F); De Groenen (NL)

Agalev (B); Ecolo (B); Green Party (GB)

The predominance of the latter parties has led some writers (Kitschelt 1988; 1989) to view green parties merely as an extension of broader New Left ideology, in which environmental themes are adopted as one theme of many. This view neglects the existence of purist parties or purist elements within green parties. More importantly, it neglects the central role of green ideology and practice that defines green parties and separates them from their leftist counterparts. Rüdig and others (Rüdig 1990; Lowe and Rüdig 1986; Franklin and Rüdig, 1995: 414) convincingly argue that green parties are best understood not merely as New Left parties, but as manifestations of an 'ecological cleavage'. In short, all green parties have broadly similar ecological concerns and demands that serve as a pivotal part of their agenda and political identity.

Another broad distinction between green parties is their strategic orientation: the extent to which they embrace parliamentary, mainstream tactics, or favour instead more radical unconventional means to achieve their aims. Generally, 'purer' parties eschew traditional forms of political activity such as party alliances or 'trade-offs' with mainstream parties. The small Dutch *De Groenen* party fits this bill. However, this match is not always the case. For example, the French Greens (*Les Verts*) have leaned towards a 'purist' or 'green–green' ideology, but have long engaged in traditional forms of political activity such as participation in presidential elections.

The green strategic conundrum

Despite differences in ideology and strategy, all green parties face similar challenges that arise from their unique beliefs and movement roots. In particular, all suffer to a certain extent under a 'green strategic conundrum': how to retain grassroots movement principles whilst adopting traditional mainstream strategies. Many of these parties began as or remain 'movement-parties' – organisations exhibiting characteristics of both traditional political parties and NSMs (Raschke 1985). Movement-parties seek fundamental change in government and society, but unlike NGOs their operating strategies include winning seats in parliaments and effecting change 'from within'. Thus movement-parties seek to maintain movement roots while pursuing political goals through parlimentary means. However, most often these movement parties end up being torn between the two poles of organisational styles and types. Whilst they typically feel compelled to evolve towards organisational centralisation, they also desire the decentralisation stressed by the movements. They therefore often drift between radicalism and reformism, unable to survive the 'parliamentary embrace' (Smith 1984: 93) or avoid the accommodation, incrementalism and compromise that come from membership in traditional party systems (von Beyme 1982).

Most literature on movement-parties suggests an inevitable slide towards the 'parliamentarisation' of movement-parties. This process means that movement-parties submit to the normalising forces of an established parliamentary system. Once in parliament, a movement-party begins to place increasingly more emphasis on parliamentary bargaining, compromise becomes more acceptable, and the party itself becomes more preoccupied with maximising votes.

Clearly, this 'de-radicalisation' has occurred in the case of many green parties, most notably the German Greens. This shift has altered but not removed the central strategic dilemma. Whilst no longer eschewing a parliamentary path, or fully embracing movement goals and strategies, green parties nonetheless are still caught on the horns of a dilemma. Their claim to be innovative and different is based on their grassroots-democratic tradition and 'their critique of the sclerotic character of the European political establishment' (Doherty 1992: 96). Any shift from radicalism undermines their distinctiveness and renders them part of the mainstream tradition. On the other hand, green parties have felt compelled to shed some of their radical cloth as more supporters have demonstrated greater willingness to practise more traditional strategies such as parliamentary participation and bargaining. Moreover, green voters have become less hostile to coalition-building with other parties, as evidenced by green party participation in the governments of several German Länder (Poguntke 1993b). The dilemma for the Greens is that failure to adapt to changed circumstances means danger of electoral decline and marginalisation of green issues. But moderating demands or strategies would disillusion many core activists and risk splitting green parties (Doherty 1992: 96; Bomberg 1992).

The German Greens

To illustrate the development and strategic dilemma faced by green parties more generally, this section focuses on one 'prototype' green party: the German Greens, or *die Grünen*. The German Greens are one of the most successful green parties in Europe. Whilst unique in many respects (see below), their development depicts key strategic tensions and conflicts faced by all green parties.[19] The rising salience of green issues has been reflected in the success of the German Greens. The 'catch all' parties in the Federal Republic of Germany (FRG) proved unable to manage effectively the new concerns and issues that arose in the 1970s (Schoonmaker 1988; Lawson and Merkl 1988). The Greens emerged as a new type of party, created by extra-parliamentary forces such as peace and environmental groups, and ideologically focused on 'new politics' issues and an alternative paradigm of politics. Officially formed as a national party in 1980, the Greens cast themselves as a 'movement-party' or 'anti-party party' (Kelly 1980).

The Greens experienced increasing electoral success throughout the 1980s, especially among the young, the highly educated, and those employed in the public sector (Dalton 1989; Conradt 1989). They started at the local level, steadily winning seats in several local and state (*Land*) parliaments. By 1989, the Greens had managed to clear the 5 per cent hurdle that they needed to jump in order to win seats in eight of the 11 Land assemblies. In three Länder (Berlin in 1985 and 1989; Bremen in 1987; Hamburg in 1986), the Greens captured over 10 per cent of the vote (see Frankland 1989a: 69–70). Campaigning on their four 'green pillars' of ecology, social equality and justice, grassroots democracy, and non-violence,[20] the Greens achieved a major victory in the 1983 national election. They entered the national parliament (*Bundestag*) for the first time with 5.6 per cent of the national vote and 27 seats. In the 1987 federal election, they received an impressive 8.3 per cent of the national vote and over 40 seats in the Bundestag.

In addition to their campaigns in domestic German elections, the Greens also campaigned in EP elections. On the European level, Greens mobilised around a 'green' critique of what they viewed as the growing influence of the centralised, bureaucratic and undemocratic character of European political institutions. In both the 1984 and 1989 Euro-elections, they captured over 8 per cent of the vote and seven to eight seats in the EP.

The German Greens' early development reflects their movement-party roots. On forming a national party in 1980, the German Green founders were determined to exploit the opportunities of electoral politics without being parliamentarised or falling into the traps of professionalisation and the detachment of party from people. Eschewing the formal structures of established parties, the Green party sought to comprise a movement in politics in which anyone could participate and which would not produce 'functionaries and professional politicians on one side and a passive herd of uninvolved followers on the other' (Kolinsky 1984: 24).

To ensure this, a number of internal rules and regulations were agreed. First, most Greens insisted on a policy of mid-term rotation of political and party posts. They believed that rotation of posts would preclude the development of an entrenched, professional political elite. The concentration of power was further discouraged by segregating party positions from positions in assemblies or parliaments. The Greens also insisted that paid party employees could not hold party office. Moreover, parliamentarians were required to relinquish part of their salaries to 'Eco-Funds'. These funds were then awarded to various ecological projects, peace camps, and numerous other citizen's initiatives.

Finally, the Greens enforced the notion of *Basisdemokratie*, or grassroots democracy. Party meetings at all levels were open to members, and minorities were guaranteed a voice. Basisdemokratie also implied a consensual decision-making procedure that would allow 'the thorough venting of the issues at all levels' (Frankland 1989b: 391–2). Greens applied these rules in an attempt to distinguish themselves from the mainstream parties. They wanted to be a political party that won enough votes to enter parliaments at all levels, where they could serve as a voice of opposition on such key issues as ecology, equality and peace. At the same time, the Greens sought to remain a core component of broader extra-parliamentary movements that acted on the same key issues outside parliaments. Indeed, they hoped to become the spearhead of these movements. The Greens, in short, wanted to serve as parliamentary opposition and extra-parliamentary opposition simultaneously (see Kolinsky 1987).

The Greens' movement-party goals and strategies were fraught with difficulties and contradictions. In their effort to translate new forms of participation and new themes into parliamentary politics, the Greens mobilised around a diverse array of issues and adopted competing ideologies (see Conradt 1989: 102–3). Acting as a movement-party also implied a pronounced need for a loose, flexible form of political organisation. Yet some of the rules intended to hamper organisational rigidity produced a rigidity of their own. For example, the practice of rotation prevented several experienced and knowledgeable office holders from continuing to serve their party in office. In the end, the practice became unworkable and was abolished on the national level in 1986.

Factional disputes emerged over issues of internal organisation and operational strategy. The most striking schism emerged in the early 1980s between 'fundamentalists' (or *'Fundis'*) and pragmatic 'realists' (*'Realos'*). The first group, nominally headed by Jutta Ditfurth and Rainer Trampert, feared any sort of dilution of movement or extra-parliamentary action. It opposed any coalition with other parties and wanted the Greens to remain critics of the capitalist system rather than 'share power . . . with the procapitalist establishment parties' (Braun-thal 1996: 96). Fundis insisted that the Greens work to change society 'from below' by mobilising social movement support to oppose the existing order.

The Realos denounced the Fundis for their utopian, unrealistic views. They felt that green goals could be realised by working within parliament and pushing for incremental governmental reforms. Realo leaders such as Otto Schily and Joschka Fischer[21] urged the party to play pragmatic politics by forming coalitions, especially with the SPD. These factional disputes harmed the party's image and effectiveness. The lack of defined functions and organisational channels meant that individual 'personalities' emerged as spokespersons for the party, sometimes without official backing and often contradicting one another.

Yet overall the Greens fared remarkably well in the 1980s. Their appeal at all levels was rooted in their ability to seize effectively on green issues. Functioning as promoters of the 'new politics', the Greens offered radical answers to questions concerning ecological problems, security concerns and issues of democratic and civil rights.

The Greens underwent a substantial change in structure and image after the late 1980s. First, die Grünen suffered a major defeat in the 1990 federal election which revolved around the issue of German unification. Adopting the unpopular stance of opposition to the pace and form of unification, die Grünen failed to cross the 5 per cent hurdle needed to enter the Bundestag. Continuing internal strife and organisational disunity also contributed to the party's defeat.[22]

Moreover, die Grünen chose not to form an alliance with the East German Greens (*Bündnis 90* or Alliance 90) which was made up of East German dissidents, human rights campaigners and environmentalists. The western Greens claimed that they did not want to swallow the Eastern counterpart as most traditional parties had. East German Greens campaigning separately won six seats in the first all-German Bundestag. Finally, following lengthy negotiations and with a view to consolidating resources for the 1994 election, the (western) Grünen and *Bündnis 90* formally joined forces in 1993 to create the current German green party, *Bündnis 90/die Grünen* (Jahn 1994).

The western Greens' electoral defeat in 1990 had a profound effect on the internal organisation and strategies of the party. At the Neumünster conference in April 1991, the party agreed to 'stream-line' and make more efficient its internal organisation, in part by abandoning certain grassroots principles such as the separation of office and mandate (Poguntke 1993b). Such moves sparked a wider strategic debate that resulted in key 'Fundis' such as Jutta Ditfurth leaving the green party. The shift towards more pragmatic and less radical strategies was underlined by the Greens' growing support for the idea of coalitions with traditional parties (especially with the SPD), even on the national level.

By the mid-1990s, the party was clearly in the hand of the Realos. This shift paid off in the electoral returns of 1994. In June 1994, the German Greens won over 10 per cent and 12 seats in the EP election, making them the largest national group within the Green Group in the EP. In the national election of the same year, the Greens re-entered the Bundestag with 7.3 per cent and 49 seats. The Greens have been routinely asked to contribute to legislative majorities in parliament and have thus found it more difficult to work for imple-mentation of their own policies and principles. They must instead 'participate in daily grind of finding consensus solutions' (Jesing-hausen 1995: 112).

Yet it would be a mistake to conclude that the German Greens have abandoned their grassroots claim or have become just another traditional party. Their 1994 national electoral platform reflected the primacy of green issues, including greater investment in mass transit, decentralisation of the energy system, dual citizenship and voting rights for foreigners, liberalisation of the existing immigration system, a commitment to pacifism, opposition of obligatory military service, and a call for eventual dissolution of the Bundeswehr (see Braunthal 1996). Moreover, in terms of organisation, the Greens are still the only German party with a collective leadership, a 'pronouncedly particip-atory and elite challenging internal political culture' and extensive opportunities for grassroots participation (Poguntke 1993b).

The Greens, in other words, still attempt to straddle the radical–reformist divide. By agreeing to play coalition politics, they have demonstrated their willingness to eschew certain radical principled positions. But they still separate themselves from conventional parties' policies and practices by adhering to green organisation principles and adopting tangibly green positions on a range of issues. Put another way, whilst certain internal reforms have 'deprived them of some of their unconventional charm ... they are still capable of keeping in touch with movement politics without being almost entirely dependent on movement mobilisation' (Poguntke 1993b: 401).

The German Greens are a unique green party in several ways. In their early years, especially, their ideological programme was tinged with radical-left, even anarchist tendencies. These tendencies had softened considerably by the late 1980s. The Greens' electoral success was also aided by particular 'opportunity structures', such as Germany's federal structure, a modified proportional representation system, and generous state funding for political parties. But the German Greens are not 'entirely singular' (Richardson 1995: 19). Rather, their emergence and development is broadly similar to that of several other green parties, especially those of a 'rainbow' variety, such as the Dutch Green-Left. In particular, the Greens' advocacy of green issues, their internal ideological diversity, and their uneven electoral performance are characteristic of green parties across the EU. More importantly, the strategic dilemmas faced by the movement-party German Greens are shared by all green parties.

Green parties' continued success depends on several factors. First, their fortunes will be determined by the relative salience of key green concerns. Second, green parties must not let other, mainstream parties 'poach' green ideas. Third, they must adapt to changing circumstances and maintain some sense of internal solidarity (see Franklin and Rüdig 1995). Finally, Greens must acknowledge and confront their unique green strategic dilemma.

CONCLUSION

This chapter has outlined the core values, emergence and development of green politics and green actors. It has suggested that green politics broadly conceived are of continuing relevance in European politics and policies. The key issues of environmental protection, sustainability, decentralisation and grassroots democracy continue to animate the public, private and government sectors.

The continuing relevance of green issues is also reflected in the development and endurance of green actors. Green NGOs have become more entrenched players in the policy-making process; in many Member States their participation is institutionalised. Green

NGOs have expanded their scope of action, and have become increasingly engaged at the transnational (EU) but also global (United Nations [UN]) level (McCormick 1995). Similarly, green parties continue to win seats in local, regional, national and transnational parliaments. They are firmly entrenched in the political landscape in several Member States and within the EP.

The political fortunes of green actors vary significantly across Member States. Working collectively, however, they have discovered rich opportunities to lobby and influence politics at the European level generally, and the EU level in particular. At the pan-European level, green parties have created a Federation (the EFGP) that represents and pursues interests shared by all member green parties. Even more visible is the Greens' role within the EU. Several aspects of the EU make it uniquely attractive to green actors: its embrace of a wide scope of environmental and related policies; its comparatively open structures; and the relative sympathy shown to green ideas by the EU's supranational institutions. Many green actors have seized upon these opportunities, yet other Greens have shunned what they see as the EU's remote, centralised structures and environmentally damaging priorities. The next chapters examine in detail the development of EU environmental policies, its attraction for green actors, and its inherent flaws according to the tenets of green politics.

2 Green issues and environmental policy-making in the European Union

INTRODUCTION

The 'greening' of European politics and the acceleration of European integration clearly have become intertwined. This chapter explores the role of the EU in this symbiotic relationship, focusing specifically on environmental policy. It argues that the EU has become an increasingly important forum for environmental agenda-setting and policy-making. It demonstrates that environmental policy is a unique area of EU policy, characterised by rapid change and fierce struggles between competing institutions and actors.

The chapter begins by analysing the pressures for transnational action on environmental protection which have led to increased powers for the EU in environmental matters. Section II provides an overview of the EU environmental policy-making process, with special reference to institutional changes mandated by the Single European Act (SEA) and the Maastricht Treaty on European Union (TEU). Section III outlines the role of non-institutional actors in shaping environmental policy. Section IV examines the policy outputs of the EU environmental policy-making process. It provides an overview of key pieces of environmental legislation and examines the extent to which environmental considerations are integrated into other EU policy sectors. Section V assesses competition between the EU and national governments for influence in environmental policy-making, and the 'implementation gap' at the national level which has limited the impact of growing EU competence. The conclusion provides a brief assessment of EU environmental policy-making and the 'greening' of EU policies.

I PRINCIPLES GUIDING EU ENVIRONMENTAL POLICY

The EU was created as an essentially 'economic' community with no firm legal basis for dealing with environmental issues. The Treaty of

Rome made no reference to the environment and made no mention of environmental policy as an integral part of a common market. More recently, especially since the acceptance of the SEA in 1987, the EU's role has expanded to the point where environmental policy is now said to be 'one of the more successful policies of the Community, both in terms of the areas of activity that it commands and the degree of popular support which it is beginning to command' (Freestone 1991: 135).

A range of political and economic factors helped expand the EU's green remit. First, beginning in the 1970s, environmental issues climbed up the political agendas of several key Member States of the EU. Particular to the development of the EU's environmental policy was a heightened awareness of the environmental consequences of unregulated economic growth. Post-war economic prosperity in the EU brought with it increased energy consumption, an extensive system of motorways, expansion of agri-business with intensive use of fertilisers, and expanded urban development intruding into natural landscapes. Concern about the consequences of economic expansion was piqued by a series of industrial and nuclear accidents, such as the Seveso accident in 1976, Chernobyl in 1986 and the Sandoz chemical spill into the Rhine in 1986. Increasing awareness amongst the European public was reflected in growing demands for environmentally sound consumer products and services and rising electoral support for green parties on the local, national and European level. In the 1989 EP elections, green parties doubled their EP contingent and increased their per cent of the popular vote in every Member State.

The second factor contributing to the EU's increasing role was a growing recognition of the *transnational* nature of environmental degradation and environmental protection in Europe. For instance, acid rain stemming from factory and power station emissions in one Member State crossed national borders and harmed forests and eroded historic buildings in another. Pollution of rivers such as the Rhine affected all countries along its banks. It became a truism to state that because EU Member States shared natural features such as air, rivers and seas, environmental problems and their solutions had to be found at the European level.

Related to the cross-national awareness was the concern over *global* environmental problems such as climate change, deforestation and depletion of the ozone layer. Member States had long realised that the EU could provide them with a stronger position in negotiations on global issues. Whilst most Member States were too small individually to play a decisive role in global negotiations, the EU, after 1995, represented 15 countries and 370 million people. A transnational actor of this size was in a powerful position to respond to environmental as well as economic global challenges, or to push others to do so. The need for global negotiations to address global problems expanded the EU's environmental role beyond EU borders.

A third reason for the increase of EU competence had little to do with rising green awareness or the salience of global environmental issues. Put simply, environmental legislation was necessary to eliminate trade distortions between Member States. Lodge (1989a: 320) argued that Member States' interest in environmental policy was spurred 'not so much by an upsurge of post-industrial values . . . as by the realization that widely differing national rules on industrial pollution could distort competition: "dirty states" could profit economically'. For instance, both The Netherlands and Germany had relatively strict national environmental standards. Fearing unfair competition from states with less stringent standards, the German and Dutch industrial lobbies argued for equal economic costs for environmental protection throughout the EU via the adoption of Dutch and German standards on an EU-wide basis (Hildebrandt 1992: 25).

The combination of these political and economic incentives spurred Member States to expand steadily the EU's role in environmental issues. The EU's continual attention to environmental issues can be traced through increasingly ambitious principles as laid down in a series of Environmental Action Programmes (EAPs). The first EAP was formally approved by Member States in 1973. This Programme is widely seen as marking the beginning of an EU environmental policy. It set objectives, stated key principles, selected the priorities and described measures to be taken in different policy sectors related to the environment. Its general objective was 'to improve the setting and quality of life and the surroundings and living condition of the Community population'. The Programme provided for action to reduce and prevent pollution, improve the quality of the environment, and encourage EU participation with international bodies in the area of environmental protection (Johnson and Corcelle 1989: 14–16).

Subsequent Action Programmes followed. The second EAP was developed in 1976 with the aim to continue and expand activities taken within the framework of the previous one. In 1983, a Third Programme remained within the general framework of policy as outlined in the previous two, whilst introducing a number of new elements. In particular it emphasised the preventive objectives of EU environmental policy and recognised the need to integrate environmental policy into other EU policies (Bomberg and Peterson 1993).

These Action Programmes expressed an increasing EU commitment to the issues of environmental protection. But any environmental legislation during this period was incidental to measures designed to harmonise laws in order to abolish obstacles to trade between Member States. There was no clear-cut *legal* basis for an EU environmental policy. Two articles relating to the common market served as the principal legal instruments for EU environmental policy. Article 100 authorised the Council to issue legislation that directly affected the establishment or functioning of the common market. Article 235 gave the Council the authority to take appropriate measures to 'attain in the course of the operation of the common market one of the objectives of the Community' where the Treaty had not provided the necessary powers to do so (Hildebrandt 1992: 18). Clearly, neither of these articles was aimed at environmental protection as such (Rehbinder and Steward 1985: 16). Moreover, both required unanimous decisions by Member States represented on the Council of Ministers. This legal base meant that the pace of environmental protection had to be directly related to the objective of economic harmonisation, and had to be unanimously agreed. Even by the mid-1980s, the EU thus lacked the ability to deal effectively with many environmental problems.

Single European Act

The SEA was a watershed in the development of the EU's environmental and related policies. Ratified in 1987, the SEA's primary goal was the completion of the internal market (the free movement of goods, services, capital and labour within the EU) by the end of 1992. The EU was mandated to harmonise product standards, including those related to the environment. If the single market was to be completed, then companies in all industries in all Member States had to compete with one another on equal terms. Completing the single market necessitated more European-wide environmental measures if economic conditions were to be standardised throughout the EU.

Trade considerations were the primary factor shaping the SEA's development. The Commission's study on the benefits of a single market (Cecchini 1988) estimated that completion of the single market would increase economic growth by over 5 per cent. But as the SEA was debated between 1985–1987, Greens and other critics raised concerns that the increased trade and economic activity generated by the internal market could have undesirable effects on the environment and public health. Moreover, there was concern over who would benefit most from the single market. Many critics claimed that the SEA would threaten workers' rights and the environment while benefiting only a small proportion of business and sectional interests (see Hey 1989; Uexküll 1989; Liberatore 1991).

The SEA addressed some of these concerns. One of the Treaty's articles dealing with harmonisation, Article 100a(3) stated that the Commission should take as a base a 'high level of protection' in its harmonisation efforts. Though not precisely defined, the message emerged that EU environmental standards would not be set at the level of the Member States with weakest laws. Moreover, the SEA's Article 100a(4) gave Member States the right to apply more stringent national regulations aimed at protecting the environment or worker health and safety, provided they are 'not a means of arbitrary discrimination or a disguised restriction on trade between Member States' (Johnson and Corcelle 1989: 344).

The SEA also added to the Treaty of Rome a special title on the Environment consisting of three articles. The title gave legal force to certain principles of EU environmental policy that already had been set out in earlier Environmental Action Programmes. Article 130r of the title stated that action by the Community relating to the environment should preserve, protect and improve the quality of the environment; contribute towards protecting human health; and ensure a prudent and rational utilisation of natural resources. As a guide to action, the title required that EU environmental policy be based on four basic tenets:

1 prevent pollution rather than simply control it;
2 use the polluter pays principle;
3 rectify environmental degradation at the source when possible; and
4 integrate environmental protection into other Union policies.

Article 130r(2) makes this last point explicit by stipulating that 'environmental protection must be a component of the EU's other policies'.

In one sense, the title did no more than provide a clear legal base for principles that had been developing since the early 1970s. But Haigh and Baldcock (1989: 20–1) stress the Article's symbolic importance. Following the adoption of the SEA, it was *de jure* correct to speak of an EU environmental policy. Previously the Commission had hesitated to propose legislation on some environmental issues, such as protecting wildlife, fearing that it would be challenged on the grounds that it had no legal competence to act in an area that was unrelated to trade. Following the SEA, that was no longer the case. The Title on the Environment gave the EU competence beyond measures simply related to trade.

The Treaty on European Union

The EU's environmental remit was furthered by the Treaty on European Union (TEU) signed in Maastricht in February 1992. The Treaty marked 'a new stage in the process of creating an ever-closer union among the peoples of Europe'. It had significant effects on environmental and green issues, both in terms of legislative substance and process. First, the Maastricht Treaty expanded the legal remit of the EU in global environmental issues. To the legal objectives of EU policy was added the aim of 'promoting measures at the international level to deal with regional or world wide environmental problems'. Thus the EU's hand in international activities related to the environment was strengthened by the force of law.

A second way in which Maastricht widened the EU's environmental remit was by adding to Article 130 a new 'precautionary principle' designed to strengthen the principle of 'preventive action' expressed in the SEA. Based on Germany's *Vorsorgeprinzip*, this principle's environmental application grew out of debates over appropriate action to be taken to counter serious international environmental threats such as acidification, depletion of the ozone layer and climate change. In short, the precautionary principle suggested the use of potentially costly measures to prevent even the possibility of serious environmental degradation. Yet the Maastricht Treaty failed to elaborate on how the principle would be operationalised in an EU context. For example, no guidance was given to clarify at what point the need to take precautionary measures takes precedence over the scientific uncertainty surrounding a potential environmental threat. Nonetheless, Verhoeve *et al.* (1992: 17–18) point out that this provision changed the nature of debate 'from disputes on "whether" action should be taken, to focus on "which" measures should be taken and "when"'.

The Maastricht Treaty also highlighted the principle of *subsidiarity*. This principle was invoked earlier by the SEA in its Title on the environment: 'The Community shall take action relating to the environment to the extent to which the objectives [of EU policy] can be attained better at the Community level than at the level of the individual Member States'. The subsidiarity principle is double-edged.

On one hand, it provides a powerful justification for the EU to develop policies where it has never done so before. Clearly, many objectives of environmental policy can be better attained at the EU level than at the national level. On the other hand, however, the principle places limits on EU action. Article 3b mandates Community action

> only if and in so far as the objectives of the proposed action cannot be sufficiently achieved by Member States and can therefore by reason of the scale or effects of the proposed action, be better achieved by the Community. . . . Any action by the Community shall not go beyond what is necessary to achieve the objectives of this Treaty.
>
> (CEC 1992b)

This passage can be interpreted to mean that the EU should be involved only in areas of policy where it can provide some sort of advantage or 'added value' to existing national policies. The Treaty leaves wide open the question of precisely where EU policies bring advantages over purely national ones. For instance, after difficulties surrounding ratification of the Treaty in Denmark and the UK, fears arose that this principle would be used to 'repatriate' environmental policies back to the national level. Off-the-cuff remarks by Commission president Jacques Delors and EU commissioner Leon Brittan elicited a flurry of press reports in the summer of 1992 suggesting that the EU might soon 'quit the green crusade' as a way to mitigate fears about the growing powers of the EU (Peterson 1994). In the event, such repatriation did not occur. But the broad implication of the sub-sidiarity principle is that the extent of the EU's competence in a range of environmental policy areas will continue to be a major bone of contention.

Finally, the Treaty gave a legal base to the EU's use of the concept 'sustainability'. The term 'sustainable development' had already been in vogue for several years, popularised by the World Commission on Environment and Development's *Brundtland Report* in 1987. The report concluded that economic growth was based overwhelmingly on exploiting finite resources and argued that policy-makers and citizens needed to consider the longer term consequences of development. At the heart of the concept of sustainable development is the idea that each generation should not close off options for the next. Sustainable development is thus defined as development that 'meets the needs of the present without compromising the ability of future generations to meet their own needs'.

The fifth EAP, published in 1992 and due to run until the year 2000, brought the term into EU parlance. Entitled *Towards Sustainability*, the fifth EAP defined sustainable development in terms of strategies to secure 'continued economic and social development without detriment to the environment and the natural resources on the quality of which continued human activity and further development depend' (CEC 1992d: 3). The Programme thus invoked the concept of sustainable development as called for in the Brundtland Report. But use of this term was inconsistent within the EAP and the TEU. The concept was attached to 'progress', 'growth' and 'development' without clarification. Despite the ambiguity, the provision did require Union policies to be environmentally sustainable. However it was interpreted, the term implied that environmental protection should be given an equal footing with economic concerns as one of the EU's objectives (Verhoeve *et al.* 1992: 15).

II   DEVELOPMENTS IN THE EU'S POLICY-MAKING PROCESS

The EU's environmental policy is formally guided by principles laid out in EAPs and in the EU Treaties. The policy-making process in the EU is a result not just of these principles, but of a wide array of actors vying with one another for power and influence.[1] This section introduces the EU policy-making process, focusing particularly on the institutional changes brought about by the SEA and the TEU.

Previous to the SEA, the basic structure of the EU's policy-making process was relatively straightforward. In a nutshell, EU proposals for legislation originated in the Commission, passed to the EP for consultation, then moved to the Council of Ministers where the actual decisions were reached. The Council needed only to seek the EP's advice on Commission proposals, advice that subsequently could be ignored. Thus, Union policy-making was dominated by the bilateral relationship between the Council of Ministers and the Commission. The policy-making process provided little formal access through which 'third' actors such as the EP or oppositional groups could exert influence.

The SEA and TEU introduced institutional changes that sought to increase the democratic legitimacy of the Union while speeding up the decision-making process. Under the SEA, the Rome Treaty was amended so that nearly all legislation related to the internal market would be authorised by qualified majority.[2] This change streamlined the decision-making process and made it impossible for one Member State to veto legislation. Implicitly, the new article also served as the

basis for environmental legislation, since many 'environmental protection measures also have objectives and consequences which are
directly linked to the functioning of the internal market' (Johnson and
Corcelle 1989: 344). For example, firms in Member States that impose
minimal penalties on polluters can receive unfair trade advantages.
The distortion is eliminated when common EU penalties are adopted.

By expanding the use of majority voting, the SEA helped speed up
the policy-making process. The SEA also sought to make the policy-
making process more democratic by increasing the powers of the
directly elected EP. Non-corporate interests such as consumer or
environmental concerns tended to be better represented in the EP
than in other EU institutions. Lobbying groups and Members of the
European Parliament (MEPs) argued that this step was essential if the
internal market was to be seen as credible from the point of view of
environmental protection and public health (Leonard 1988).

The SEA increased the powers of the EP in Union policy-making by
putting into force the 'co-operation procedure'. This applied to
limited – but important – policy areas, including specific research
programmes, regional fund decisions, and most legislative harmonisation necessary for the single market. EU environmental policy *per
se* was not covered by the cooperation procedure. But again, because
the procedure refered to legislation related to the internal market,
environmental considerations featured prominently.

Under the cooperation procedure, legislation started in the usual
way with a Commission proposal, a parliamentary Opinion and the
Council of Ministers' decision. However, in cooperation procedure
cases, the Council's decision was not final. It adopted a 'common
position' which was returned to Parliament for a 'second reading'. The
Parliament then had a three month deadline in which it could take
one of three actions. First, it could approve it (silence and inaction
counted as tacit approval). Second, it could propose amendments by
an absolute majority of its members. Third, the EP could reject the
Council's position. If the proposal was rejected, the Council could
carry it through only by a unanimous vote. The cooperation procedure
gave the EP greater influence in Council decisions. The Council still
had the final say on policies, but previously the Council's decision on
amendments proposed by the Parliament was final. The cooperation
procedure gave the EP a second opportunity to put them forward.

Institutional changes introduced by Maastricht altered further the
environmental policy-making process. First, the Treaty extended
considerably the areas where qualified majority voting applied. For
instance, the Maastricht treaty sanctioned majority voting rather than

unanimity on the 'cross-border aspects' of environmental policy (i.e. the transport of toxic wastes). As Verhoeve *et al.* (1992: 26) concluded, majority voting 'can now be regarded as standard procedure for [EU] environmental measures'. Moreover, a new process of 'co-decision' gave the EP a right to negotiate amendments directly with the Council and to veto outright certain types of legislation, thus granting the EP equal standing with the Ministers for the first time. Environmental strategy, consumer protection and public health were among the areas covered by co-decision. Under the cooperation procedure, the EP required the Commission's backing in order to get its amendments through the Council. With co-decision, the EP had the right to negotiate directly with the Ministers the changes it wanted and ultimately to reject bills that did not contain them.

However, in terms of the EP's role in environmental policy, the results of Maastricht were mixed. MEPs felt only limited powers had been ceded to the Parliament. The EP still did not have the power to initiate legislation. Moreover, the text of Maastricht's Article 130s was not clear as to when each of the decision-making procedures (consultation, cooperation or co-decision) should be followed, and arguments between the EU institutions over the appropriate procedure inevitably occurred (see Corbett 1994: 208). A related problem was the enormous complexity of the new co-decision procedure. It proved unduly complicated and in some cases involved 13 separate stages extending over many months. This complexity in certain cases led to more protracted decision-making, thereby nullifying the aims of increased majority voting and transparency.

Yet, overall, treaty changes increased significantly the EP's institutional powers generally, and its role in environmental policy-making particularly. As the EP's own visibility and influence increased, conflict among the EU's institutions became a much more common feature of EU politics. The increased structural and political power of the EP forced both the Commission and Council to take EP views more seriously and to engage in substantial inter-institutional bargaining. By expanding the areas covered under co-decision, the Amsterdam Treaty, signed in 1997, promises to increase the EP's role further. Because of its tendency to champion environmental causes, the EP's enlarged role served both green issues and actors.

III ENVIRONMENTAL POLICY-MAKING: NON-INSTITUTIONAL ACTORS

EU policy-making is extraordinarily complex. One of its most enduring features is the inclusion of a wide array of non-institutional members and interests, particularly in environmental policy-making. First, it reflects the competing interests expressed by civil servants and governmental officials from 15 Member States with widely varying environmental priorities (Sbragia 1996).

Second, the EU's environmental policy-making process includes non-state actors such as scientific experts, environmental NGOs and business interest groups. Their participation stems from the dependence of the Commission, who proposes legislation, on a wide variety of sources for information. The European Environmental Agency (EEA), which came into operation in 1993, can provide the Commission with objective, reliable and comparable information at the European level on the state of the environment. But the highly technical nature of environmental policies accentuates the Commission's need for outside experts. Moreover, given the restricted size of its permanent staff, the Directorate General (DG) for the Environment, DG XI, must rely on a wide array of participants from outside its department for technical and political advice.[3] In particular, it depends on experts and officials on secondment from other EU institutions, private organisations and foundations. One official in DG XI claimed that 'we have more officials on loan than any other DG'.[4]

The prominent role of temporary scientific experts was underscored by Ken Collins, MEP and Chairman of the European Parliament's Environment Committee:

> [EU] policy-making in the environmental area is curious in that it is made up of the normal political folk but is also made up scientists of various kinds. They might be biochemists, biologists, or physicists . . . but they're all mixed up with the political types and this makes for a very disparate network.[5]

DG XI has been generally considered to be more open to lobbyists than any other DG. In particular, it is relatively open to a wide array of pressure groups and environmental NGOs anxious to exert influence. However, many Greens argue that this tradition of openness was challenged in the 1990s by a desire on the part of DG XI to dismiss its label as 'nest of green radicalism'. Green MEPs and NGOs argue that the DG succumbed to a 'techno-managerial ethos' and became intent on introducing lowest common denominator environmental policy (Ehrlich 1996: 18).

Finally, the EU's environmental policy is distinctively influenced by the EP. The Commission welcomes the Parliament's view precisely because the EP is democratically elected and thus can legitimate EU environmental policy. An official in the UK's Department of the

Environment unit responsible for European affairs confided that 'the Parliament carries a lot of weight with the Commission because the Commission knows that even if [the EP's] powers are primarily advisory, it is democratically elected and the Commission is not'.[6]

The open and crowded nature of the environmental policy-making process has led some analysts to describe it as taking place in a series of loose 'issue networks' (see Mazey and Richardson 1993; Bomberg 1998). A large number of actors vie for influence and access, and the array of effective actors differs considerably according to the specific issue under consideration. According to this model, EU environmental policy-making incorporates a wide range of decision-making centres and a diverse array of actors who move in and out of policy arenas and have different views of desired policy outcomes. Compared with other EU policy sectors, environmental policy features relatively *ad hoc* policy-making structures in which not only a large, but to a certain extent unpredictable number of conflicting interests participate (see Heclo 1978).

In short, environmental issues comprise an especially dynamic policy area in the EU. Unlike more entrenched policy areas such as agriculture, where the EU's Treaty powers are longstanding, patterns of EU policy-making in the environmental arena are still relatively new and fluid. This very complexity makes it possible for new actors to challenge, change or shape EU policy in areas related to green issues.

IV POLICY OUTPUTS: ENVIRONMENTAL AND RELATED LEGISLATION

'Policy outputs' refer here to EU legislation in the areas of environmental and related policies. The loose and complex nature of EU environmental policy-making renders these policy outputs variable and unpredictable. EU legislation takes several forms: *regulations*, which apply directly to all; *decisions*, which are binding only on the Member States, firms or individuals to whom they are addressed; *recommendations* and *opinions*, which are not binding; and *directives*, which stipulate the ends to be achieved but leave the means open (see Johnson and Corcelle 1989: 338–41). Most environmental policy relies on the use of directives. Since it first took the initiative in the field of environmental policy in the early 1970s, the EU has agreed over 200 pieces of environmental legislation. An outline of some key environmental measures reveals a broad range of areas and issues covered.

Several major pieces of legislation concern *water* quality. The main thrust of the EU's water policy involves setting minimum standards for water, depending on its usage. In the 1970s, the EU adopted directives setting water quality standards for bathing water (76/160/EEC), drinking water (75/440/EEC) and freshwater fish (78/659/EEC). In addition to adopting minimum standards, the Commission put forward proposals concerning pollution by emission of dangerous substances (76/464/EEC). Despite extensive legislation and investments made in the area of water quality, the Commission conceded that 'Over the last 20 years, the state of the Community's water resources has not improved. . . . Far more examples exist of deterioration in quality than of improvements . . .'(CEC 1993). More recent and proposed water legislation is concerned primarily with revising existing legislation to clarify standards and enable more effective implementation. To this end, the Commission began in the mid-1990s an attempt to consolidate diverse pieces of water legislation under a single framework directive. This initiative met with grave resistance from green campaigners who saw it as likely to repeal existing rules without replacing them with comparably tough policies.

EU legislation to curb *air* pollution has proven more successful. In the area of general air quality, standards have been set for sulphur dioxide emissions, smoke and nitrogen dioxide. Limiting motor vehicle exhaust has been a key focus. The Union has issued a series of directives aimed at limiting the sulphur content of certain fuels as well as the lead and benzene content of petrol. For instance, in 1989 a directive was passed limiting emissions of small cars and requiring cars to be fitted with catalytic converters by January 1993. Related directives under discussion by 1997 sought to amend current legislation by focusing on collaboration with the automobile and oil industries.[7]

In the area of *chemicals,* early EU legislation focused on controlling specific substances. More recently, the EU has restricted the import and export of certain dangerous chemicals (Regulation 2455/92/EEC). Related EU environmental legislation has aimed to prevent industrial accidents which can have devastating environmental consequences. For example, the 1982 Seveso Directive, enacted in the wake of an industrial accident in Italy, required that: industry prepare safety reports and on-site emergency response plans; local authorities produce an off-site emergency plan; and the public be informed periodically of what to do in the event of an accident.

The EU's *waste* policy has three main environmental objectives: to recycle and reuse waste to a maximum extent; to reduce the quantity of unrecoverable waste; to dispose of as safely as possible any unrecoverable waste. EU waste legislation was first introduced in 1975 (75/442/EEC). It required Member States to draw up plans for environmentally sound methods of waste disposal and to encourage waste recovery and recycling. Since then the EU has gradually moved towards an EU-wide waste management regime, placing progressively stronger controls on transnational shipments of toxic and hazardous wastes. A packaging waste directive, modelled on German legislation, was adopted by the Council and EP in December 1994. The directive was designed to reduce the amount of packaging waste (nearly 50 million tonnes) from the industrial, business and private sectors.[8]

Finally, the EU has adopted a range of legislation aimed at the protection of *wildlife and habitats*. More specifically, the EU has issued directives protecting whales, seals, wild birds and their habitats. Recent legislation has acknowledged the importance of preserving 'biodiversity' within the Union, after the EU as a whole signed the Convention on Biodiversity agreed at the 1992 UNCED summit. The 1992 Habitats Directive (92/43/EEC) established 'sites of Community importance', which are designated as those that contribute significantly to the maintenance of a 'natural habitat type' or 'biological diversity within the bio-geographical region concerned'.

Taken together, this body of legislation represents a movement towards EU-wide standards on a wide array of environmental issues. In many cases, EU policy simply has codified legislation already in place at the national level in many Member States. In other cases (e.g. small car emissions), EU policy represents a genuine raising of standards across the EU.

Related policy outputs

In addition to the EU's environmental policy *per se*, measures taken in a wide variety of other policy sectors have implications for environmental quality. Any assessment of the 'greening' of EU policies needs to take into account energy, agriculture and the internal market. An overview of these policy areas reveals that whilst in some instances progress has been made in integrating environmental concerns into related policy spheres, only minimal integration has occurred in other areas.

Energy policy is inextricably linked with environmental policy, owing to the EU's reliance on fossil fuels, and the environmental consequences of nuclear energy production and waste disposal. Early EU action in energy policy was based on the 1957 European Community of Atomic Energy (Euratom) Treaty, which sought to encourage the production of cheap, plentiful and guaranteed energy for the Community through nuclear power. Although the Commission has expressed its eagerness to improve the safety standards of nuclear power plants, EU legislation has not reflected this goal. By the mid-1990s, there were still no uniform standards for safety and discharges, no clear provisions for storage and transport of nuclear fuels or waste, and no agreed emergency procedures in case of major malfunction (Budd and Jones 1991: 124; Haaland Matlary 1996). Confusion over EU competence in this area continued into the 1990s. The resumption of French nuclear tests in the Pacific Islands in September 1995 raised international concern that the EU was unable to control its Member States' nuclear policies.

However, environmental imperatives have to a certain extent compelled the EU to confront with greater vigour the environmental implications of nuclear power and energy conservation. In the early 1990s, the Commission began to lay the foundation for a new energy policy framework. It has put forward a variety of proposals, including one in May 1992 for a CO_2/energy tax. This tax would apply to all forms of energy except renewable energy and energy used as a raw material in industry. The main thrust was to shift demand away from the most polluting fuels and to encourage energy efficiency. This proposal foundered on opposition led by the UK, which consistently resisted the introduction of any EU-wide tax. Eventually, the Commission was forced – as it rarely is on environmental matters (Wurzel 1996: 278) – to reissue a much less ambitious proposal for minimum rates of taxation on all forms of energy.

In other areas of *industrial policy*, the Commission has developed proposals to ensure that environmental considerations are integrated into all industrial operations and decisions. For instance, a voluntary Eco-Management and Audit Scheme (EMAS) was approved in 1993. This scheme enables companies that sign up to the scheme to demonstrate high levels of environmental performance. Environmental concerns have also been integrated into *consumer* policy. An example of such integration is the Ecolabel scheme (880/92/EEC), launched in summer 1993. This voluntary scheme promotes the design, production, marketing and use of products that have the least impact on the environment. The aim is to provide a consistent, EU-wide label to counter the rash of 'eco-friendly' labels appearing on products, many of which make questionable claims. However, progress in labelling products has been slow, not least because criteria are decided on a product-by-product basis.

The integration of environmental concerns into other policy areas remains inadequate, as is evidenced clearly by the *Common Agricultural Policy* (CAP). The CAP is still *the* dominant EU policy, consuming about half of the Union's budget. The CAP has traditionally provided guaranteed prices for farmers, which in some cases meant that farmers could sell their products irrespective of levels of production and demand. Farmers were thus encouraged to produce more, often by intensive use of fertilisers and 'reclaiming' uncultivated land or wetlands. Despite recent attempts at reforms (see Rieger 1996), the continuing legacy of the CAP is over-production and environmental degradation caused by the large-scale use of chemical fertilisers and pesticides.

In the related field of *biotechnology*, the Council has adopted several directives aimed at controlling the use of genetically modified organisms (GMOs). Environmental concerns are often not addressed in these directives. For instance, a directive passed in 1991 by agricultural ministers regulating the sale of new types of pesticides clearly conflicted with an earlier directive approved in 1990 by the Environmental Council of Ministers. The Environment Directive stipulated that genetically modified organisms (GMOs) designed for use as pesticides could be sold only after a detailed assessment of their environmental impact. The later directive contained no such provisions for assessing GMOs and mandated that a committee of agricultural experts – not environmental authorities – would license new pesticides. Both DG XI and Green MEPs argued that leaving such decisions to a committee associated with agri-business amounted to the inmates taking over the asylum (MacKenzie 1991).

Decisions on *regional* policy also impact the environment. The conflict between EU environmental directives and decisions on EU regional funding for peripheral regions is widely documented (see Baldock and Wenning 1990; Mazey and Richardson 1994). In several instances, EU Structural Funds[9] are being used to finance infrastructure projects (such as roads and dams) that seriously degrade the environment. A growing awareness of this problem prompted an investigation by the EU's Court of Auditors in 1990–1. The resulting report offered a damning critique of the poor coordination between environmental and regional policies and the environmental degradation such non-integration had caused (Court of Auditors 1992).

Finally, the possible impact of *internal market policy* on environment has received considerable attention. Some see the potential for a stronger EU environmental policy in the 1992 project. The drive for an internal market gives the EU an ideal forum for creating an integrated policy in which ecological and economic goals are effectively integrated (see Keyes 1991: 8). But others point out the extent to which internal market goals contradict rather than complement the goals of environmental protection, and argue that the two cannot be integrated. Two possible negative effects of the 1992 project stand out. First, any significant increase in economic activity generated by the single market is likely to have an impact on the environment by increasing pressure for road-building, fuel consumption and waste disposal. Second, the removal of physical barriers has eased the way for increased road haulage and road traffic more generally. Moreover, removal of border controls means the abandonment of the easiest ways of controlling and monitoring certain sensitive commodities, including endangered species or hazardous waste.

Thus, overall progress towards integrating an environmental ethos into other EU policies has been slow and difficult. Whereas environmental policy has become more stringent in its own traditional domain, the impact of environmental considerations on other areas of policies often remains weak. The problems caused by deficient integration have been recognised for some time. The third EAP asserted the need to integrate concerns for the environment into the planning and development of a wide range of economic activities. The fifth EAP, *Towards Sustainability*, stated that '[g]iven the goal of achieving sustainable development, it seems only logical, if not essential, to apply an assessment of the environmental implications of all relevant policies, plans and programmes' (CEC 1992d: 66). The fifth EAP resulted in the creation of an Environmental Consultative Forum which advises the Commission on various environmental issues. Made up of 32 representatives from industry, consumer and environmental NGOs, and national and local authorities, the forum was designed to allow an exchange of information among the public and private sector and the Commission. Yet the Commission's mid-term review of the fifth EAP conceded that progress on integration has been slight (CEC 1996).

The Maastricht Treaty further promoted the integration of environmental and other policies. Whereas the SEA simply stated that environmental protection requirements are 'a component of the Community's other policies', the Maastricht Treaty's Article 130r(2) went further, stipulating that these requirements 'must be integrated into the definition and implementation of other Community policies'. More specifically, the Treaty went some way towards integrating regional and environmental decisions by establishing a 'Cohesion Fund', part of which assists southern Member States in meeting the costs of implementing EU environmental standards.

'Environmental integration' was also discussed during the 1996–7 Intergovernmental Conference (IGC) convened to revise the Maastricht Treaty. Member States considered proposals to integrate environmental protection requirements into all Community policies; to strengthen and clarify internal market provisions as they relate to the environment; and, most ambitiously, to make sustainable development one of the explicit objectives of the Union.

It is still too early to assess the durability of these good intentions. Efforts to incorporate environmental concerns may constitute fundamental change, or they may amount to nothing more than empty promises. It should be noted that past institutional or constitutional changes have done little to bring about policy integration.

The international dimension

A final area of environmental policy involves legislation and agreements that reach beyond EU borders. Because of the growing concern over global environmental issues, the Commission has been drawn into world wide discussions of transboundary environmental issues. EU environmental policy now has an inescapable international dimension.

In its early years, the EU was deemed competent to conclude an international convention only when this was expressly provided for in Treaty (i.e. in trade negotiations). But in a 1971 case, the European Court of Justice held that whenever the EU had passed legislation in a particular area, it had the right to handle external affairs relating to that field (Haigh 1992). Still, ambiguity remained regarding the proper competences in international environmental agreements. For example, the Commission played a major role in the drafting and implementation of the 1987 Montreal Protocol on Substances that Deplete the Ozone Layer. In a 1990 meeting in London at which amendments to this Protocol were agreed, Member States accepted that the EU Commission should have competence for negotiating the percentage reduction in the quantity of ozone depleting substances that could be produced, because the EU had already passed an EU regulation covering this. But it was also agreed at the same meeting that the EU had *no* competence over the related question of funds for developing countries, since it had not adopted any legislation in this area (Haigh 1992).

Currently, the EU is party to a wide array of international agreements, including those aimed at protecting regional seas, regulating the transport of hazardous chemicals, ensuring that timber brought into the EU is sourced from environmentally sound suppliers, and financing conservation projects. The EU is also involved in continuing international negotiations to halt the increasing emissions of greenhouse gases, especially carbon dioxide. At the United Nations Convention on the Environment and Development (Earth Summit) held in Rio de Janeiro in June 1992, the EU accepted a commitment to stabilise emissions of carbon dioxide at their 1990 levels by the year 2000. In the run-up to the 1997 International Conference on global warming in Kyoto the EU pushed for reducing greenhouse emissions in 2010 to a level 15 per cent below that of 1990. The EU's efforts to curb carbon dioxide emissions have been hindered so far by the inability to agree an EU-wide CO_2 tax (Zito 1995). The case of the CO_2 tax illustrates that the Commission has moved on from reconciling needs of Member States to playing a role at the global level, but that intense disagreements remain in determining when the EU has negotiating rights in international environmental negotiations and when those rights override national prerogatives.

V   EU AND MEMBER STATES – PROBLEMS OF IMPLEMENTATION

The preceding section suggested that EU policy-making is often marked by substantial political conflict about the proper line to be drawn between national and EU powers. The consequences of such conflict is seen most clearly in difficulties surrounding the implementation of environmental policies.

Member States are formally involved in the formulation of EU policy at the level of COREPER[10] and the Council of Ministers. But Member States are also the key players in the successful incorporation and implementation of EU environmental and related policies. As mentioned, the EU's most successful policy tool generally has been the directive. Because directives are binding only as to the result to be achieved, leaving national authorities to choose forms and methods of application, EU environmental law can be applied flexibly by developing proposals that accommodate existing national legislation and administrative practices. The price of such flexibility is often policy incoherence, lax implementation and even outright non-compliance (Liberatore 1991: 290; Collins and Earnshaw 1992). It is widely agreed that EU environmental law is 'environmentally stringent, comprehensive and far-ranging, but ... also widely flouted' (Anderson 1991: 182). To illustrate the point, in 1995 no Member State had successfully implemented all environmental legislation. Denmark and The Netherlands came the closest with a 98 per cent implementation rate; Belgium brought up the rear with a success rate of 83 per cent.[11]

One difficulty is that the Member States vary widely in their experience of adopting and implementing environmental legislation on the national level (Keyes 1991; Sbragia 1996). For instance, Denmark, Germany and The Netherlands have developed strong environmental protection policies independently of EU influence and are often the leading forces behind strict environmental standards. Poorer EU states such as Spain, Greece and Portugal usually adopt environmental legislation only when prompted by EU directives. Generally, the position of the poorer states is that the stringency of EU regulations stymies economic growth and development. Thus, a basic cleavage in EU environmental politics is between northern countries who stress legislative, standards-setting measures and the southern countries who favour more expensive spending programmes to remedy problems such as soil erosion, forest fires and coastal pollution (CEC 1990: 17).

When Member States do formally adopt EU legislation (i.e. incorporate it into national law), actual compliance is often patchy. First, relations between different levels of government within Member States represent a potential obstacle (see Bomberg 1994). The Commission has limited powers for directly ensuring that sub-national units implement EU environmental directives in a timely and satisfactory way. Second, administrative styles influence the chance of successful implementation. The Member State that most often has resisted the Commission's incursions into new realms of environmental policy has been the UK. The 'British problem' has had as much to do with style as the substance of new proposals. For example, in worker and product safety related to the environment, the notion of enforcing stringent and mandatory pan-European standards of the sort proposed by the Commission is alien to the British civil service, which is used to regulation based on voluntary agreements and 'gentleman's understandings' between government and industry.

The key problem, however, is that the Commission's position in enforcing EU legislation is weak. It is a small bureaucracy that is chronically understaffed in parts of many DGs, especially DG XI. Moreover, the Commission lacks any 'green' force of environmental inspectors. This lack was the motivation behind the attempt of the EU's former Environment Commissioner, Carlos Ripa Di Meana, to ensure that the European Environmental Agency develop an 'inspectorate' arm to monitor implementation and compliance by

Member States. His request was denied; the EEA, at least for the time being, has no enforcement powers.

The Commission usually learns of violations of EU environmental law – or laws related to the environment – only if it receives a complaint from an individual, NGO or other interested party (such as a rival industrial firm). These reporting 'agents' are more vigilant in some countries than in others. While the Commission received more complaints about the UK than any other Member State in 1990, the UK actually ranked fourth among Member States in having the lowest number of outstanding cases pending for violation of EU environmental rules.[12]

In many cases, public complaints provide the impetus for infringements proceedings by the Commission against Member States. But the lengthy information-gathering process, combined with the heavy caseload of the European Court of Justice (ECJ), explains why an average of about four years separates the arrival of a complaint about an alleged violation of an environmental directive and a ruling by the ECJ.

Before resorting to the Court, the Commission may, in some cases, accept a government's case for delay. This step is usually taken because of the high costs that full implementation would entail. For example, in September 1992, British car manufacturers were given a 12 month exemption from environmental legislation requiring cars to be fitted with catalytic converters by January 1993. The depressed state of the car market left manufacturers and dealers with a large number of unfitted cars. To save the costs of unsold cars, 160,000 new cars not fitted with catalytic converters were allowed to be sold during 1993.[13]

A final implementation problem involves what happens when the Commission is *successful* in proposing and imposing the controls that are decided upon. The Commission is frequently criticised for interfering in an unnecessarily high-handed way. The British media in particular is fond of stories about the British 'way of life' under threat from Brussels bureaucrats. This portrayal particularly affects the image of the Commission and ultimately damages its authority. This image problem has become much more serious since the difficulties surrounding ratification of the Maastricht Treaty. In response, the Commission has adopted a less active role in initiating legislation and a less assertive role in enforcing legislation, including that related to the environment (Fitzmaurice 1994: 186).

In sum, implementation of EU environmental policy is inhibited by wider disagreements between the EU and its Member States over policy scope, content and direction. It is further complicated by disparities in levels of environmental priorities in different Member States, considerable differences in institutional structure, different styles of policy implementation, and lack of effective enforcement procedures.

VI CONCLUSION: ASSESSING EU ENVIRONMENTAL POLICY

This chapter has shown how the growth of green movements in Europe was paralleled by the steady expansion of the EU's competence in the area of environmental protection. From an essentially economic community with no firm legal basis for dealing with such issues, the EU has taken on an increasingly central role in policy sectors related to the environment and quality of life. Over the past 20 years, the EU has built up a substantial body of environmental law and has even embraced some green ideals such as the notion of sustainable development. Behind the 200 environmental directives that tackle particular policy issues lies a strategic policy framework, provided by EAPs and Treaty articles. EU environmental policy can also be credited for having pushed a significant proportion of EU Member States further than they would otherwise have gone in areas of environmental protection, while creating provisions that allow other Member States to pursue stricter environmental standards than mandated by EU law. Moreover, the Union's environmental regulation has provided obvious advantages in combating transboundary pollution. In short, it is not inaccurate to say that the EU has 'greened' environmental policy by increasing both its scope and strength in areas related to pollution control.

Yet Greens and other critics would highlight several factors that inhibit the success of an effective environmental policy and preclude the label of 'green' being attached to the EU. The first barrier to 'greenness' might be termed the 'integration gap', that is, the failure of environmental considerations to be integrated into decisions made in other policy sectors such as regional funding, transport or agriculture and the internal market.

The second factor inhibiting policy development in environmental and related issues is the 'implementation gap' described above. Whilst an impressive legislative framework has been built up, there is no corresponding structure for environmental management. As a result, the degradation of the EU's environment has continued.

Third, whilst EU legislation might raise standards of 'laggard' states, it might also effectively pull down or weaken the environmental legislation of 'leader' states such as Denmark, Sweden or The Netherlands. This is a real concern of Greens in these 'leader' Member States. Indeed, fears that Sweden would have to accept diluted environmental regulations was a primary reason for the Swedish Greens' opposition to EU membership (Burchell 1996).

More generally, EU policy-making structures and processes remain far from meeting green goals. The subordinate position of the EP to the other institutions of the EU highlights the 'democratic deficit' of the entire EU structure. The EP – the EU's only directly elected body – wields the least amount of authority in a policy-making process dominated by the Commission and Council. For the Greens, this is an untenable situation: 'a monopolistic legislative process from which the public is excluded'.[14]

Similarly, EU policy-making can appear technocratic, bureaucratic and remote – features anathemic to green values. EU policy-making appears 'technocratic' because it depends on the participation of unelected technical and scientific experts. It also necessarily relies on interaction between the national and EU bureaucracies to formulate and enact policies. To Greens and other critics, the result is an EU run by an 'unaccountable technocracy'.

In conclusion, despite its comparatively strong record of environmental legislation, the EU has not 'gone green'. But this conclusion hardly diminishes the EU's fundamental importance in determining the environmental future and quality of Europe. In particular, the growing role of the EU has prompted a wide variety of green actors to seek access to and reform EU institutions and policies. These actors and their visions of Europe are analysed in the next chapter.

3 Green visions of Europe

INTRODUCTION

This chapter explores alternative conceptions of Europe and notions of a true European 'community' or 'union' as embraced by green parties on both the national and EU levels. Invoking principles from ecological and regionalist movements, the Greens offer a provocative critique of current EU structures, which reflects wider concerns about centralisation, bureaucratisation and degradation of the natural environment. They propose a 'Europe of the Regions' as an alternative construction. Yet this chapter reveals that a general ambivalence and lack of agreement among the Greens in European policy has precluded the formulation of a coherent 'green' Euro-political alternative.

Section I outlines the central concepts that underpin the Greens' vision of Europe. Section II introduces the notion of a 'Europe of the Regions', which the Greens put forward as their alternative to the current structure of Europe. In Section III, the inherent contradictions and problems that beset this alternative view are examined. Section IV analyses attempts by green parties to forge and act upon a common view. The conclusion considers the opportunies and challenges represented by green visions of Europe.

I GREEN CONCEPTIONS OF EUROPE

Five overlapping 'green tenets' provide the foundation for the Greens' alternative conceptions of Europe. The most important include: decentralisation, ecological sustainability, community/grassroots democracy, the 'global–local nexus', and diversity. These concepts derive much of their character from earlier movements and political forces in Europe. Drawing primarily on the European platforms of several different national green parties,[1] this section underlines the historical precedents and continuing relevance of these concepts.

Decentralisation

All green parties express the need for decentralisation. Fears of political centralisation in Europe and concomitant calls for decentralisation date back centuries (see Rokkan and Urwin 1982). The works of radical federalist writers such Denis de Rougemont exercise a particularly powerful influence on the Greens. A fervent supporter of decentralisation and champion of European culture and federation, de Rougemont pushed for the decentralisation of the modern nation-state and the establishment of multi-functional 'participation entities' in the 1960s. De Rougemont (1966: 423) viewed the nation-state as the main hindrance to a peaceful European order:

> The division of modern Europe into nations . . . does not translate our true regional, religious, ideological, linguistic diversities, does not make them fruitful. On the contrary, it accounts for the feeling of paralysis and decadence that prevailed in the first half of this century.

In the 1970s, the decentralisation philosophy expressed by de Rougemont became increasingly popular among student activists and youth groups. For groups such as the Young European Federalists, a federation of regions accorded with basic aspirations for enhanced participation in smaller political units (Marks 1992: 213). Young federalists demanded a comprehensive democratisation of society through decentralisation and direct citizen access. These groups differentiated their demands for integration from both the 'top-down' neofunctional view of integration, in which integration was driven by elites (see Haas 1965; Lindberg 1963), to a realist-intergovernmental view of integration focused on national interest and leaders (see Moravcsik 1991; Keohane and Hoffmann 1991).

One notably strong advocate was German Green co-founder Petra Kelly. As early as 1979, Kelly made clear her support of the regionalist, federalist conceptions put forth by the Young European Federalists. She emphasised that federalist philosophy meshed well with the green priorities of decentralisation, wide co-determination and grassroots democracy. According to Dierker (1987: 15–16), Kelly's support helps explain the ease with which these federalist concepts made their way into the German Greens' 1980 party platform.

Throughout the 1980s, the principle of decentralisation featured prominently in green conceptions of Europe. Like the federalists before them, the Greens argued that industrialised states were over-bureaucratised and too hierarchical in structure. They opposed tendencies in industrial nations towards centralisation, which thwarted the initiative of citizens, and instead advocated decentralisation and a simplification of administrative units. For example, French eco-logists viewed the deterioration of the environment as the 'inevitable consequence of . . . an overcentralised French state' (Dalton 1993: 51). The German Greens were among the first green party to express these sentiments. In their first national party programme, the Greens asserted that 'it would be quite contrary to the principles of an ecological policy if we were to try and solve all problems uniformly and through centralisation' (die Grünen 1980: 24–5).

Echoing de Rougemont, the Greens argue that the modern nation-state is inherently dangerous because its centralised power 'is in-evitably used for economic competition, large scale exploitation and massive wars' (Spretnak and Capra 1986: 48). Thus, the German Greens officially opposed German unification and instead advocated a rethinking of the relationship between East and West Germany (see Gransow 1989: 143–4). They argued that Bonn's insistence on one German nation was a primary source of inter-German and European tension. In 1986, the Greens charged that:

> The present federal government refuses to draw the consequences from nearly 40 years of different development and to recognise the existence of the two states. Doggedly it persists with the claim to be the sole political representative in all things German. By insisting that the German question has remained open – an issue which has hardened into an ideology – it has obstructed all progress in German–German relations.
>
> (die Grünen 1986: 2)

Instead, the German Greens emphasised the need to restructure both Europe and 'global society' so that unification would become un-necessary and the borders between the two Germanies would lose their divisive effect. Pushing for a new European order, the Greens 'abandoned the ghost of a German Reich, and with it, the goal of reunification' (Vaughn 1988: 84). More generally, Greens argued that not larger, but smaller, decentralised, units of population would result in a safer world on all counts.

In contrast to other advocates of European unity and integration (see Butler 1986; Cecchini 1988), the Greens warn against the danger of a 'United States of Europe' or a 'Superpower Europe'. The British Greens (Green Party 1994: 3) instead demand a loose confederation: 'Our objective is a European confederation of culturally diverse and economically self-reliant regions.' For some Greens, even the peaceful federation envisioned by de Rougemont and other federalists is not decentralised enough: 'We want a regional network rather than a federation. That is, we want to see the competence of the regions enlarged rather than the power of the centralised Community' (Schwalba-Hoth quoted in Ricketts 1986: 2–3).

Ecological sustainability

Ecological sustainability makes up the second plank of the Greens' European vision. Essentially, ecological sustainability is based on the belief that 'our finite Earth' places limits on industrial growth and consumerism (Dobson 1995: 72). Greens argue that human aspirations of ever increasing industrial growth and consumption cannot be fulfilled. Moreover, '[t]he concept of scarcity is fundamental' and resistant to technological fixes: 'It is rooted in the biophysical realities of a finite planet, ruled and limited by entropy and ecology' (Irvine and Ponton 1988: 26; see also die Grünen 1984b: 15–16).

The term 'ecological sustainability' became fashionable in the 1970s and 1980s (see O'Riordan 1981). However, antecedents are found in earlier conservationist and ecology movements. One important precursor was the German *Naturschutz* movement (1890s–1930s) which sought to protect nature, cultivate rural landscape, and preserve the environment of the traditional village (Merkl 1987: 134). The British Greens have a similar historical attachment to conservationist movements. In the late 1800s, several British groups were organised as part of a wider movement to protect landscapes, ancient monuments and wild birds (Young 1993: 17).

For the Greens and their forefathers, the 'natural world' ought to help determine the political, economic and social life of communities. Kirkpatrick Sale (1985: 42) identifies a sustainable 'bioregional paradigm' in green thinking which requires that inhabitants 'get to know the land around them, respect it, and work with it'. Greens attempt to realise this paradigm by minimising resource use and aiming at sustainability through self-sufficiency.[2]

British green party manifestos have underlined this point: 'The Green vision of Europe will mean the rejection of the economics of "more and more" and the adoption of the economics of "enough"' (Ecology Party 1984: 4; see also Green Party 1989). The French Greens have been even more adamant. Their vision of Europe 'implies a critique of a civilisation founded on the thirst for power and accumulation of material things, plundering the resources of the planet and menacing the survival of humanity' (Les Verts 1993: 2).

Ecological sustainability is central to the Greens' view of Europe in general and EU policies in particular. Greens have consistently urged that the 'current economic priorities such as the control of inflation and the creation of economic growth will have to take a back seat to the goal of ecological sustainability' (Green Party 1993: 15; see also Les Verts 1994a: 18). More specifically, the French Greens have insisted that market policies must include the 'integration of social and environmental costs in the price of goods, most notably through specific eco-taxes, the most important of which is a tax on non-renewable energy' (Les Verts 1994a: 17).

The importance of ecological sustainability is also evident in the Greens' position on the EU's Common Agriculture Policy (CAP). From a green perspective, current agricultural practices in Europe are unsustainable and unacceptable. Intensive chemical-based farming pollutes waterways, encourages erosion and upsets ecological balances through insensitive pest control (Dobson 1995: 115). In their 1984 manifesto, the British Greens described the EU as:

> a profoundly unecological body. It promotes an agricultrual system that relies on the heavy use of fossil fuels and artificial fertilisers; a system which is damaging the long-term fertility of the soil and steadily destroying the countryside.
>
> (Ecology Party 1984: 3)

Or, as expressed more vehemently by the German Greens:

> After 30 years of CAP the results are disastrous. . . . The use of nitrogen fertilizers has increased fivefold and the use of pesticides threefold since [the] CAP was introduced. . . . [The CAP] destroys ecologically sound ways of farming, decentralised distribution systems and healthy food.
>
> (die Grünen 1989c: 8–9)

Instead, the Greens demand a sustainable agriculture involving less machinery, more hands, and more respect towards the ecological needs of the region.

Community and grassroots democracy

The introduction of a 'community' different from that embodied in the European Community/Union is of utmost importance to the

Greens. For the Greens, the concept of community is compatible with decentralisation and grassroots democracy. The Greens see a sustainable society on the European level as one operating through numerous grassroots communities. For instance, German Green co-founder Rudolf Bahro (1986: 94ff) envisions a political life founded on 'communitarian decentralisation'. At the centre of this alternative lifestyle are smaller communities or communes which would rely on their own resources and would instil a sense of local loyalty and participation. Whatever their precise label or form, these communities imply a major shift in the loci of authority to smaller decision-making units.

The Greens admittedly were not the first movement to emphasise the importance of community. Dalton (1993: 42–3) traces the roots of the French environmental movement to a romanticist trend developed in the mid-1900s. Writers such as Chateaubriand, Hugo and Vigny shared a romantic fascination with strong pastoral traditions (*champêtres*) and rural communities. In Germany, many earlier movements valued the idea of community, or *Gemeinschaft*. Indeed, detractors of the German Greens are quick to draw parallels between the Greens and the earlier Romantic movement, the *völkish-bündish* movement of the nineteenth century, or the 'blood and soil' tendencies of the Nazis (Bodeman 1985–6: 149–51; Bramwell 1989). Parallels do exist. Like the Greens, these precursor movements not only emphasised feelings of brotherhood and *Gemeinschaft*, but also shared the Greens' awe of nature and protest against industrialisation.

Yet the Greens distinguish themselves from these earlier movements in important ways. Whereas the Romantics were preoccupied with defending the social order and institutions of aristocracy, Greens stress egalitarianism and grassroots participation (Merkl 1987: 132). Moreover, the notion of 'brotherhood' espoused by the Romantics must encompass 'sisterhood' if it is to be acceptable to the Greens. Whereas the *völkish-bündish* organisations emphasised a strict hierarchic order, the Greens decry the same. Green movements and parties' internal organisation attests to their laboured efforts to remain anti-hierarchic and democratic. In short, the Greens claim that community without grassroots democracy is not a green community.

This green sense of community is expressed in numerous aspects of green European policy. Precisely because Europe is so large, argue the Greens, more emphasis on community representation and grassroots input is imperative. The Greens charge that the increasing centralisation and 'bureaucratisation' of Europe has betrayed any sense of community: 'For what actually developed in Brussels – far away from the people and their regions – was an inflated bureaucracy, costly, incomprehensible and unchecked by any kind of democratic control' (die Grünen 1984a: 6).

The Greens criticise the EU for its lack of communal emphasis and embrace the notion of subsidiarity as a way to encourage grassroots democracy. Along with many regional authorities and politicians, Greens interpret subsidiarity as 'the devolution of powers from Brussels and Strasbourg not to a national but to a subnational or regional level' (Harvie 1994: 1). The British Greens (Green Party 1993: 17) object that 'the EC project is being shaped exclusively for the benefit of large corporations and the banking systems: the needs and concerns of ordinary people are being sold short'. Similarly, Les Verts (1994a: 4–5) warn against the development of a 'Europe of merchants' at the expense of the common (wo)man. They argue that whereas rules on the free movement of people within the single market are not always adhered to, toxic waste circulates freely.

The Greens contend that the European Community/Union is neither 'European' nor a 'Community'. They reject a Europe dominated by the common market, arguing that 'Europe is more than the EC', and that 'demands for cooperation and solidarity don't stop at bloc borders' (die Grünen 1989c: 3). Greens across Europe therefore embrace enlargement of the EU to include Eastern European countries and 'anyone else who wanted to join' (Green Party 1994: 7).

Global–local nexus

According to the Greens, a new global order is needed to deal with cross-national concerns of peace, social welfare and the environment. Key to this new global order is the recognition of the obsolescence of the nation-state. For the Greens, the nation-state is both too large and too small. They fear not only the 'omnipotence' of the state (in, say, the case of censorship and police power) but also its 'impotence' in solving environmental problems such as the pollution of rivers and the atmosphere (see Les Verts 1989: 18).

To a certain extent, these criticisms draw from earlier internationalist and anti-imperialist movements. As early as the 1930s, de Rougemont had argued that as a colonial power Europe had spread the formula of the nation-state through the entire world: 'It is therefore Europe's duty, in these closing years of the twentieth century, to show through the living example of the regions that the

Nation-State is an obsolete, murderous and colonising formula, imperialist by its very nature' (1983: 206).

For his part, Italian Green Alexander Langer saw nation-states as:

> both too big and too small. They are too big to allow real participatory democracy, to respect the requirements and the powers of local communities. . . . And they are too small to be able to deal effectively with some of the great contemporary problems such as the environment or peace and disarmament.
>
> (quoted in GGEP 1991c: 3)

British Greens are equally critical of the nation-state:

> If we are serious in our desire to tackle the problems of planetary abuse which characterise industrial societies then we have to reject the idea that there is any hope to be had from a 'unity' based upon the defence of national sovereignty.
>
> (Ecology Party 1984: 3)

The British Greens insist on the need to

> promote and develop a sense of international responsibility based on the common understanding that it is only by determined joint action that we will begin to solve the problems of ecological destruction and lay the foundations of a sustainable future.
>
> (Ecology Party 1984: 3)

The German Greens echo this sentiment: 'The existing political decision-making structures are completely inappropriate as a means of solving European and international problems in a way that accords with the principles of ecology and grassroots democracy' (die Grünen 1984b: 9).

What distinguishes the Greens from earlier internationalist groups is their emphasis on the link between international and local events. As the Greens see it, a new 'global order' 'cannot be prescribed from above. It can only be brought about through the responsible efforts of all people, beginning at local and regional levels in accordance with the motto "think globally, act locally!"' (die Grünen 1984b: 39). Thus, unlike some of their internationalist precursors who called for a world federation or government, the Greens abhor the idea of a centralised authority to deal with transnational problems. Indeed, Greens fear the overwhelming power of a European super-state. In particular, the Greens criticise the EU's post-Maastricht increased powers in the areas of justice and home affairs. Instead, the locus of power needs to be devolved to the grassroots rather than national or supranational institutions. The Greens feel that it is 'important that grassroots movements in Europe have begun to cooperate beyond borders and blocs without reference to their governments' (die Grünen 1989b: 7).

Greens envision a new global order which recognises the link between local and international events and economies. This 'nexus' in the Greens' vision is reflected in their view on aid to the developing world. Greens argue for a full-scale revamping of EU development aid. In particular, they demand that aid be 'linked with ecologically sustainable development, not with economic restructuring in order to meet the needs of the global market. We want a renegotiation of trade agreements to promote ecological sustainability, social justice and self-reliant local economies' (Green Party 1994: 2).

Greens desire an alternative Europe in which power is devolved to local communities. Yet, their 'think globally, act locally' maxim is fundamentally problematic as a guide to European action. Because the EU is neither global nor local, it is often neglected as a forum for the pursuit of green objectives. At least from a philosophical point of view, many Greens find the idea of political action at the EU level – where power continues to accrue – fundamentally unexciting.

Diversity

Advocating a 'holistic multicultural society' (die Grünen 1989c: 29), the Greens consider their celebration of diversity a primary factor separating their views from those put forth by more conventional parties on the one hand, and extreme right protest parties on the other. For the Greens, respect for individual rights and diversity is a prerequisite for the holistic multi-cultural society they desire. Peaceful coexistence among and between societies is only possible with mutual tolerance of ethnic, social, political and sexual minority groups.

This positive stress on diversity was derived in part from the writings of earlier European philosophers, historians and federalists. Writers as diverse as Jose Ortega y Gasset, Jean-Paul Sartre and Ernst Jünger agreed that tolerance for diversity was predicated on respect for individual rights (see Loose 1974; Gerdes 1984). For these writers, the promotion of diversity was a path to guaranteed human rights, protection from state encroachment of liberties, and a check on virulent nationalism. Ernst Jünger argued further that liberty thrives among the cultural diversity found in a people's history, speech and race, customs and habits, art and religion. As he expressed it: 'Here there cannot be too many colors on the palette' (1948: 46).

For federalist de Rougemont, the values of diversity and unity were inseparable. He pushed for the unity of Europe 'in so far as it aims at federating our differences, not ironing them out [and] making life uniform through the continent' (1965: 63). De Rougemont blamed the nation-state system for transforming diversity into 'rigid, morbid divisions' (1965: 64). Instead, argued de Rougemont, the diversities should be recognised, even celebrated. This would allow antagonisms to be resolved by practical compromise, which would be 'embodied in an institution or method which overcame the tension without suppressing it' (de Rougemont 1965: 48). In short, the only unity possible in Europe was a strong yet flexible union that promoted 'unity in diversity'.[3]

Views remarkably similar to these are expressed in green parties' political platforms. For the German Greens (die Grünen/Bündnis 90 1994: 48), a peaceful world order must be based on individual freedoms, democratic self-determination and the safeguarding of human rights at all levels. This sentiment was echoed by Agalev spokesman Ludo Dierickx, who warned against allowing regions to be 'annexed by the extreme right' and reminded his compatriots that 'there has never been a multicultural fascism' (quoted in GGEP 1991c: 8).

The French Greens' critique of EU single market policy also underlines further the importance of diversity: 'The actual working of the single market does not permit the achievement of objectives of regional solidarity, reductions in inequality, and a Europe of diverse languages and cultures' (Les Verts 1994a: 19). In fact, Les Verts go so far as to push for more widespread use of the transnational, polyglot language 'Esperanto', which is mostly a curiosity for language students. The use of Esperanto would allow 'communication between citizens on an equal footing, without prejudice to regional or national languages' (Les Verts 1994a: 19).

More generally, the phrase 'unity in diversity' became a touchstone of green politics, and the principle was later incorporated into the parties' European campaign platforms and speeches. The title of the French Greens' 1989 Euro platform – '*Les Verts et l'europe. Pour une Europe des regions et des peuples solidaires*'[4] – underlined the need for solidarity and embrace of diversity. The German Greens were even more explicit. In their 1984 election to the EP, they campaigned for 'the recognition and promotion of the cultural diversity of the different nationalities and historical regions of Europe' (die Grünen, 1984b: 39). In 1989, their campaign brochure insisted that 'diversity in Europe must precede unity and, indeed, build unity. Unity in Diversity!' (die Grünen 1989b: 11).

As a further example of their intent, the German Greens nominated a Stinti, a Gypsy without any citizenship, as their top candidate in the 1989 EP campaign. As a non-citizen, the candidate was entitled neither to vote nor to take office if elected. The nomination of a Stinti was thus a symbolic gesture. The Greens sought to spotlight and oppose what they saw as the xenophobia of West German society. Green member Daniel Cohn-Bendit remarked that this was a 'conscious move'. The party wanted to declare themselves 'proponents of a social vision'.[5] Similarly, many candidates on French Green's 1989 Europe list were selected specifically to represent the cause of second generation immigrants (Hainsworth 1990: 96).

Taken together, the five principles analysed in this section underpin the Greens' alternative conceptions of Europe. In their statements and speeches, green parties standing for EP election have delivered a scathing critique of established parties' conceptions of European integration and structures. In the eyes of most Greens, the structures of the EU and European integration violate all of the key principles of their alternative vision of Europe. The result is a centralised non-ecological body incapable of bringing about the social and ecological transformation necessary for the survival of Europe and the globe (die Grünen/Bündnis 1994: 23).

II   EUROPE OF THE REGIONS: THE GREENS' ALTERNATIVE

The green alternative to the European Union as presently constituted is best described as a 'Europe of the Regions' (EoR). The EoR conception respects each of the key green tenets that inform green visions of Europe. It also requires a redrawing of the map of Europe. First, it demands radical decentralisation. At its core, an EoR features a loose confederation of regions. Europe would not be administered from a central power. Instead, power would be distributed throughout a confederation of regions that were 'culturally defined, historically developed, self-determined but intertwined' (die Grünen 1984a: 38; 1989b: 11; Green Party 1994: 7).

Second, the notion of ecological sustainability would serve as the guiding principle. The French Greens noted that:

In the face of the meaninglessness which has seized our European societies and at the moment when the recent surprises of history have rendered possible a new foundation of Europe, ecology in all of its dimensions can constitute a path towards a unified and pluralist continent.

(Les Verts 1994a: 66)

Third, an EoR would feature grassroots communities as its base. Stressing the grassroots character of their conception of Europe, Petra Kelly said of the Greens: 'We seek an ecological, decentralised, self-administered, nonmilitary Europe of the regions. . . . Long live Europe from below!' (quoted in Stuth 1984: 64).

The Green's vision would also be guided by recognition of the global–local nexus. 'We need a new vision for building a global consensus that will deal with the growing divide between rich and poor, the degradation of the ecology of the planet and the increasing instability of the global economy' (Green Party 1993: 19).

The EoR conception also features the principle of 'unity in diversity'. The Greens believe that the wealth and potential of Europe lies in the cultural diversity of the various regions. In an EoR, cultural communities would determine the boundaries of these regions. In other words, the Greens consider nation-state borders as arbitrary; boundaries in an EoR would be determined on the basis of cultural and linguistic communities. These boundaries would, however, remain fluid. Close cooperation between communities would 'transcend all borders and blocs' (die Grünen 1989b: 7).

In their 1994 EP election programme, the German Greens argue that reconstructing Europe along the lines of an EoR would bring three grassroots advantages. First, it would strengthen regional decision-making for issues that crossed local boundaries but did not require national or supranational action. Second, an EoR would create a base of decision-making more accountable to citizens. Third, it would protect diversity by providing a level at which people felt 'connected' without reverting into jingoism (die Grünen/Bündnis 1994: 10)

In sum, the Greens view the EoR as their official alternative to an 'EC of bureaucracies, bombs and butter-mountains' (die Grünen 1984a: 38). Invoking principles of decentralisation, community, globalism, sustainability and 'unity through diversity', the EoR promises to be a 'peaceful, nonaligned decentralised Europe made up of manageable administrative areas' (die Grünen 1989b: 7).

Politically, the concerns addressed by the EoR are widespread among Green supporters and non-supporters alike. In particular, the Greens' conception of Europe appeals to regionalist sentiments and fears of centralisation and unchecked state power. Dirk Gerdes (1984) asserts that, throughout the post-war era, regionalism has appeared as a protest movement against political, administrative and socio-economic centralism in Western Europe. By the mid-1980s, over 50 regional movements were active in Europe (Heuglin 1986: 439). This number had increased by the mid-1990s, as regionalism sometimes dominated national political debates, as it did in Scotland, Belgium and Spain (Scott *et al.* 1994; Hooghe 1995; Heywood 1996). Ascherson (1992: 31) highlights 'myriads of struggling local identities and linguistic pockets which now feel that their cultures will not survive unless they have political home rule to protect them'.[6]

Other public fears and political demands are embodied in the Greens' alternative conception of Europe. Many Europeans share trepidation about ever more complex industrialisation, especially the large-scale technologies and environmental dangers it may produce (see Lodge 1990: 214; Sarkar 1986: 237). Leaving aside environmental concern, the EoR taps into fears over the growing distance between European citizens and elites. The difficulties surrounding ratification of the Maastricht Treaty on European Union were widely acknowledged to stem from public fears that echo the green critique of an EU 'far from its citizens and out of touch from the common people' (die Grünen 1984a: 6). Several unlikely allies of the Greens are also attracted to aspects of the Greens' alternative conception. For instance, the EoR's emphasis on decentralisation and small-scale, sustainable farming methods, as well as its implicit critique of the CAP, has appealed to some smaller farmers. The CAP favours larger farmers, while '[t]he farmer with little to sell, either because his farm is small or because he is situated in difficult farming country, benefits proportionately less' (Marsh 1989: 156).

The political importance of regionalism and regional identities is recognised in the Maastricht Treaty. It provides for a Committee of the Regions which consists of 189 representatives from local and regional government. The Committee is designed to increase substantially the consultative role of regional and local interests in the EU decision-making process. The Treaty enables the Committee to present proposals for directives to the Commission and requires that the Committee be consulted on relevant proposals for legislation. Whilst its powers are still only advisory and its early performance disappointing, the Committee represents an important step towards more systematic regional representation within the EU (see Bomberg and Peterson 1998).

Conceptually, the EoR model offers a historically grounded, potentially relevant framework for a rapidly changing Europe. The Greens present – albeit vaguely – a contending model of Europe based on regionalism and decentralisation. In the mid-1980s, Heuglin (1986: 439) criticised the lack of conceptual attention to regionalism in Europe: 'Due to a centrist *Weltanschauung*, both politicians and political scientists have been slow to recognise decentralisation as a general trend.' Since that time, scholarly literature on regionalism, territoriality and center–periphery relations has increased dramatically.[7] These new studies of territoriality indicate a growing interest in the importance of regionalist notions, including those originally put forth by the Greens. In short, the rapid, dramatic changes occurring in Europe, many of which are linked to regionalist or centrifugal forces, suggest a need for discussion of alternative, contending models of Europe. The Greens' EoR conception offers one such alternative blueprint.

III CONTRADICTIONS, CONFLICTS AND NEGLECT

Despite its innate appeal, the Greens' concept of an EoR is marred by internal and external conflicts. The first major weakness of the Greens' notion is that its building blocks or major tenets are themselves problematic or contradictory. For instance, decentralisation is perhaps the primary tenet of a green EoR. That political responsibility be devolved to local communities is a fundamental, but problematic principle of green thinking. It is never made clear how such a decentralised society would be coordinated, i.e. how relations between and within communities would be universalised and regulated. Critics accuse the Greens of overestimating the intrinsic value of decentralisation. Boris Frankel (1987: 56) asks whether economies in decentralised entities would not simply 'grow into capitalist markets with all the inherent qualities of inequality, exploitation, and so forth'.

The theme of diversity is also problematic. The Greens believe that their alternative Europe will not merely tolerate the diversities of human culture, it will thrive on them. The Greens thus embrace uncritically the implicit tension between the goals of collective unity and individual diversity. They feel they can reconcile this tension by balancing the egalitarianism of modern individualism with an organic holistic view of nature and the community. This balancing act is visible in the German Greens' 'unity in diversity' campaign theme, and also in green parties' internal organisation. The Greens pride themselves on the alternative, open structure of party conventions and meetings. Their consensual decision-making process respects dissenting views and minority opinions. Yet the Greens underestimate the tension between their call for diversity, and the potential rigidity of norms and standards they seek to achieve. They attempt to paper over what Dobson (1995: 25) flags as a fundamental contradiction: 'how to have a conception of the Good Society that requires people behaving in a certain way, and yet advertise for diverse forms of behaviour'.

This contradiction is also problematical for the French Greens, who on the one hand call for diversity but on the other hand find it hard to resist the French nationalist backlash against foreign 'cultural imperialism' stoked by the clash between the US and EU over trade in audio-visual products within the General Agreement on Tariffs and Trade (GATT). In their 1994 manifesto, the French Greens critique 'in a fundamental manner the ideology of free exchange which is at the base of the GATT. Free exchange signifies . . . the disappearance of economic, geographic and cultural diversity. It's the uncontested reign of a "McDonald's/Coca Cola" civilization' (Les Verts 1994a: 27).

A second factor damaging the Greens' European vision is the near total neglect of 'Europe' by national green parties. The alternative concept of an EoR has been neither widely accepted nor prominently featured in the platforms of European green parties. At the national level in particular, the concept remains vague or unexplored. A closer look at the German Greens' European and national elections illustrates this general point.

In the German Greens' first national party programme in 1980, the EU was not even mentioned. The Greens were able to agree on a general stance towards Europe only in March 1984, at the national assembly in Karlsruhe. Bemoaning this 'provincial' slant of the Greens, co-founder Petra Kelly noted that 'most of us have wasted a lot of energy on our own (domestic) problems instead of tackling problems outside'.[8] The idea of an EoR was advocated by the German Greens in its 1984 EP election campaign. But this portion of the Greens' European programme met with widespread disinterest, was inadequately discussed, and lacked concrete formulation. Presenting 'Europe of the Regions' to the party base and public, the Greens limited themselves to a critique of the EU and an extremely general exposition of the future 'Europe of the Regions'. In an internal party memo outlining her thoughts on Europe, Petra Kelly wondered aloud about this lack of agreement: 'We strive for an alternative Europe – but which one?? We must be clear on this' (Kelly 1984a: 3).

Although Green representatives such as Vollmer (1984) had much to say about the positive cultural and geographic diversity emphasised in an EoR, they offered no clear alternative structural or procedural strategies for delivering it. 'Europe of the Regions' thus remained an overly vague abstraction. Later attempts to make the EoR conception more concrete confronted the same obstacles of disinterest and disarray on the national level, and were no more successful. As green member Brigitte Heinrich noted in 1986:

> What in the world might a green-alternative 'Europe of the Regions' look like concretely? Obviously, a decentralisation of the decision-making process, regional energy programmes, etc.... But it's been ... years and we are still facing these same vague conceptions.
>
> (quoted in Wolf 1986: 68)

These 'same vague conceptions' were still present in the 1989 European election campaign. The German Greens promised to campaign for: 'a Europe of dissolution of military alliances, of self restraint, of cooperation between regions and international solidarity. Above all, we campaign for a common restructuring of Europe' (die Grünen 1989b: 9). Yet the discussion in 1989 remained as obscure as before. Nowhere, for instance, was a 'region' defined.

By late 1989, political events sweeping Europe rendered the Greens' regionalist conception more compelling. The dismantling of the Berlin Wall, the disintegration of Soviet Union, vociferous demands for regional sovereignty in Eastern Europe, and the nearing of a single European market all focused world attention on 'a new Europe'. It was hoped that the events of 1989–91 might provide the needed thrust to make more concrete and prominent (among the Greens themselves if not society at large) an alternative conception of 'Europe of the Regions'. But no such conception emerged. For example, the German Greens' 1994 EP campaign programme devoted only a half page (out of 48) to the notion of an EoR.[9]

The third problem besetting the Greens' notion of an EoR is more predictable, and results from disagreements among green parties over the precise shape of a European alternative. While forming the basis of shared beliefs among green parties, the five tenets outlined in section I are not given the same interpretation or priority by different green parties. For instance, the French Greens have always emphasised the importance of ecological sustainability and decentralisation, but downplay the danger of nationalism and the importance of diversity and community (especially the social community as envisioned by Germans). The notion of diversity, on the other hand, was seized upon by the German Greens, not least to differentiate them from other parties on the far right that were also levelling a harsh critique at the EU.

Another key difference surrounds the extent to which different green parties highlight an explicit critique of capitalism. All green parties are critical of the consequences of a capitalist system. But whereas the German Greens use the term 'imperialist system' in their critique, 'purer' green parties are careful to critique both capitalism and socialism, both left and right. As expressed in the British Greens' 1989 European platform: 'Whether you call it capitalism, indus-trialism, socialism, liberalism or communism, every national economy in the world is based on the belief that more consumption is inevitably and incontrovertibly a Good Thing'.

Finally, a key and contentious issue is the desirability of federalism. The Italian and German Greens stress the importance of federalism as a building block for a green, decentralised Europe. Others, especially the British Greens, voice reservations about a federal superstate and push instead for a confederation, the looser the better. Ideological differences among national parties have thus plagued attempts to form a common green vision of Europe.

IV   FORGING A COMMON VISION

Attempts to agree a common vision of Europe have long preoccupied European green parties. The first attempts to construct a common statement of a 'Green Europe' emanated from the Coordination of European Green and Radical parties, which was set up following the 1979 EP elections. Green parties participating included die Grünen, Agalev (Belgium), Mouvement d'Ecologie Politique (forerunner of Les Verts in France), The UK Ecology Party, Politieke Partij Radikalen (The Netherlands) and Partito Radicale (Italy). Attempts to formulate a common statement or manifesto were stymied by major dis-agreements among the Greens, especially between radical-leftist Greens (such as die Grünen) and purist types (such as the French Greens). In the end, no offical pan-European platform was agreed in 1979.

Over the next five years, the original Coordination of European Greens was joined by the green parties from Sweden, Ireland and Austria. In addition, another French Green grouping – Les Verts–Confederation Ecologiste – had joined in 1983.[10] These 'purer' parties pushed out the two radical parties from The Netherlands and Italy. The new group removed 'Radical' from its title and changed its name to simply 'Green Coordination' or 'The European Greens'. In January 1984, the Coordination presented a *Joint Declaration of the European Green Parties* in Brussels. Many participants hoped that this Brussels declaration would serve as a base for a common pan-European platform (see Parkin 1989: 258).

The Brussels Joint Declaration was a broad statement of goals that set out the Greens' common vision of an alternative Europe. In particular, it called for the replacment of nation-states with regions because:

> a truly democratic Europe will be made possible only through decentralisation of institutions, constant dialogue between citizens and those making decisions at various levels, open discussion of problems, free access to all official documents and files, referenda at the will of the people and the granting of the vote to immigrants.[11]

The Greens' common platform also called for civilian based, non-violent defence, a stop to the arms trade, and for a unilateral first step towards multi-lateral disarmament. The green notion of sustainability and 'community' were also apparent: 'We favour regenerating the economy from the bottom up, making it human and sustainable, creating a system of community-based self reliance, giving priority to respect of the ecosystems'. Although the document included references to the need for economic redistribution, they added up to a 'purist' as opposed to rainbow green vision: 'We wish to break totally from the liberal capitalism of the West and the state capitalism of the East and want a third path which is compatible with an ecological society.'

This 'purer' stance was unsatisfactory to many of the green parties active on the European level. Leftist green parties from Germany and The Netherlands in particular felt that the document insufficiently covered wider concerns of social equality and justice (see Parkin 1989: 260). Disagreements over vision spilled over into nasty disputes over the proper composition of the European Green group. As the 1984 EP election drew nearer, a decision was reached to replace the European Greens with a loose technical alliance of green, radical and leftist parties. The loose alliance abandoned the 'purer' Brussels Declaration and issued instead a formal common platform in April 1984, in time for the upcoming EP campaign: the *Paris Declaration.*

The vision of Europe as expressed in the Paris Declaration reflected its loose technical character. Compared with the earlier Brussels Declaration, the Paris Declaration was much weaker in its demands and much vaguer in its vision. It consisted of several short points or planks, including opposition to the stationing of nuclear weapons;

opposition to 'the pollution of the air, water and earth, and ...
the concreting of nature and countryside'; demands for measures
against unemployment, and a recommendation of an 'ecological form
of agriculture'. Moreover, whereas the Brussels Joint Declaration had
emphasised non-socialist green goals (decentralisation, ecological
sustainability), the later document reflected the inclusion of leftist
radical critique. For instance, the Declaration called for 'the free
expression of fundamental rights of the people, one of the conditions
most important to bring us to an emancipated, ecological society'. The
influence of the women's movement, which was subdued in earlier
Coordination efforts, was also evident: 'We are for the equality of
women in all sectors of social life.'

In sum, early common visions of Europe reflected difficulties of
green groups to forge a common platform. Radical and leftist Greens
felt that the Brussels Declaration inadequately addressed wider social
issues. The subsequent Paris Declaration included left libertarian
elements, but was too vague to serve as an effective guide to common
action.

The GRAEL and the GGEP

The election of Green Members of the European Parliament (MEPs)
in 1984 provided an opportunity to turn a common vision into
concrete actions on the European level. Following the 1984 elections,
a loose collection of green parties formed the Green Alternative
European Link (GRAEL). The GRAEL was dominated by German
Greens MEPs and its platform was consequently left libertarian. The
GRAEL embraced the Paris Declaration as its guiding principle for a
vision of Europe. It was suitably vague, and incorporated leftist
elements. Statements and pronouncements put out by the GRAEL
stressed non-ecological issues as well as 'straight' environmental
issues. Peace, human rights and social equality were seen as key
components of a new Europe (see GRAEL 1984). Overall, however,
not much attention was paid to an alternative vision of Europe. No
effort was made to forge a common vision beyond that laid out in the
Paris Declaration. Little attention was paid to the notion of a Europe
of the Regions.

Following the 1989 election, a new cohort of green MEPs entered
the Parliament. Dominated by the 'purer' French and Italian Greens,
the new Green Group in the European Parliament (GGEP) promised
to develop a more coherent vision of Europe and a European Union.
In its early years, the GGEP seemed to take seriously the need for a

coherent European policy. It embraced the concept of an EoR and used it as an overarching blueprint for action. In early 1991, the GGEP chose 'regions' as a priority theme for the year. Its first bulletin stated that the notion of European regions 'is a theme that can draw on the various fields of our work. Our work groups are preparing programs on various aspects of ecological, balanced, sustainable development centered on Europe's varied regions' (GGEP 1991a).

One French Green claimed that the new influx of French MEPs ensured that the EoR would receive more attention: 'The Europe of the Regions has been around in the French language for a long time. Just think of [federalist Denis] de Rougemont. We Greens use it today as a concept to guide our work.'[12] A German GGEP MEP underscored the point, stating that the GGEP

> takes this regionalism stuff seriously. For us, democratisation of the Community must mean strengthening regional and local rights of self-determination ... [by] creating direct independent access to the Community's legislative process for grassroots groups and individual initiatives.[13]

The practical application of regionalism was seen also in the GGEP's position on agricultural policy. In May 1991, the GGEP sponsored a conference on EU farm price policy with the explicit intention of incorporating regional imperatives into the CAP. According to the GGEP, any common agricultural policy that does not take into account regional diversity is fundamentally flawed. German MEP Graefe zu Baringdorf opened the conference with the hope that it would 'foster our idea of regions, against bureaucratic centralised growth' (GGEP 1991d: 2). The Cestona Declaration that emerged from the conference stressed the need

> to construct policies that have the power to correct current imbalances and encourage regional initiatives. . . . Single markets will obliterate regional identities. What matters is to look not at the needs of the market but at the needs of the people. Power over agricultural policy should be decentralised to the regions.
>
> (GGEP 1991d: 6)

But problems of conceptualisation and coordination increased throughout the GGEP's first term. All could agree on the faults of the EU in its current construction. Similar to the critique expressed by several national green parties, the GGEP argued that 'the EC is not "Europe". Intended as a pole of the world economy, the EC is absolutely not the vehicle for the alternative model of development sought by all Greens' (GGEP 1991c: 4). Yet a positive alternative vision – as opposed to a shared critique – failed to emerge due to national and ideological differences among green parties.

GGEP's position on the *Maastricht Treaty* illustrated both the Greens' shared critique and disagreements over the best alternative. All Greens agreed that Maastricht violated the green vision of Europe. Ecological sustainability was not adequately addressed by the Treaty: 'The agreement signed in Maastricht did not bring to the general system of EC treaties the basic changes ... necessary to combat the ecological crisis' (GGEP 1992c: 5). Greens also pointed out that environmental policy did not become one of the common policies, as called for by the EP, but was 'relegated among other policies, as an appendix to the communities' economic policy' (GGEP 1992c: 5).

Greens felt that the Treaty violated grassroots democracy by 'taking more powers away from national parliament without passing them on to the EP' (GGEP 1992c: 2). The notion of subsidiarity as outlined in the Treaty was viewed as little more than a ruse and did little to strengthen grassroots democracy.

> The definition provided by the new Treaty for the principle of subsidiarity confirms the governments' concern to maintain their power while limiting on the one hand the role of the Community institutions (the Commission and EP) and on the other that of the regions, which continue to be marginalised when it comes to European policy choices.
>
> (GGEP 1992c: 3)

The assurance of peaceful global order, one which linked global and local concerns, was also undermined by the Treaty's provision for a Common Foreign and Security Policy (CFSP). Greens argued that the CFSP 'is linked strategically to NATO and operationally to the WEU [West European Union], giving a priori privilege to the military dimension and completely marginalising questions of disarmament and human rights' (GGEP 1992c: 3).

Finally, the protection of diversity was endangered by the Treaty. In particular, the Treaty's emphasis on intergovernmental decision-making 'demonstrates a dangerous supremacy of national interests ... and risks opening a phase of dangerous political fragmentation in the Union'. GGEP spokeswoman Adelaide Agliette put the point more flamboyantly, warning that:

> At the very moment when clouds of racism, of ethnic and religious intolerance are gathering in the skies over Europe ... Maastricht

gives a negative answer to those countries which have placed in Europe their hope of progress and the concrete opportunity to dissolve in the common European home their hereditary, national, ethnic and religious conflicts.

(GGEP 1992e: 11)

Concerns about the Treaty's violation of key green principles led the GGEP to call on the EP to ratify Maastricht reluctantly and 'only after . . . correction of manifest flaws in the Treaty' (GGEP 1992c: 2).

Despite general agreement on the faults of the Treaty, the GGEP could not agree on an alternative or shared strategy to confront these flaws. For instance, Greens disagreed as to the EU's proper role in formulating a common foreign policy. The French warned against the emergence of new military blocs, but they generally welcomed the idea of joint foreign and security policy-making. Italian and Belgium Greens, headed by Alexander Langer and Paul Lannoye, were even more sanguine about the prospects for cooperation. Langer argued that Greens should press for a pan-European security policy, and even a common policing, although he noted that this would require institutions for democratic monitoring. But his advocacy of CFSP was strongly opposed by the German Greens, who feared the growth of a European military superpower. The German Greens specifically criticised Maastricht's CFSP arrangements as 'opening the door to the militarisation of the EU' (die Grünen/Bündnis 1994: 46).

More generally, the Greens were faced with divisions over strategy, as well as content. They could not agree whether to support the Treaty – warts and all – or to adopt a 'purer' stance and oppose the Treaty because of its faults. As MEP Boissiere summed up, Maastricht

divided even the most ardent champions of a democratic federal Europe between those who believe that the treaty must be rejected to make way for an improved version, and those who fear the rejection would play into the hands of the adversaries of European Union and would trigger a return to narrow nationalism.

(GGEP 1992e: 11)

In short, the Maastricht debate underlined a more general point: European Greens could agree on the EU's flaws but not on positive alternatives.

In the run up to the 1994 EP election, another attempt to agree a common vision was made. The Greens' efforts were aided by the development of the European Federation of Green Parties (EFGP) in 1993. The EFGP grew out of earlier attempts at cross-national cooperation, such as the European Coordination mentioned above. Although the EFGP included parties from countries outside the EU, its guiding principles (see EFGP 1993) served as the basis for Greens' EP election platform. The subsequent 1994 'Election Platform of the Green Parties of the European Union' reflected the progress and limitations of green conceptualising. On the one hand, the document differed significantly from earlier common statements. It was clearer, more detailed and much more comprehensive (over 40 pages). The platform was less polemical and placed greater emphasis on pragmatic policy alternatives, especially in the economic sphere (such as the use of specific eco-taxes). But on the other hand, like earlier common platforms, the 1994 document suffered from internal conflicts and lack of vision. It reflected inevitable bargaining among over a dozen different parties.

Discussions of the document began in early 1993, but were soon bogged down in internal disputes about the priorities, tone and purpose of the document. In particular, conflicts surrounded the issue of whether the platform should be used to 'bind' incoming green MEPs. In the end the document was deemed a 'guidebook' for the next group of Green MEPs. As such, it featured primarily pragmatic suggestions – about committee work, parliamentary rules, use of staff, etc. – rather than a blueprint for an alternative vision of Europe. Indeed, the EoR vision aspect was virtually absent. It received only a brief paragraph near the end of the text (p. 37). Thus, despite early attempts, the Greens were unable or unwilling to devote the time and energy necessary to construct a coherent alternative vision of Europe.

V CONCLUSION: GREEN AMBIVALENCE

This chapter has examined attempts by green parties to construct a common vision of Europe. Despite agreeing on basic principles and a shared criticism of Europe in its current construction, the Greens have been unable or unwilling to construct a coherent vision of Europe. The Greens' lack of coherent theorising on Europe can be explained by the inevitable difficulties surrounding attempts to forge a common vision from many diverse parties. But the lack of theorising can also be explained by the Greens' ambivalence towards Europe and the EU more generally. Amidst attempts to 'think globally, act locally', the Greens neglect this middle sphere: the regional level of Europe. For many Greens emerging from the peace, ecology or local citizens' movements, Europe is an uncomfortable halfway house, neither international nor local and for that reason uninteresting.

As Kolinsky notes (1990: 73), many supporters of the Greens had been anti-European in the past as part and parcel of their left wing orientation. Whilst this opposition stance was found particularly among 'rainbow' green parties, it was also evident in the UK Greens' position on Europe. Indeed, early platforms of the British Greens called for immediate withdrawal from the EU. Only in the late 1980s did the British Greens qualify their demand that the UK withdraw from the EU (Rüdig 1995). Even so, ambivalence towards EU and 'Europe' remains among British Greens. A member of the executive board confirmed that every few years a motion is tabled advocating British withdrawal from the EU.[14]

Moreover, for many Greens the notion of 'Europe' immediately conjures up the EU. It appears that for some green members their refutation of the EU carries over to a more general refutation of (or at least ambivalence towards) European policy in general. As a consequence, the green's European policy (and their policy towards the EU in particular) has suffered from a history of neglect on both the national and European levels.

In sum, the Greens' movement-party character provides them with distinctive possibilities and problems when formulating their European policy. On one hand, the Greens put forth a vision of Europe significantly different from those of established parties and actors. Their particular emphasis on decentralisation, democracy and diversity stems from their unique link to grassroots and protest movements. On the other hand, the Greens' movement-party character also leads to an ambivalence and confusion towards Europe in general, and the EU in particular.

4 Green transnational strategies and electoral performance

INTRODUCTION

The Greens' vision of a 'Europe of the Regions' represents an alternative blueprint of a European community or union. Transforming this European conception into political strategies and action has proved difficult for Greens across the EU. The present chapter focuses on the transnational electoral strategies and performance of green parties in EP elections. It illustrates a steady shift away from grassroots-based strategies and towards a more professional, parliament-oriented approach. However, tensions between radical and reformist imperatives continue to plague green parties, especially at the European level.

Section I examines early attempts by green parties to wage a European electoral campaign in the run-up to the 1979 EP elections. Section II examines these parties' more professionalised strategies in the EP elections of 1984 and 1989. The application of the more pragmatic approach during the 1994 EP campaign is analysed in Section III. The conclusion assesses the extent to which strategic debates have overshadowed more fundamental questions about the content of an alternative green European policy.

I EARLY ELECTORAL ACTIVITY: THE 1979 EP ELECTION

Before 1979, the main environmental protest activity in Europe was conducted by movements and pressure groups rather than parties. A significant impetus for more formal transnational activity occurred in spring 1979. The first direct elections to the EP held in that year served as the necessary catalyst for formal coordinated activity of Green and alternative groups in Europe. Green candidates were fielded in France, Belgium, the UK and West Germany. Radical movement-parties that incorporated anti-nuclear issues also ran in The Netherlands and Luxembourg. The electoral activities of these various parties and lists represented a first attempt at formal transnational activity on the part of green parties as opposed to spontaneous coordinated protests. But the 1979 campaign illustrated the emerging conflict among Green actors over the desirability of parliamentary versus street action. This latent conflict was visible in the election campaign of all four green parties fielding candidates for the 1979 EP election.

Under *German* electoral rules, movements had to constitute themselves as a national political party to participate in EP elections. In March 1979, a heterogeneous national alliance of citizens' action groups, green lists, minor parties and alternative groups formed the SPV: '*Sonstige Politische Vereinigungen, Die Grünen*' ('Other Political Alliances, The Greens') in Frankfurt. Five hundred delegates, representing several positions along a left–right continuum, participated in the conference. The ideological diversity of the assembly was striking. On the right was Herbert Gruhl's *Grüne Aktion Zukunft* (GAZ) or 'Green Action Future'. Gruhl had left the Christian Democrats earlier because he felt his environmental ideas and initiatives 'fell on deaf ears' (Gatter 1987: 24). Launched in 1978, Gruhl's GAZ highlighted environmental issues while emulating the functions and structures of the major parties. The *Aktion Unabhängiger Deutscher* (AUD) or 'Action Community of Independent Germans', led by August Haussleitner, combined populist and rightist themes in what Stöss (1980) has termed 'populist conservatism'. On the left came a group from Hamburg, *die Bunte Liste*, made up primarily of members from women's, gay rights and communist groups (Langguth 1986: 8; Gatter 1987: 24ff). Ideologically positioned in the middle was the GLU (*die Grünen Liste Umweltschutz*), which had already contested a local election in lower Saxony in 1977. Despite ideological differences, these various groups agreed to contest the first direct election to the EP under the SPV banner.

The 1979 campaign of the SPV reflected the heterogeneous background and contentious character of die Grünen. Naturally, ideological conflicts erupted between those positioned on opposite poles of the left–right continuum. More interesting, however, was an incipient debate distinct from the left–right conflict. In this campaign, an argument began to develop that centred on the merits of parliamentary versus direct action strategies to achieve green goals. For instance, members of Hamburg's *Bunte List* viewed the election primarily, if not purely, as a way of attracting publicity to the movement. The GLU, on the other hand, viewed it as a way to introduce parliamentary strategies into the environmental movement.

This incipient conflict was also apparent within green parties of other countries. Agalev and Ecolo – the two *Belgium* green contenders for the 1979 EP election – were both loose collections of citizens' initiatives and green movements. In the French-speaking Wallonian region of Belgium, Ecolo existed as a group of environmentalist lists, but not as a formal green party. An inchoate collection of these environmentalist and regionalist groups came together to consider the possibility of fielding candidates under a common 'Europe Ecologie' banner. Disputes within the list were intense, and focused on the extent to which Ecolo should be opened up to parliamentary strategies and radical elements on the left. However, despite internal conflict, a common 'Europe Ecologie' list was presented to field EP candidates in the Wallonian region (Derschouwer 1989: 43).

Ecolo's Flemish counterpart, Agalev, also fielded candidates in its region. The rationale expressed by Agalev's political secretary, Johann Malcorps, was typical of both Ecolo and Agalev at the time. According to Malcorps, the intent of Agalev in fielding candidates in 1979 was simply 'to raise consciousness in the existing parties' rather than to win seats (quoted in Feinstein 1992: 258). Agalev's 1979 campaign reflected these alternative goals; its campaign literature consisted of a single pamphlet with the slogan: 'if you have the nerve, vote for Agalev'. The intent was to keep close to movement roots and avoid traditional stances of conventional parties.

Similarly, in *Luxembourg*, environmental activists formed an anti-nuclear electoral list called the Alternative List–Resist (AL–WI – Alternative Leescht–Wiert Ich). Yet members made it clear that the AL–WI was not a party but rather a temporary electoral formation set up for the national and European elections in 1979. Its main objective was to use the election as a platform to publicise their opposition to plans to build a nuclear power station in the country (Rüdig 1985: 61).

In *France*, participation in elections was more readily acceptable as a legitimate form of ecologist action. French ecologists had already campaigned in national elections for the presidency and thus were less reluctant to tread the parliamentary path. Moreover, the 1979 EP election offered new hope for ecologists after a poor (2 per cent) showing in the 1978 national election. Nonetheless, the movement-party strategic debate was also present here. Green groups and lists were fearful of falling into what they viewed as the trap of centralised party activity. Activists eager for European action shunned any structures remotely reminiscent of centralism and followed instead the loose organisation patterns demonstrated by French ecologists in earlier national and municipal elections. The fear that the ecology movement might be led or coordinated from Paris contributed to a very individualised approach towards local national and EP elections. Local control was designed to preserve the independence of each local group and their grassroots supporters.

Lengthy negotiations between various groups had to take place before the EP election. After much discussion among several green lists and activists, a 'Europe Ecologie' list was set up to field candidates for the 1979 election. The list was headed by Solange Fernex, an anti-nuclear activist who had helped found the *Ecologie et Survie* group in Alsace in the early 1970s. Yet strategic conflict among environmental groups remained (see Prendville 1994: 24). The tension was evidenced by *Amis de la Terre's* (Friends of the Earth) decision, under the leadership of a future French presidential candidate, Brice Lalonde, to boycott Europe Ecologie's EP campaign.

In the *United Kingdom*, the Ecology Party's 1979 EP campaign resembled in form and content its national election campaign of the same year. Attempts were made prior to the campaign to link various local anti-nuclear movements, such as the Scottish Campaign to Resist the Atomic Menace (SCRAM), into larger umbrella organisations. The hope was that these umbrella organisations could serve as a base for the Ecology Party's election campaign. However, these movements generally remained separate and distinct from the Ecology Party. Although there was some overlap in membership, the Ecology Party could not count on full support from social movements active in the 1970s. For instance, unlike the German Greens, the UK Ecology Party did not necessarily represent the most obvious political channel for the aims of the UK peace movement. Members of the Campaign for Nuclear Disarmament (CND) either viewed the British Labour Party as offering a suitable vehicle for their goals, or preferred to stay 'out of party politics' altogether (Parkin 1989: 222).

In the event, the Ecology Party ran an 'awareness campaign' designed to educate rather than win seats. Candidates were fielded in only three constituencies. Enthusiasm for a full-fledged campaign was limited, both within the party but especially among its potential movement supporters. The 1979 election thus clearly reflected the independence of movements from the Ecology Party, and the reluctance of movement members to embrace electoral strategies.

In all of these Member States, the 1979 composition of green parties or lists was loose and informal. In most cases, lists were composed not of existing parties but of a combination of green movements and organisations considering – but still undecided about – a parliamentary path to parallel their street action and protest. Generally, the

1979 campaign was dominated by movement activists and movement sentiments. Environmental activists, peace marchers and members of alternative movements formed 'technical' alliances to contest the upcoming election. But as activists stated continually and vehemently, they did so only for logistical reasons, i.e. as a way to publicise movement demands and educate the public. Most candidates did not expect to gain a seat. Moreover, movement activists insisted that the 1979 parliamentary campaign had not eroded the pre-eminence of extra-parliamentary strategies and protests. The purposefully un-professional ('grassroots') and inexpensive campaign in several coun-tries suggested the dominance of movement influence. It was assumed that after the election the movements would go their separate ways, far away from government structures and back to the grassroots.

Table 4.1 1979 EP election results

Country	Party	%	Seats
Belgium	Agalev	2.3	0
	Ecolo	5.1	0
FRG	SPV-die Grünen	3.2	0
France	Europe Ecologie	4.4	0
Luxembourg	AL–WI	1.0	0
UK	Ecology Party	3.7	0

Source: European Federation of Green Parties

1979 results

As Table 4.1 indicates, no green parties or lists won seats in the 1979 election. The French came the closest. The Europe Ecologie list polled 4.4 per cent, thereby just missing the 5 per cent hurdle necessary to win a European seat.[1] The German SPV/Grünen, receiv-ing 3.2 per cent of the vote, failed to meet a similar 5 per cent hurdle required to win a seat under German electoral law. In Belgium, Agalev won 2.3 and Ecolo 5.1 per cent. This was not enough to clear the 7.2 threshold and gain EP representation. The UK Ecology Party won 3.7 per cent of the vote (in the constiuencies it contested) and no seats. The Luxembourg AL–WI list polled 1 per cent.

For many movement activists the poor showing of green parties in the election seemed to illustrate the need to stay close to the grassroots and not abandon movement strategies for parliamentary ones. None-theless, for others the electoral result seemed to vindicate parlia-mentary strategies as an effective strategy to parallel street protest and action. Despite the small percentage gained, the 1979 election campaign and results highlighted several advantages of parliamentary participation.

First, even though they gained no seats, many green parties enjoyed other benefits available to an established party. Non-monetary resources such as media access and publicity served as an impetus for further parliamentary activity and increased publicity. For example, in the UK and Belgium the result served to attract more public attention and party members from environmental groups and other parties (Rüdig 1985: 59). Membership of the British Ecology party shot up to 5,000 (from 650) immediately following the national and European 1979 campaigns (Young 1993: 37). In the case of the French 'Europe Ecologie', the level of local support for green candidates was particularly encouraging. The EP results indicated impressive local support for list leader Solange Fernex who won 10.6 per cent in her own area of Alsace, the Haut-Rhin (Parkin 1989: 98).

The advantages were even clearer in the German case. According to German campaign laws, all parties who polled at least 0.5 per cent of the total vote were entitled to a cash reimbursement. The amount given was not related to actual campaign costs, but was instead determined as a flat rate in relation to the party's share of the vote. The Greens' 3.2 per cent of the vote entitled them to a reimbursement of election expenses of DM 4.8 million. Because they spent only DM 300,000, this resulted in a net gain of DM 4.5 million, which could be used for the SPV's future activities.

The advantages of party existence, in other words, were becoming increasingly appealing. Whilst not leading to seats, the returns of several parties made more feasible the prospects for future collaboration and expanded political activity on the European level. Yet access to these resources by no means solved the movement-party strategic debate. As promised, several movement activists turned back to their specific movements following the 1979 elections. But an even greater number now focused on the task of forming or strengthening a national party. Bolstered by the publicity and funds garnered from the EP election, the official West German Green Party was founded in 1980. In Belgium, the unforeseen success of the Wallonian 'Europe Ecologie' list (5.1 per cent) was the immediate cause for the creation of a permanent green political party in Wallonia (Ecolo), which was officially created as a political party in March 1980 (Derschouwer 1989: 43). Agalev's formation followed soon thereafter. In short, the 1979 electoral results altered the parameters of movement-party debates. What began as largely a movement-dominated campaign to publicise movement demands, ultimately promoted continued parliamentary activity.

Yet if the 1979 European election prompted a strategic debate, it contained no comparable debate over European objectives. Enthusiasm for 'Europe' quickly dissipated among the Greens after 1979. Greater coordination of green parties' transnational goals also fell off the agenda as parties turned their attention towards domestic concerns. Greens in France and Belgium concentrated on the task of building up national parties or attempting to resolve internal disputes. In the UK, the lack of European goals and vision was more evident. The 1979 election had been primarily an extension of the national campaign, with only slight differences in issues and platform put forward. Little effort was made to generate interest in a European as opposed to a national programme. Moreover, unlike some of its green counterparts in other European countries, the UK Ecology Party did not gain financially from the European election.[2] Indeed, because of the costs of deposits, the campaign 'emptied the party's coffers as well as the pockets of many members' (Parkin 1989: 222). In terms of financial and conceptual opportunities, Europe held no special appeal for the UK Ecology Party.

In Germany, the neglect of Europe was just as pronounced. Despite the participation of several 'Euro-minded' party co-founders, such as Petra Kelly and Roland Vogt, the issue of Europe or *'Europapolitik'* received scant attention from the Greens as a whole. To the dismay of those who felt the movement-party should think both 'globally and locally' (Kelly 1984b), the Greens consciously decided to direct their energies towards the domestic concerns of the next federal election in 1983. When in 1983 the Greens successfully entered the federal parliament with 5.6 per cent of the national vote, the importance of Europe seemed to decrease further. Only a small core of European activists kept their eye on Europe and the next EP election to be held in 1984. In the early 1980s, a few interested members formed a loose 'working group' (*Bundesarbeitsgruppe*, or BAG) on European issues. Yet, from the beginning, the BAG was seriously neglected by the rest of the party. In matters of European policy, wrote one frustrated BAG member, there was 'not a trace of enthusiasm to be found' (Horst 1984: 32).

In sum, strategy had come before substance for most Greens in 1979. Fundamentalist movement activists had concentrated on ensuring that movement strategies were not endangered by the experiment with parliamentary strategies. Parliamentary advocates, on the other hand, used the 1979 election as a forum in which they could push for increased green parliamentary activity at all levels. Put bluntly, the candidacy of the Greens in 1979 had little to do with European policy *per se*. It was much more an affirmation of the parliamentary route to be taken by Greens in the 1979 election and afterwards.

II THE 'PROFESSIONALISATION' OF GREEN CAMPAIGNS: 1984 AND 1989

1984 election campaign

The 1984 EP campaign provided an opportunity for revived green party activity in Europe. The run up to the 1984 election witnessed a growing interest in transnational cooperation and coordination among green and radical parties. Greens from Germany, Belgium, France and the UK, and leftist and radical leftist parties in The Netherlands and Luxembourg stepped up contact and discussed collaboration.[3] A transnational working group composed of a wide range of parties and movements was established. With an eye to the 1984 EP election, this loose and informal working group was able to hammer out the Paris Declaration (discussed in Chapter 3), a common but vague programme that acted as their coordinated campaign platform for the upcoming June 1984 election.

Yet the common platform did little to iron out differences in European electoral strategies. Instead, the 1984 campaign intensified the movement-party conflict. In Germany, the achievement of national representation had been followed by a growing split between Realos and Fundis within the party. A year of experience inside the German Bundestag had sharpened the contours of the movement-party debate and raised further questions about the proper balance between parliamentary and extra-parliamentary strategies.

In Belgium, a similar split was seen in both regional parties, although it was not as acute as elsewhere. Both Belgian parties achieved a national electoral breakthrough in 1981 when four green candidates were elected to the national parliament. However, fears arose about the danger that an extended parliamentary strategy might hurt the movement. Several members of Agalev in particular voiced concern about an 'over-professionalisation' of green politics (Derschouwer 1989: 41).

In Luxembourg, hesitation towards a more parliament-based approach was also evident amongst anti-nuclear acitivists within the AL–WI. But the 1984 campaign served as an impetus for the transformation of the AL–WI list into the Green Alternative Party, made up of many AL–WI members as well as members from environmental, peace and women's groups. Rüdig (1985: 61) argues that the new party was less radical and less leftist than the AL-WI electoral list, and also more willing to play parliamentary politics. Several Green Alternative candidates for the EP election had stood as AL–WI candidates in 1979, but other AL–WI members boycotted the new party entirely.

In the UK, the Ecology Party was beset by similar tactical problems. A heated debate ensued in the run up to the 1984 election when pragmatists within the party claimed that a more efficient organisation and office were needed to cope with the increased membership that followed the 1979 election. According to Sara Parkin (1989: 222), arguments about office organisation reflected wider confusion about the actual role of the party: should it contest elections at all, or concentrate on movement tactics and actions? 'Was party political activity an ecological activity in the first place? How should it relate to other parts of the movement?' .

In France, too, internal green divisions marked the period between subsequent EP elections. Here, the movement-party split was manifest in conflict between 'purer' Greens with stronger links to movements, and more pragmatic Greens willing to form coalitions with leftist and centrist parties. From the start, several movement activists were wary not only of collaboration with the left, but of electoral activity more generally. Polls carried out among green activists in 1983 indicated that nearly a quarter believed that *'presence sur le terrain'* (presence at the grassroots level) was the best way of converting people to ecological ideas (see Chafer 1984: 39).

Yet, as in 1979, the upcoming 1984 European election campaign served to unite the various groups into one green party to stand in the EP elections. In January 1984, several green lists and movements joined together to form *Les Verts* (The Greens). They claimed close movement roots and shunned 'contamination' from leftist activists or pragmatists willing to form coalitions with leftist or centrist parties. This pure stance was reflected in Les Verts' refusal to grant 'pragmatist' and former presidential candidate Brice Lalonde a high place on a green list of candidates for the 1984 election. Aside from disagreeing with his strategic plans, many in the movement saw him as a careerist exploiting the EP as a platform for his own political ambitions. Lalonde thus joined a new list especially set up for the 1984 EP election, the *Radical Ecologist Concord* (ERE), which also included members from the radical left and liberal centre (Rüdig 1985: 63).

A similar split among leftist pragmatists and purer fundamentalists was developing in The Netherlands. Until the early 1980s, new social movement interests had been represented by the Radical Party (PPR) and the Pacifists-Socialists (PSP), who had traditionally polled around 2 per cent of the vote. Dutch electoral law stipulates that parties gain at least 4 per cent of the total vote to obtain a seat in the EP. In preparation for the 1984 election, the Radicals initiated discussion of possible electoral cooperation among several other small leftist parties as well as with environmentalists of no party affiliation. The idea was to reorganise left wing radical politics by founding a party alliance that included the PPR, the PSP and the Communists (CPN). However, the Radicals also hoped to attract non-affiliated movement activists, especially environmentalists (Müller-Rommel 1985a). After a series of critical debates, the Green Progressive Accord (GPA) was formed out of these various parties and activists.

In common with fundamentalist members in Les Verts, several 'purer' elements within the Dutch green movement abhorred the possibility of joining forces with leftist parties, especially the Communists. Dissidents from the recently formed GPA, together with other environmentalists, thus formed a new political party called *De Groenen* (The Greens). The split was followed by bitter debate about the respective green credentials of both parties. De Groenen saw themselves as a fundamentalist green party with close links to grassroots environmental concerns. They were to act as a counter to the pragmatist GPA coalition of radical leftist parties. According to De Groenen, the GPA was merely using a green cover to further their leftist ends. The GPA, on the other hand, accused De Groenen of being a one-issue party with no concern for social and economic questions (Rüdig 1985: 64–6). As result of this split, two different lists laid claim to the green label in the 1984 EP election. Both lists canvassed green parties in other countries for support. The leftist-rainbow German Greens strongly backed the Accord, but most other green parties, especially Les Verts in France, favoured De Groenen as the 'purer' expression of green politics.

Thus, in both France and The Netherlands, the movement-party debate became superimposed on the debate between leftist-rainbow and purist factions. In both cases, the purer faction (Les Verts or De Groenen) represented more closely the fundamentalist demands and strategies, whereas the leftist-rainbow alliances (ERE, GPA) expressed a greater willingness to embrace parliamentary and coalition strategies.

Table 4.2 1984 EP election results

Country	Party	%	Seats
Belgium	Agalev	7.1	1
	Ecolo	9.9	1
FRG	die Grünen	8.2	7
France	Les Verts	3.4	0
	ERE	3.3	0
Luxembourg	GAP	6.1	0
Netherlands	GPA	5.6	2
	De Groenen	1.3	0
UK	Ecology Party	2.7	0

Source: European Federation of Green Parties; GGEP (1994)

1984 results

Despite green ambivalence over the desirability of parliamentary participation, four green parties from three countries gained representation in the EP. In total, 11 MEPs were elected to represent green parties in the EP. With 8.2 per cent of the German vote, die Grünen won seven seats – the most of any green party. In Belgium, both Agalev and Ecolo won one seat each after polling 7.1 and 9.9 per cent respectively. The Dutch GPA gained 5.6 per cent and two seats. Whilst the Luxembourg Green Alternative Party did not win any seats, they did poll an impressive 6.1 per cent. The UK's Ecology Party won an average of 2.7 per cent in the constiuencies it contested, and no seats.

These results showed that rainbow parties continued to dominate their purer counterparts in France and the UK. The result also illustrated the electoral consequences of domestic movement-party splits. For instance, in France, the split between leftist parliamentary factions (ERE) and purer green factions (Les Verts) was particularly consequential. The French Socialist Party had welcomed the emergence of the ERE as a way of splitting the ecological vote and attracting centrist voters away from its rivals. To a certain extent, their hopes were realised: Les Verts won 3.4 per cent, a slip from the 4.4 per cent green return in 1979. Lalonde's competing list of ERE won 3.3 per cent. Neither party gained seats. Clearly the split weakened the ecological vote and helped account for the failure of Greens to win any EP seats (Rüdig 1985: 62–3).

In The Netherlands, the split between rainbow-pragmatists and purist-movement parties was also apparent. De Groenen's hopes of attracting the votes of unaffiliated and purer Greens were disappointed; they polled only 1.3 per cent. The GPA fared better with its Realo embrace of parliamentary participation and coalition-building. Yet voter ambivalence about this strategy was also evident in the returns. The 5.6 per cent received by the GPA represented only slightly more than a combination of the votes that its constituent parts (PSP, Radicals, Communists) might have received separately. In other words, neither De Groenen nor the GPA attracted the votes of non-affiliated Greens in the 1984 EP election. Clearly many Dutch green activists – and European Greens more generally – remained wary of electoral participation in any form.

1989 election campaign

The tension between parliamentary and grassroots strategies continued in the next EP election in 1989. Played out primarily within individual parties, the strategic debate overshadowed efforts to forge a more coherent cross-national green strategy towards EP elections or green European activity more generally. In 1989, this strategic debate was sharpened by two new factors. First, green members had now spent four years working within the EP, and had solid experience of parliamentary participation. A second factor was the increased electoral saliency of green issues which made an increase in seats more likely. Green parties fielded candidates (alone or on combined lists)[4] in every country except Greece.[5] The movement-party debate was present in all.

On one hand, movement activists again raised fears of the inevitable compromise required of parliamentary actors. First, movement 'energy' and vigour would be neutralised once the movement had gone through the necessary compromise and cooperation required of any parliamentary actor. For example, German environmental activists warned that continued parliamentary participation would 'pollute' grassroots goals. The Greens' defining principle of democratic decision-making would not survive the parliamentary process undiluted, particularly on the European level. Grassroots activists pointed out that the EU's decision-making process allowed precious little direct parliamentary or public access. German Green members Maier and Schulz (1988: 6) reminded their colleagues that the EU's Council Ministers, though in theory accountable to their respective parliaments, in practice did business through 'secret and impromptu horse-trading'. Participation in the EP thus meant that the MEPs were taking part in a 'dubious community' (the European Community) in which the EP functioned merely as a 'shadow parliament', or 'alibi' to cover the EU's lack of democracy (Nostitz 1986: 4). Key members of

Agalev remained equally wary of EU involvement. They warned that the richest and most powerful EU Member States were transforming the EU into a powerful superstate, 'thereby rendering the rest of Europe, particularly the East, into another version of the Third World' (Malcorps quoted in Feinstein 1992: 258).

Some movement members were even harsher. They charged that the Greens' participation in the EP effectively legitimised the structures and operation of the EU. Leggewie (1989: 9) summarises these critics' demands: 'Why legitimize European institutions which continue to exist in a scandalously pre-constitutional, undemocratic condition?' Or as expressed by two British Greens in *A Green Manifesto for the 1990s*: 'If Westminster is distant, Strasbourg is farther away still. If MPs are unrepresentative, how much more unrepresentative will be Euro MPs?' (Kemp and Wall 1990: 178). In short, many green members were intent on protecting their political integrity through strict and fundamental abstinence from conventional politics (Schoonmaker 1988).

In some cases, the concern of more fundamentalist members led to the formation of separate green parties competing with one another. In Italy, for instance, two separate parties or lists represented divergent strategies: *Verdi Europa* (Greens Europe) represented 'purer' ecological politics and feared contamination from leftists or radical parties; *Verdi Arcobaleno* (Rainbow Greens), on the other hand, espoused a more explicit left wing agenda and demonstrated a willingness to merge with leftist groups and parties. In Luxembourg, a similar split existed between two small green parties: the Green Alternative Party (GAP) and the Green Left Ecological Initiative (GLEI).

Responding to the fundamentalist critique, 'parliamentarians' already active in the EP, such as Grünen MEP Undine Bloch von Blottnitz, argued that parliamentary infiltration by Greens was precisely what was needed to reform the EU's 'undemocratic condition'. Bloch von Blottnitz insisted (1986a: 36) that 'this regrettable situation will only change when, finally, capable ecological and radical democrats are present at the European level'. The MEPs were there, after all, to represent the green consciousness of the grassroots, even if they received little attention or support from them.

For parliamentarians, the fears voiced by grassroots activists amounted to a 'real phobia ... about being dominated by parliamentary concerns' (Hülsberg 1988: 209). They argued that influence on agenda-setting would outweigh the costs of participation in the EP.

Little could be gained by obstructionism from the outside. To have a long term impact, the Greens needed to raise problems and provide practical solutions. Realos in the British Green Party argued that the party needed to divest itself of the symbolic radical commitments and shake off its qualms about professionalism in politics (Doherty 1992: 111). Others pointed out that EP elections posed particular opportunities because some voters viewed them as 'second order elections' (Reif 1984) and thus might be more willing to 'risk' their vote on a party unlikely to receive a plurality. Moreover, the impressive returns of German and Belgium green parties in earlier EP elections had served as a 'springboard to national respectability' (Franklin and Rüdig 1992: 130).

Finally, parliamentary advocates stressed the accomplishments of the Green European parliamentarians' in the preceding four years. Working through the EP, these Greens presented themselves as the European 'mouthpiece' of movement ideas and demands. The Agalev MEP Paul Staes underscored this point by holding frequent sessions to inform supporters of his activities in the EP. In Germany, parliamentary advocates distributed a special edition of the party newsletter which heralded the 'Green MEPs' Success in Strasbourg' (die Grünen 1989a). These parliamentary advocates expressed the hope that parliamentary participation would force important issues into parliaments and into the public consciousness. They viewed parliaments as a tool for consciousness-raising, and the Greens as the 'yeast in the dough' (Jäenicke 1982). For parliamentarians, 'it was crucial to enter the political arena ... only if you actually threatened their votes will you force other parties to act' (Uexküll 1991: 345).

The advantages of parliamentary participation were especially important on the European level. Coordination across nations in Europe would be made easier by adopting supranational electoral strategies. Moreover, collaborative activities within the EU would highlight the cross-national imperative on environmental issues. This cross-national aspect held particular appeal for green parties not yet represented in the EP. In the case of Spain and Portugal, the prospects of green seats in Strasbourg made compromise and coalitions with left wing parties more palpable. The Spanish Greens (*Los Verdes*) joined a small left wing party, *Izquierda de los Pueblos*, to contest the EP election. Similarly, the Portuguese Greens' candidate stood on a combined list with the Communists. In short, by 1989 most green parties had opted for professional, pragmatic campaigns and greeted eagerly the chance to contest and hold seats in the EP.

Table 4.3 1989 EP election results

Country	Party	%	Seats
Belgium	Agalev	12.2	1
	Ecolo	16.6	2
FRG	die Grünen	8.4	8
France	Les Verts	10.6	8
Ireland	Comhaontas Glas	3.7	0
Italy	Verdi Europe	3.8	3
	Arcobaleno	2.4	2
Luxembourg	GAP	4.3	0
	GLEI	6.1	0
Netherlands	Groen Links	7.0	2
Portugal	Os Verdes (w/Communists)	14.9	1
Spain	Los Verdes (w/Izquierda de los Pueblos)	1.1	1
UK	Green Party	14.9	0

Source: European Federation of Green Parties; GGEP (1994)

1989 results

As Table 4.3 indicates, green parties enjoyed spectacular success in the 1989 EP election. The EU-wide green vote increased from 2.5 to 7.5 per cent, reflecting a clear transnational 'green trend' in European voting behaviour (Kolinsky 1990; Lodge 1990; Curtice 1991). The most spectacular result was the British Greens' poll of 14.9 per cent of the vote, the highest share a green party had ever received in a nation-wide election anywhere (Franklin and Rüdig 1992: 129). Despite their high per cent of the vote, however British Greens captured no seats because of the UK's single majority voting system.

New Green MEPs from France (eight seats),[6] Italy (five seats), Portugal (one seat) and Spain (one seat) entered the EP, where they joined the German, Belgian and Dutch Greens already comprising the Green Alternative European Link (GRAEL). The German Greens slightly increased their share of the German vote to win eight seats. The Dutch maintained their two seats; and the two Belgian green parties increased their MEPs from two to three (one from Ecolo, two from Agalev).

The Greens' success underscored the electoral importance of pragmatic strategies. For the Spanish and Portuguese, in particular, the necessity of compromise and coalitions with 'non-green' lists allowed them to secure seats in the EP. Similarly, the more professionalised campaign of the Germans and Belgians paid electoral dividends. But within and across green parties, ambivalence towards

Realo strategies and parliamentary participation remained. This ambivalence would continue into the next EP election.

III THE 1994 ELECTION CAMPAIGN

The 1994 campaign was fought under changed circumstances. First, Greens suffered from flagging public support due to a downturn in the economy. Second, the elections took place at a time of waning support for European institutions and European integration more generally. But the trend towards Realo or parliamentary strategies within the green movement continued. By 1994, the supremacy of the parliamentary, professional wing of green parties was unquestioned. On the European level, the shift towards practical politics was reflected in the near complete embrace of the EP as an institution. The tone of the joint party manifesto[7] of green parties clearly indicated an intent and desire not only to play a constructive role within the EP, but also to strengthen it. Individual party manifestos also reflected this shift.

In short, by 1994 the conflict was no longer one of *identity*: it could no longer usefully be called a 'movement-party' conflict because Greens had chosen definitively to tread the parliamentary party path. Movement sentiments were decisively marginalised. Nonetheless, a 'core', central, *strategic* dilemma remained: how to reconcile radical, alternative politics with mainstream, traditional institutions and practices. Despite a general acceptance of the parliamentary means, ambivalence towards EU institutions and EP participation was apparent in most parties.

For the British Greens, a clear expression of Realo sentiment came from FoE founder and Green Party member Jonathon Porrit, who endorsed a Plaid Cymru (Welsh Nationalist Party) candidate over the Green candidate in the Mid and West Wales EP constituency. In defence of his decision, Porrit adopted a Realo line, arguing that the Plaid candidate would serve the wider Green agenda in Europe 'better than any other'. Porrit felt that the Greens would not win 'come hell or high water', and pushed for greater realism and more alliances in green politics.[8]

Porrit's action illustrated the continuing tension between purist and pragmatic strains within the party. Many green members were outraged by Porrit's 'Machiavelli' stance and some charged him with being a 'Green Tory'.[9] Meanwhile, the 'purist' strain of the British Greens was reflected in a strategy that was aimed to influence public debate rather than win seats. The Greens fielded candidates in all 84

British EP constituencies, but they had few illusions about winning any seats or matching their 1989 poll of 15 per cent. Party spokesman John Cornford underlined the point that the campaign was less about gaining parliamentary power and more about influencing other parties. He felt that without significant green presence 'the other parties will shelve their green-tinged policies they adopted post 1989'.[10] Moreover, in certain respects the style of the Greens' election campaign resembled the grassroots, low-key campaigns of earlier decades. For instance, the British Greens failed to inform journalists of the launch of their campaign, so that when the announcement came only one or two journalists were there to report it.[11]

For the German Greens, four years out of national parliament had rendered them more pragmatic and mainstream. The party had undergone a series of internal reforms designed to streamline and professionalise party organisation. In 1993, the West German Greens had united with the loose coalition of citizen initiatives that had contested the 1990 East German elections under the banner *Bündnis 90* (Alliance 90). This pragmatic alliance was more willing to compromise on an array of issues, including the possibility of joining a coalition with the Social Democrat Party (SPD). By the time of the 1994 election campaign, prominent Fundis, including Jutta Ditfurth, had been driven out of the green party.

On the European level, the Realo tendencies were also present. Whereas past manifestos had been used to attack the EU, the 1994 manifesto outlined precise strategies to be carried out once elected. The composition of the Greens' Euro-list also reflected a Realo emphasis. Gone were the symbolic candidates of earlier elections such as ineligible gypsies and imprisoned radicals. Instead, the list was headed by prominent Realos and parliamentarians such as Elisabeth Schrodter and Edith Müller. It contained several sitting MEPs, a representative from an Eastern citizens' movement and a Land government official (Daniel Cohn Bendit). Party spokesman Ludwig Volmer called the list a 'supreme integration achievement', and felt that the party could now enter the European stage with greater coherency and unity.[12]

The manifesto of the *French Greens* (Les Verts) also underlined a more pragmatic stance towards the EU and its institutions. It included a clear demand for strengthening the EP's legislative and appointment and budgetary powers (1994a: 31). But ambivalence towards the EU remained, and the limitations of the EP were recognised. Les Verts (1994a: 10) criticised the EP as 'too timid' and bemoaned its 'limited desire for revolt'. The party further characterised the EP as a place where 'words substitute for action'.

Adopting a far more Realo stance was a rival green list formed in 1990, Generation Ecologie (GE). Led by Brice Lalonde, GE was formed as a more pragmatic, mainstream green party. From 1990 onwards, the two green parties were continually involved in factional fighting both within and between themselves. After an unsuccessful merger (*entente ecologist*) to contest the 1993 national legislative elections, the two green lists decided to contest the European election separately. Thus in France the strategic conflict was played out not within but between competing parties. Les Verts represented a more radical, purist green politics; GE represented a Realo list willing to compromise, strike deals with other parties and absorb issues outside of green politics.

1994 results

Table 4.4 1994 EP election results

Country	Party	%	Seats
Belgium	Agalev	13.0	1
	Ecolo	10.7	1
FRG	B'90/die Grünen	10.1	12
France	Les Verts	2.9	0
	GE	2.0	0
Greece	Politiki Oikologia	1.1	0
Ireland	Comhaontas Glas	7.9	2
Italy	Federazione dei Verdi	3.2	3
Luxembourg	GAP/GLEI	10.9	1
Netherlands	Groen Links	3.8	1
	De Groenen	2.4	0
Portugal	Os Verdes (w/Communists)	11.2	0
UK	Green Party	3.2	0

Source: European Federation of Green Parties

The Greens' strategic dilemma overhung the 1994 EP campaign. The election results (see Table 4.4) indicate that at least the German Greens' more pragmatic stance paid off. By shifting to the centre, the Greens profited from the left wing Social Democratic Party's unpopularity among their traditional supporters. The Greens increased their vote to 10.1 per cent, and their seats to 12.

But Realo strategies were not universally successful. In Belgium, both Agalev and Ecolo returned one seat, but their percentage of the vote dropped by 2 (Agalev) and 3 (Ecolo) per cent. The Belgian

Greens failed to benefit from a widespread protest vote that went instead to far right parties such as *Vlaams Blok*.[13] The Belgian green parties felt the full thrust of the green strategic dilemma. For many voters, Agalev and Ecolo had become established mainstream parties. This perception was strengthened by the Greens' decision in 1992–3 to support the majority parties in federalisation reforms in exchange for support for the introduction of certain eco-taxes. For the Belgian Greens, this compromise may have had a negative impact on their electoral performance. On the other hand, the loss of votes was not decisive; a green core of support remained even without protest votes (Carter 1994: 497).

In The Netherlands, the Greens kept one of their seats but were harmed by internal divisions between two competing green parties. The GPA's successor, 'Green Left' (Groen Links), was led by Nel van Dijk, a long serving Green MEP. She was able to retake her seat with 3.7 per cent of the vote. But another Green MEP, Herman Verbeek, ran under the ticket of the rival, purer green party, De Groenen, instead. De Gronen did not gain enough votes to secure Verbeek another term in the EP. The competition between the leftist Green Left and purer De Groenen parties deprived the Dutch Greens of one of their previous seats.

Internal divisions also hurt the French Greens, whose vote collapsed leading to the loss of all nine of their EP seats. The decision of Les Verts and GE to run separately backfired, with feuding clearly denting voter loyalty (Carter 1994: 500). Many previous green voters supported either the socialists or the new left wing Energie Radicale list, which was headed by Bernard Tapie and included former GE activists.

Less surprising losses occurred in the Mediterranean Member States. In Greece, ecological politics and parties remained marginal; a loose, last minute ecology list (*Politiki Oikologia*) failed to win any seats. Spain and Portugal both lost their Green MEPs. The strong anti-government mood in Spain benefited conservative opposition parties rather than the Greens. The Portuguese Greens retained an uneasy alliance with the Communists, but the alliance was uneven; the Green candidate was too far down the combined list to win a seat. Italian Greens fared better. The *Federazione dei Verdi* (Green Federation), headed by former Environment Commissioner Carlo Ripa di Meana, garnered 3.2 per cent of the vote and three MEPs. But their overall support was lower than in 1989 when they sent five MEPs to Strasbourg. Former members of the 1989 Italian green list had since defected to the far-left list or to the Radical party.

The most crushing, although not surprising, defeat was borne by the British Greens, whose share of the vote sank from 14.9 per cent in 1989 to 3.2 per cent in 1994. Their number of MEPs – zero – remained the same. The Greens never expected to match the success of 1989, when the environment had been a key issue and the major parties were split. The party claimed that they were not intending to win seats but rather to educate. Yet public displays of disunity did little to educate the public and much to harm the Greens' appeal. Because only three of the 84 candidates achieved the 5 per cent necessary to save their deposits, the election was a financial disaster as well.

More encouraging results for the Greens emerged from Luxembourg and Ireland. In Luxembourg, the two small green parties – GAP and GLEI – had previously feuded and campaigned separately. In 1994, however, they joined together on a single list headed by Jup Weber, a well-known and charismatic politician who also served as an MP in the national parliament. In addition to Weber's popularity, the green list also benefited from widespread opposition to a joint French–Luxembourg agreement to build a nuclear waste disposal facility on the border.

The success of the Irish Greens (Comhaontas Glas) came as a surprise. Media coverage of their campaign was minimal and the party had limited resources. Yet the Comhaontas Glas gained two of Ireland's 15 EP seats. Compared to many of their counterparts, the Irish Greens were not as plagued by internal disputes. Moreover, public concern about particular environmental issues helped their campaign. The party actively campaigned against a range of cross-national environmental dangers, such as the commissioning of the Thorp reprocessing plant at Sellafield, England, just across the Irish Sea. They also targeted what they viewed as misuse of EU structural funds for large construction projects in rural areas.

For all green parties, the debate over strategy had significant bearing on the electoral outcome. Clearly, the ability of certain green parties to put aside strategic debates and put forth a united front (Germany, Luxembourg) helped them in the polls. The factionalised campaigns of the French, British and Dutch Greens resulted in a poor showing. Moreover, the strategic dilemma – to what extent should green parties embrace mainstream political structures? – continued to plague most green parties, most notably in Belgium.

Although played out on the domestic level, the strategic debate confronting individual green parties had repercussions for the Greens' European policy. On the European level, the decision to tread the parliamentary path implied acceptance of the European Parliament and its role within the EU. By 1994, all green parties had officially reconciled themselves to working within the EP and had actively sought participation in it. European green parties had agreed to a joint manifesto that stressed reform 'from within' rather than the anti-EU stance of some earlier campaigns. Ironically, this stance came at a time of wide disaffection with the EU, reflected in a particularly low voter turnout (56 per cent) and support of nationalist or anti-EU parties in Denmark, France and Belgium. The Greens' earlier strategy of opposing EU institutions was now fashionable, but their strategy had since become more pragmatic and accepting of EU institutions, warts and all.

V CONCLUSION: STRATEGY VERSUS CONTENT

Green NGOs and social movements were among the first European actors to develop transnational, extra-parliamentary strategies in pursuit of political goals. Informal protests and direct action campaigns prepared the ground for more formal European parliamentary action, which began with the first direct election to the EP in 1979. This election sparked a strategic movement-party debate among the Greens, as early movement tactics soon gave way to more organised parliamentary methods. The merits and risks of continued parliamentary participation was the subject of heated and sustained debate, as parliamentary advocates vied with radical movement activists over the 'best' European strategy.

The 1984 and 1989 campaigns led to the widespread acceptance of reformist/parliamentary strategies. The 1994 election witnessed the marginalisation of movement tendencies and the acceptance of EU institutions, and the EP in particular. By 1994, general acceptance of the EU and EP was official green policy. Parties agreed on the need to reform the Union 'from within', and the value of the EP as vehicle for such reform. Yet the campaigns illustrated that green ambivalence towards the structure, operation and goals of the EU remained acute.

This ambivalence underscores the continuing dilemma faced by green parties. The Greens grew out of various social movements and inherited their predecessors' discourse, values and strategies. At the European level, the Greens were caught in the crossfire of conflicts between the demands of alternative, radical politics and movements and institutional, parliamentary structures. In addition, the playing field of Europe was particularly complex and distant, exacerbating an already difficult balancing game between movement and party (or, subsequently, between radical and reformist politics). On one hand, Europe offered electoral opportunities not readily available on the national level. On the other hand, the EU's image as a remote, non-democratic body rendered green parliamentary participation especially problematic.

In all four EP elections analysed here, strategic disputes overshadowed any discussion of the content of a green European policy. Preoccupied with strategic questions, both sides neglected the 'end goal' of green participation, i.e. achieving a decentralised, ecological 'Europe of the Regions'. On one hand, grassroots activists lacked an institutional vision, a practical concept of what Europe should be and what methods could best achieve it. Additionally, radical proponents were unable to specify how transnational goals could be achieved, if not through a supranational body like the EU. Put another way: 'Radical charm will only turn into radical politics when the Greens realize and reflect upon the conditions and feasibility of their demands' (Nostitz and Merkel 1986).

The parliamentarians or reformists, on the other hand, could be accused of putting method before aims, strategy before content. On the European level, Green members advocating participation in the EP election often considered these means to be ends in themselves. As a result, the substantive issues of the desirability of integration, or formulation of an alternative European 'community', were neglected. In both cases, the need for and improvement of transnational coordination of green party aims and goals were also neglected, as individual parties focused on domestic strategic debates.

The conflicts analysed here have consequences for the implementation of a green European policy. The dominance of parliamentary strategies in most green parties indicated that, to a certain extent, Greens were attempting to act as a party, or at least exploit governmental structures as would a party. But all green parties lacked some of the traditional qualities of a party, such as the ability to elaborate policy collectively.

Moreover, parties traditionally define ends and then collectively seek means to achieve them. Parties depend on consensus, but in the fight for EP representation, consensus proved elusive. Even more difficult was the problem of agreeing on a clear green *strategy*. All four elections demonstrated that the Greens had not yet decided whether to exploit institutional advantages fully or maintain their 'political chastity' as representatives of alternative politics. They thus occupied the unique 'middle ground' of a green party – between the street and the parliamentary chamber – but at the expense of strategic coherence and unified collective action.

5   Greens and the European Parliament: an inside look

INTRODUCTION

This chapter examines the internal structure, organisation and politics of the Greens within the EP. The internal coherence of the Green faction has improved significantly since green parties first entered the EP in 1984. However, the Greens' European activities have been hampered by two conflicts: a) between radical (movement) and pragmatic (parliamentary) imperatives; and b) between different types and styles of national green parties.

Section I introduces the first group of Green MEPs, comprising the Green Alternative European Link (GRAEL). The internal conflicts besetting this group – and leading to its dissolution – are explored in Section II. Section III examines the subsequent 1989–94 Green Group in the European Parliament (GGEP), and highlights their more pragmatic approach to EP politics. In Section IV the second GGEP (1994–9) is analysed. Section V assesses the strategic dilemmas facing Green MEPs and outlines their opportunites and challenges within the EP.

I THE GREENS ENTER THE EP

In 1984, public support from an electorate increasingly concerned with environmental issues helped propel green parties into the EP. German Greens fared the best, capturing 8.2 per cent of the German vote and seven seats. 'Non-green' movement-parties also made gains. Radical federalist and regionalist parties from Belgium and Italy won several seats, and an anti-EC movement in Denmark received 20.8 per cent of the Danish vote and four seats in the EP (Buck 1989: 169).

EU rules for the 1984–9 parliamentary term stipulated that official party groups within the EP needed to comprise at least 10 MEPs from a minimum of three different countries.[1] Through the building of factions, the representatives of smaller parties were able to enjoy the significant financial, structural and procedural advantages offered to larger, more established parties in the EP. For example, factions or party groups were given the resources to employ office staff, convene conferences and provide translation services. Moreover, leaders of the party groups took part in drafting the EP's plenary agenda and allocating committee chairs (Müller-Rommel 1985a: 394).

Following the 1984 EP election, green parties from Germany, Belgium and The Netherlands technically had gained enough mandates to form a green faction or political group. The Germans resisted. An incipient cleavage between European movement-parties emerged that rendered coordination among different national groups extremely difficult. Green MEPs were like any others in one respect: they inevitably reflected national concerns and preferences. In this case, national differences caused tension between the more conservative 'purist' ecologists, as represented in Belgium's Ecolo, and leftist 'rainbow' parties like the German and Dutch GPA. Whereas the latter parties attempted to represent a broad alliance of ecological, feminist, peace and New Left groups, the former 'purist' parties tended to shun connections with the New Left and focused more specifically on ecological issues.

The Germans were afraid that with only the bare minimum of delegates in the faction, the group as a whole would be vulnerable to the minority wishes of single faction members. Put another way: 'in a . . . ["purist"] green faction the Dutch and German Greens would have been vulnerable to political blackmail by the minority vote of the Belgians' (Müller-Rommel 1985a: 393). Instead, the Germans insisted that a future parliamentary group in the EP should incorporate radical leftist movement-parties. In the view of German Green MEPs, this inclusion was desirable for two reasons. One was that increasing the size of the faction would give their parliamentary group more clout within the EP. For instance, because speaking time in EP plenary sessions is allotted in relation to the strength of the political faction, a larger group would receive more time to voice their views in Strasbourg. Second, and more importantly for the Germans, was that the enlargement would act as a safeguard against the 'blackmail tactics' of the purist ecologist Belgian parties.

The political differences among these groups was palpable to the new MEPs. Differences arose not just between the various national parties or lists, but within the lists as well. For instance, the Dutch GPA was itself composed of four different parties. One newcomer described the competition among different groups as 'a rainbow in which one color is continually attempting to cover or blur into another color' (Ennich 1986: 29). But after several fierce rounds of negotiation among both green and non-green movement-parties, the 'Rainbow Group' was formed as a parliamentary group in the EP.

Upon its formation in 1984, the Rainbow consisted of 20 elected members of the EP. Of the eight political groups constituting the EP in the 1984–9 term, the Rainbow was the second smallest. It was also one of the most diverse. In both its conception and structure, the Rainbow was designed to be a purely technical group. It was an extremely heterogeneous assemblage made up of three sub-groups that rarely worked or met together. The main group within the Rainbow, and the one that represented green issues in the EP, was the Green Alternative European Link (GRAEL) (see Table 5.1). The two other sub-groups in the Rainbow were the European Free Alliance (a collection of regionalist groups) and the Danish movement against the EC.

Table 5.1 GRAEL seats in the EP, 1984

FRG	7
Belgium	2
Netherlands	2
Italy	1
	12

In 1984, the GRAEL included a total of 12 parliamentarians: seven from West Germany, two from Belgium, two from The Netherlands, and one from Italy.[2] As their common platform, the GRAEL used the Paris Declaration that was agreed by European green parties in April 1984. It will be recalled that the platform was an extremely vague set of principles setting forth the GRAEL's vision of a 'new, neutral, decentralised Europe'. It was based on opposition to deployment of nuclear missiles in East and West Europe; a no-compromise policy on the environment; equal rights for women and minorities; a new economic policy on employment and social benefits; reorganisation of economic relations between Europe and the Third World; free exercise of fundamental civil rights; and ecological forms of agriculture (GRAEL 1984). Because the group was so diverse, the Declaration was inevitably vague. The intention (and hope) was that GRAEL members would develop the specifics of these broad principles during their first term.

As a representative body of several different movement-parties, the GRAEL's organisational structure was purposefully kept loose and non-conformist. Strategies were designed to encourage internal democracy and grassroots control within the GRAEL. Its meetings were generally 'accessible to the grassroots' (open to the public). New working groups were established to research political issues relevant to the grassroots movements (Buck 1989: 170). Moreover, German MEPs were expected to accept revenues roughly equivalent to that of a skilled worker, with the remainder of the rather generous MEP allowance and salary re-routed back to the party for various projects and ecological causes.

In its first term, the GRAEL employed 18 staff members in Brussels. All staff members received equal wages and were responsible for preparing the political work within the working groups. No staff member was employed to do strictly auxiliary work such as typing, photocopying and similar services, since the GRAEL's policy was 'not to separate manual and intellectual work' (GRAEL 1988b: 5).

In addition, several specific measures were taken to encourage wide and equal participation within the GRAEL. Most important was the emphasis placed on equality between the MEPs and their alternates, or 'co-deputies' (or, in German, *Nachrücker*). All GRAEL MEPs and their alternates participated in the political work of the group with 'equal rights and duties' (GRAEL 1988b: 5). GRAEL members and their deputies drew the same salary and both were entitled to vote within the group. For the German and Dutch members, equality between MEPs and alternates was also enforced through the rotation policy. Halfway into their first legislative period, these Green MEPs were expected to step down from their posts and be replaced by their alternates. The former members (*Weggerückten*) continued to work within the group as 'elder statespersons'. Only four of the seven Germans and one of the two Dutch MEPs delivered on their commitment.

II CONFLICTS WITHIN GRAEL

National and ideological differences

Despite the consensual character of the GRAEL's internal organ-isation, relations within the GRAEL were difficult from the start. Even the supposedly minor issue of what to name the faction was resolved only after long and agonising debate. According to German GRAEL members, the German acronym for the original name, Grün-alternative Europäische Bündnis (GRAEB), was too similar to the German word *Grab* (grave) and thus not appropriate for the 'new beginning' of the green party in Brussels (GRAEL 1988a: 7). MEPs from other countries, however, disclosed another reason for changing the name from GRAEB to GRAEL: they preferred a 'more neutral, non-Germanic' acronym.[3]

Nor did conflicts among the different national groups fade over the 1984–9 term. In particular, the underlying tension between 'purist' Belgium and 'rainbow' Germans continued unabated. Reflecting back on her term in the GRAEL, one German MEP remarked that

> We [the German Greens] should have taken more care in our relationships with Greens from other countries, especially France and Belgium. Then we would have achieved a lot more. Instead, we put forth the impression of a house divided, a family at feud.[4]

Throughout the GRAEL's 1984–9 term, the West German Greens enjoyed clear numerical dominance within the GRAEL: over one-third of GRAEL MEPs were German. A majority of staff members were also German, since distribution of staff by nationality was roughly equivalent to that of the countries represented in the GRAEL. Green MEPs from The Netherlands and Belgium expressed concern that the Germans, given their relative financial and organisational potency, tended to lean towards the 'arrogance of the mighty'.[5]

Concerns and resentment over German dominance within the GRAEL were shared by green parties within and outside the EP. Indignant about the conduct of German GRAEL members, spokes-woman for the British Greens, Sara Parkin, complained that 'there is no real excuse for the arrogant and often contemptuous behaviour of some members of the German party' (Parkin 1989: 259). German MEPs themselves admitted that this was a problem: 'Yes, well the Germans are known as rather addicted to self-promoting themselves. That took some time to work out' (Ennich 1986: 29).

Movement-party conflicts

A more serious source of disputes stemmed from the measures pursued to try to ensure internal democracy. The internal organ-isation of the GRAEL – designed to strike a proper balance of movement and parliamentary imperatives – was a constant theme of conflict and dissatisfaction among MEPs. For instance, the division of manual and intellectual work was described as 'utterly disastrous' by one German Green fulfilling his second term as an MEP.[6] According to another GRAEL member serving as an alternate, the main impression of GRAEL internal relations was of an ongoing power struggle among MEPs and between MEPs and alternates. The most important issues seemed to be 'who's "The Greatest"; who's taking what from whom; who's poaching on whose estate?' (Nitsch 1986: 55).

The rotation policy caused particularly bitter disagreements within the GRAEL. In an official account of his GRAEL activities (*Rechnenschaftsbericht*), MEP Schwalba-Hoth (1988: 2) reported that the principle of rotation – and, specifically those who refused to abide by it – hurt both the operation and atmosphere of the GRAEL. When the first rotation deadline arrived, he and three other of the seven German MEPs agreed to step down. Other Green MEPs argued that strict adherence to principles of grassroots democracy was not always possible if Greens were to assume positions of political responsibility. They emphasised further the need for experienced, qualified people to deal with the complex institutional and bureaucratic apparatus of the EC (Bloch von Blottnitz 1986b: 39). In other words, MEPs continued the debate between 'parliamentarians' and 'movement-oriented' Greens that had emerged in the early stages of Green activity in Europe.

Overall, the Greens' first EP electoral success sharpened rather than mitigated the movement-party debate. In effect, the 1984 European election results shifted the movement-party debate from the theoretical to the practical plane. The debate was no longer limited to the question of whether green parties should field candidates for the EP, or whether they should join forces with leftist or radical parties. The question became whether the MEPs sent to the EP could balance extra-parliamentary demands with the imperatives of parliamentary politics.

Strategic and ideological differences had consequences for the Greens' European policy. In party politics, a diversity of views often produces creative alternatives to policy problems. In the Greens' case, however, a coherent set of Euro-political goals and strategies was blocked by trenchant antagonism among the Greens and, specifically, 'between those who believed reform of the EC was possible and those who believed the EC system was neither tolerable nor reformable in its current state' (Scheuer 1989: 191).

More concretely, Green MEPs were either unwilling or unable to agree on fundamental measures before the EP. For instance, the Greens had no position on Community enlargement (accession of Spain and Portugal) in 1986. In the event, the GRAEL put in votes both for and against enlargement. They also put in contradictory votes on resolutions concerning increased competence for the EP. Green

MEPs could not agree on a common position towards the Single European Act. In short, divided by national, ideological and personal splits, the GRAEL was a weak and divided political force.

III   FROM THE GRAEL TO THE GGEP: 1989–94

The 1989 EP election heralded a high point of green awareness in Europe. In almost all EU Member States, green parties managed to increase their share of the vote. Green parties already represented in the EP were able to maintain or increase their seats. The German Greens slightly increased their share of the vote, winning 8.4 per cent of the German vote and eight seats. The Dutch Greens also increased their share of the vote to 7 per cent and sent back two veterans of the GRAEL. The two Belgium parties also retained seats. Agalev's incumbent, Paul Staes, returned with 12.2 per cent of the vote. The highest per cent of any green party was gained by Ecolo, which won 16.5 per cent of the Belgian French-speaking vote and two seats.[7] GRAEL veterans were joined by new Green MEPs from France (eight seats),[8] Italy (five seats), Portugal and Spain (one seat each).

But the Greens' electoral success did not resolve internal tensions. Instead, existing conflicts were exacerbated by new ones. With the entry of the French, Portuguese, Spanish and Italian Greens into the EP for the first time, the latent conflict re-emerged between more conservative or 'purist' green parties, as represented by the French Greens, and 'rainbow' green parties such as the German Greens. Whilst this conflict first threatened at the time of the GRAEL's formation in 1984, it had remained muted because of the Germans' clear domination. Moreover, 'purist' green parties were under-represented in the GRAEL, as none of the Mediterranean green parties gained entry in 1984.

By contrast, 'purist' green parties held the majority following the 1989 election. Many German Greens felt outnumbered and discriminated against by the French and Italian green representatives. Several Germans complained that the French and Italian Greens had sent their 'conservative elites' to Europe (Bullard 1990: 5). These Mediterranean 'elites', moreover, held a particularly low opinion of the current status of the GRAEL, which they viewed as too leftist and quarrelsome.[9] One incoming French MEP offered his explanation for GRAEL's problems: 'There was so much fighting and squabbling with others and themselves. . . . You see, the Germans [in GRAEL] were decidedly leftist and didn't want to work with other green parties. . . . And of course they completely ignored the French.'[10]

The new contingent of 'purist' parties meant that the composition of the GRAEL would change dramatically. The new parties were not interested in being part of the larger Rainbow Group. French and Italian, as well as several new Belgium MEPs, sought instead to form a 'purer' green political group. While GRAEL veterans, especially from Germany, sought to maintain a left rainbow group, they were outnumbered by 'new blood' seeking new opportunities (GGEP 1994: 8–9).

Had the GRAEL been a more cohesive, coherent body it might have withstood these external challenges. But by the end of its first term, the GRAEL still had made no firm decision for or against parliamentarisation; the movement-party dilemma had not been resolved or even tackled. Moreover, the GRAEL had no agreed collective goals to be pursued in Europe. It was beset by vastly different conceptions of and attitudes towards Europe and the 'best' green European policy. The body GRAEL could not withstand the push-and-pull of these multiple conflicts. Under the pressure of both internal and external demands, the GRAEL dissolved in summer 1989.

Green group in the European Parliament (GGEP)

The defunct GRAEL was replaced by the Green Group in the European Parliament (GGEP) on 25 July 1989. The GGEP was significantly different from the GRAEL in composition, organisation and attitude. At its conception, the GGEP consisted of 30 MEPs (see Table 5.2) and was the fifth largest of the 11 EP political groups in the 1989–94 session.[11] In addition to those countries with elected GGEP MEPs (Belgium, France, Italy, Portugal, The Netherlands, Spain and the Federal Republic of Germany), the GGEP added two

Table 5.2 GGEP seats, July 1989

France	8
FRG	8
Italy	7
Belgium	3
Netherlands	2
Portugal	1
Spain	1
	30

Note: The GGEP also included an observer from East Germany and one from the UK.

honorary members. First, to counter what the GGEP viewed as Britain's unjust first-past-the-post electoral system, they included one British Green representative, Jean Lambert, who was given full voting powers within the group. Also, Hans Meisel, a member of the former East German citizen initiative group, *Neues Forum*, joined as an observer in February 1991.

Unlike the GRAEL, the GGEP formed its own parliamentary group and was not a part of the Rainbow Group. Because it no longer included the anti-EC or regionalist parties that helped make up the Rainbow, the GGEP was a more cohesive green collective rather than just an expedient coalition of leftist alternative groups. The new group did include three 'non-green' members: a Basque regionalist, Juan Maria Bandres Molet; a member of Italy's Democrazia Proletaria, Eugenio Melandri; and Marco Tardash, elected on the Italian Anti-Prohibition list, an off-shoot of the Italian Radical Party. Compared to the Rainbow Group, however, the GGEP was much more a 'political rather than a technical group' (Lannoye 1991: 1). The basis for membership of the new group included acceptance of the principles laid out in the March 1989 'Common Statement of the European Greens'. The Statement emphasised the pre-eminence of environmental protection, criticised the single market as 'profoundly un-ecological', and called for 'a Europe of autonomous regions without any borders' (GGEP 1994: 8).

German Greens comprised the second largest national contingent in the GGEP. But numerically and otherwise, the Germans no longer enjoyed a position of leadership. Structurally, the GGEP's primary decision-making body was an executive committee (Bureau) with eight members and two presidents. Compared to the German-dominated GRAEL, the GGEP was clearly 'Mediterranean-led'. The GGEP's first executive committee was led by one Portuguese and one Italian president; the only German member served as a 'co-vice president'. The second executive (formed 15 months into the term) was similar, featuring one Belgian and one Italian president, and one French and one German vice president. Moreover, whereas key administrative posts in the GRAEL had been held by Germans, the GGEP's staff was headed by three secretaries-general representing three different nationalities. A final indicator of the German's lost dominance was that whereas German had been the working language of the GRAEL, the GGEP embraced French as the primary tongue.

Thus, at its inception, the GGEP was a larger, more coherent group influenced more by French and Italian Greens than the German-dominated GRAEL. Yet, despite the GGEP's increased electoral support and size, it encountered the same opportunities and dilemmas that had faced the GRAEL. Internal conflicts relating to national and strategic differences plagued the new group from its early days.

National differences

Because it comprised representatives from seven different nations, the GGEP was far more riven by national differences than was the German-dominated GRAEL. First, national ideological differences between purer French ecologists and left rainbow Germans became more intense after 1989. German and Dutch GGEP members remained much more concerned with non-environmental issues such as feminism and neo-colonialism, whilst their French and Belgian counterparts hoped to focus primarily on issues directly related to the environment, such as eco-regionalism and eco-development. Other tensions related to different national attitudes towards European integration. Several new Italian and French representatives were committed to an 'ardent defense' of federalism and welcomed further moves towards European integration (GGEP 1994: 9). Dutch members, on the other hand, preferred to retain their wholesale critique of European integration in its current form (GGEP 1994: 18).

These national differences were most apparent in the first few years of the new group. On one hand, the different national priorities often formed a wide basis for constructive discussion concerning the GGEP's main goals within the EP. But more often such differences were manifest in petty personal disputes or disagreements over staff matters. Reflecting on the early days of the GGEP, British observer Jean Lambert recalled that:

> the overall period of staff recruitment was immensely long and complex. It was necessary to respect gender parity at all levels and to ensure a broad national base. . . . there was a certain degree of internal maneuvering to ensure particular candidates were appointed.
>
> (Lambert 1991: 5)

Unhappy about the recruitment process, the German contingent within the GGEP complained that 'a severe and dishonest battle for political influence took place. National political interest predominated and not the search for common political projects' (quoted in Lambert 1991).

Movement-party conflicts

National differences aside, the GGEP was also faced with the movement-party or 'radical-reformist' dilemma and the conflicts it engendered. Whereas some MEPs were more comfortable emphasising radical movement goals and strategies, others embraced more fully their reformist parliamentary role. The GGEP as a whole attempted to straddle the radical-reformist divide by representing the best of both traditions.

Emphasising its grassroots movement links, the GGEP, like the GRAEL, sought to be different from 'traditional' political groups. In particular, they attempted to avoid the rigid structure of established party organisations. Instead, the GGEP emphasised its support of alternative politics and grassroots principles. The group's structure was intended to allow gender parity, a diversity of views and multinational representation. Whilst adopting a more formal structure than the GRAEL, the GGEP still embraced grassroots-style organisational policies. For instance, French MEPs agreed to rotate half-way through their term and make way for their co-deputies. The French co-deputies shared work, salary and voting rights. The idea was to guard against the creation of a parliamentary elite.[12]

In addition, many MEPs retained some contact with movements or groups outside the EP. As one German MEP noted:

> Those pressure groups and movements not representing powerful interests are still provided a platform by us. For instance a French colleague and I are putting on a work-shop in alternative economics and others are planned. . . . The European coordination of various projects remains an important part of our political work here.[13]

Moreover, GRAEL veterans such as Wilfried Telkämper and Hermann Verbeek retained close links to radical roots and continued to regard extra-parliamentary representation as one of their primary roles within the EP.

But the majority of GGEP members took a different stance. In comparison to the GRAEL, most GGEP members limited their formal and informal contact with movements outside the Parliament. An internal document adopted by the group in 1990 explicitly stated the need to form a coherent political force rather than a composite of various social movements:

> Our identity in the institution of the EP is that of a Parliamentary Group representing a party, not the totality of all the means of

political action available to the international environment, eco-pacifist, non-violence, freedom and emancipatory movement. . . .
We cannot confuse our role with that of particular constituencies from which we come. We have, instead, to take up the role entrusted to us by the electorate, to construct a new Europe.[14]

In other respects, the GGEP also consciously embraced parliamentarisation. First, the GGEP devised conventional and cooperative strategies of a sort shunned by the GRAEL. For instance, it pushed hard for the use of economic incentives as a tool for environmental policy. The GGEP embraced a report by Dutch staff member Alexander de Roo (1990) advocating a tax on non-renewable energy sources. The author of the report explained that the GGEP was developing a whole array of economic tools because 'legislative norms alone won't do. You have to acknowledge – but not concede to – the concerns of governments and industries'.[15] This was a marked departure from the 'no compromise' stance of the GRAEL.

An Italian GGEP member underscored what he saw as the more 'rational' approach of the GGEP on environmental and energy issues: 'We're different than GRAEL. It's time we came up with concrete alternative energy proposals. We need to demonstrate – scientifically – that this transition to regional energy programs makes environmental and economic sense'.[16]

Reflecting on the GGEP's priorities in the EU, a co-president of the Group underlined the importance of a new approach:

I think it's right to focus on new rules for the economy, including the GATT. We need new rules inside and outside the EC. Economics must internalise environmental [concerns]. To realise this aim it is necessary to have concrete things like eco-taxes, CO_2 tax, civil liability. This is my priority.[17]

More generally, the GGEP's overall attitude towards parliamentary participation was more accepting than the GRAEL's. Instead of the confrontational tactics employed by the GRAEL within the EP, the GGEP chose to work more closely with other parliamentary groups, even if this meant compromise and accommodation. One Belgian Green MEP compared the two groups in this way:

The earlier group was essentially a German group which played very hard politics. They were not really integrated into the Parliament. They were essentially formed for the movements and were not [part] of the EP.[18]

Whereas the GGEP shared the GRAEL's criticism of the EP's limited power *vis-à-vis* other EU institutions, its co-president, Lannoye, ultimately argued for green participation within the EP: 'Nevertheless, [the EP] is the only supranational parliamentary body where such fateful matters are debated. For that reason alone the voice of the Greens should make [itself] heard with conviction, coherence and strong arguments' (Lannoye 1991: 2).

By mid-term, GGEP members were deeply entrenched in the EP's parliamentary committee structure and held the chair or vice-chair of five committees (Bowler and Farrell 1992: 133). Reporting back on a conflict between the Commission and the Parliament over parliamentary powers, French Green Didier Anger went so far as to claim that 'the Greens are the only ones to have defended to the end the powers of the Parliament' (GGEP 1991d: 3).

The point is that the GGEP appeared to have planted its green roots more firmly in the parliamentary sector. Under the leadership of Paul Lannoye, a skilled conciliator, the Group established itself as a more coherent, integrated parliamentary player. But the movement-party tension remained throughout the term and was expressed in the internal differences, conflicts and politics of the GGEP.

First, moves to 'professionalise' and parliamentarise the group were not unanimously accepted. Nor was the pace at which such parliamentarisation should occur. Whereas most of the serious GRAEL 'Fundis' had not been re-elected to the EP, a few remained in the group, at least initially. One such member, Dorothee Piermont, left the Group in dramatic fashion in October 1989 to join the looser Rainbow Group. For those that remained, the proper balance between parliamentary and extra-parliamentary strategies was a constant source of disagreement.

These strategic debates manifest themselves in a variety of specific prolonged conflicts concerning the statutes of the group and nomination of group staff. A 1990 memo from the German members of the GGEP outlined ways in which the GGEP was violating green principles agreed in the Group's Common Statement. In particular, German members criticised the division between the GGEP Bureau and MEPs on the one hand, and staff on the other. The authors of the memo asserted that in the GRAEL such a 'non-green' hierarchy would not have existed, and bureau members, MEPs and staff would all have had equal standing.

Whilst nominally about specific items of GGEP structure, these disagreements were indicative of larger strategic differences within the Group. In an internal memo,[19] German members of the

Group summed up (in exaggerated form) the strategic differences in this way:

> The majority [of the GGEP] seems to believe that hierarchy . . . and traditional institutional power positions characteristic of parliamentary representation are exclusively effective to implement green policies. We believe this is a serious error . . . institutional participation has to be linked to extraparliamentary movements.

The Germans were joined in their critique by other members. Dutch MEP Nel van Dijk reminded the Group of the continuing strategic dilemma. She outlined the strategic choices facing the Greens, beginning with the 'movement' strategy that could be followed by the GGEP:

> We can use Parliament as a forum to express our indignation at the inability of politics to contribute towards a world in which the environment is taken into consideration to a great extent. If this is our aim, whether we achieve anything in parliament is immaterial. All that counts is our public image.

She then went on to outline parliamentary goals:

> We want to be involved in the decision-making process, to influence its outcome as far as possible and to steer it in our direction. To achieve this, we shall have to enter into (temporary) coalitions and make compromises. . . .[20]

Compared to the GRAEL, the GGEP had made clear its willingness to head down the latter parliamentary path. However, the dangers of this parliamentary route were clear. In the same memo, van Dijk warned her colleagues that if the parliamentary route were taken, 'we must take care not to betray our principles in the process'.

Strategic differences aside, conflicts also arose on specific issues. In one particularly bitter dispute, Greens both within and outside the GGEP clashed over issues of the Group's representation, autonomy and accountability. The dispute began in 1990 when three Italian members of the GGEP (themselves former Italian Radicals) signed an EP resolution by Italian Radical Party leader Marco Pannella calling for the removal of sanctions against South Africa and attacking the African National Congress for still having not renounced violence.

A concerned memo from Jürgen Maier, a member of the German Greens federal executive, claimed that the resolution was 'full of racist spirit' and was signed by 'well known right wingers' as well as the three members of the GGEP. He regretted the fact that the GGEP was associated with such company and with such a resolution.

The Bureau's reply to Maier's memo noted that the GGEP Bureau did:

> not want to engage in discussion with representatives of committees of parties, even if this affects parties or lists whose members belong to the parliamentary Group. We would otherwise come into the difficult situation [of being] held accountable to secretaries of executive committee member of die Grünen, Liste Verdi . . . Les Verts, etc. . . .
>
> (quoted in Feinstein 1992: 381)

The Bureau's response was motivated by the need to assert the GGEP's autonomy and independence from national green parties. But for other members of the Group, the response raised the wider issue of the role of grassroots representation and accountability within the GGEP. Some non-Bureau members resented the high-handed manner in which the Bureau members dealt with party concerns. Such aloofness by the Bureau was not deemed appropriate for a green party (Feinstein 1992: 381). The sarcastic reply from Maier to the Bureau underlined the problem:

> Your honour, who does the Right Honorable Bureau deem import-ant enough to engage in a discussion? . . . . I devotedly take the liberty to ask how Your Excellencies in the Bureau think democratic accountability of representatives of the people should work if not by discussion and by being held accountable?
>
> (quoted in Feinstein 1992: 381)

Eventually this particular conflict subsided, but it left in its wake the thorny movement-party dilemma: how green or 'unique' could the GGEP be whilst simultaneously acting as a competent, independent parliamentary actor?

In short, the strategic debate plagued the GGEP as it had the GRAEL. Greens in Parliament still wished to remain 'different' from conventional parties. They sought to represent specific green parties, but also the wider green movement. Summing up the GGEP's ecological mandate, GGEP co-president Paul Lannoye explained that the chosen strategy of the GGEP was 'a constant pedagogy of political ecology . . . Fulfilling this demanding task in coordination with the whole ecological movement is a constant challenge – a challenge we must take up' (1991: 2). Yet the difficulty of meeting this challenge was perhaps underestimated.

Moreover, personal squabbling and national differences further disrupted the work of the GGEP. Internal disputes between different national and ideological sects were predictable and common within the EP's political groups. But such conflicts were costly for the GGEP, as it had formed itself as a coherent whole, a political entity in and of itself. More importantly, many Green MEPs and supporters felt that conflicts came at cost of constructive progress towards the 'greening' of the EU.

IV   GGEP2: 1994–9

The 1994 election brought mixed fortunes for the Greens. Green parties fared well in Germany, Italy and Ireland, but failed miserably in France and Great Britain (see Chapter 4). After a month of heated discussion concerning possible alliances, the second Green Group (GGEP2) formed in July 1994 (see Bomberg 1996). It consisted of 22 members from six Member States. The most fundamental change was the absence of the French Greens (who failed to win a single seat) and the entry, for the first time, of one Luxemburger and two Irish Greens. With the accession to the EU of Austria, Finland and Sweden in January 1995, the GGEP gained another three MEPs (one from each new entrant). Three additional Greens joined the GGEP following Sweden's first EP election in September 1995.[21] In December 1996, MEP Noël Mamere (France) left the European Radical Alliance to join the GGEP but left to serve in the French National Assembly in 1997. By late 1997, the number of Green MEPs stood at 27 (see Table 5.3).

In national make-up, strategies and ideology, the second Green Group represented a mix of both GRAEL and GGEP1 tendencies. In terms of its national make-up, it was similar to the GRAEL. First, like the GRAEL, the Group lacked a strong 'Mediterranean' element to counter-balance the northern European (especially German) presence. Although Italians were represented, there were (initially) no French, Spanish or Portuguese members of the GGEP2.[22] The Mediterranean presence, according to several current members of the Group, was 'sorely missed'. Remarked one (non-German) member: 'The Group is so heavy and earnest now; the French lightened things considerably. The Germans take things much more seriously.'[23]

Like the GRAEL, the Group was clearly dominated by German members. German and non-German MEPs agreed that this imbalance had a significant effect on the style and substance of the Group. But whereas the Germans dominated numerically, they seldom shared common positions or views. Rather, a recurring problem was the

Table 5.3 GGEP MEPs, 1994–9

Name	Member State	Party
Magda Aelvoet	Belgium	Angalev
Adelaide Aglietta	Italy	Fed. dei Verdi
Nuala Ahern	Ireland	Comhaontas Glas
Undine Bloch von Blottnitz	Germany	B'90/die Grünen
Hiltrud Breyer	Germany	B'90/die Grünen
Daniel Cohn-Bendit	Germany	B'90/die Grünen
Nel van Dijk	Netherlands	Groen Links
Per Gahrton	Sweden	Miljöpartiet
Fiwi Graefe zu Baringdorf	Germany	B'90/die Grünen
Heidi Hautala	Finland	Vihreät Liittoo
Ulf Holm	Sweden	Miljöpartiet
Wolfgang Kreissl-Dörfer	Germany	B'90/die Grünen
Paul Lannoye	Belgium	Ecolo
Malou Lindholm	Sweden	Miljöpartiet
Noël Mamere (until 1997)	France	Energie Radicale
Patricia McKenna	Ireland	Comhaontas Glas
Edith Müller	Germany	B'90/die Grünen
Leoluca Orlando	Italy	La Rete
Carlo Ripa di Meana	Italy	Fed. dei Verdi
Claudia Roth	Germany	B'90/die Grünen
Inger Schörling	Sweden	Miljöpartiet
Elisabeth Schroedter	Germany	B'90/die Grünen
Irene Soltwedel-Schäfer	Germany	B'90/die Grünen
Gianni Tamino	Italy	Fed. dei Verdi
Wilfried Telkämper	Germany	B'90/die Grünen
Wolfgang Ullmann	Germany	B'90/die Grünen
Johannes Voggenhuber	Austria	Grünen Österreich
Frieder Otto Wolf	Germany	B'90/die Grünen

inability of German members to agree amongst themselves, and their tendency to use the Group as a platform to play out internal battles and personal disputes. One non-German Green MEP complained that the Germans continually fought 'amongst themselves and tr[ied] to get the rest of us to take sides'.[24]

In terms of strategic orientation, the structure of the GGEP2 revealed the Group's desire to work efficiently whilst satisfying 'purist' demands for decentralisation and openness. In an attempt to reflect national and gender diversity, the GGEP2 continued its tradition of an executive bureau including two co-presidents (one female, one male) and vice-presidents from different Member States.[25] MEPs could have their own assistants, but several additional staff or 'collaborateurs' worked for the Group as a whole. Policy issues were covered by working groups organised around subject areas. Administratively, the GGEP was assisted by a secretariat-general and a press attaché.

Yet compared to its predecessors, the GGEP2 has softened its radical grassroots structure in order to streamline its operations and, in the words of an administrative staff member, to 'run a tighter ship'.[26] For instance, the idea of a 15-month rotating Presidency – proposed to avoid entrenchment of an elite – quietly slipped off the agenda: German Claudia Roth has served as President since 1994. Like the GGEP1, the majority of the second Group adopted reformist rather than radical strategies. Most MEPs exploited the opportunities afforded by EP membership, whilst implicitly accepting the basic parliamentary 'rules of the game'.[27] But important exceptions existed, and several individual GGEP members continued to eschew conventional parliamentary behaviour and focused instead on movement goals. For instance, one Irish MEP highlighted the need for the Greens to act as 'trouble-makers':

> Our most effective role so far is giving people at home information about what is going on, informing them of the ways they can object to things or protest and try to get their point of view across . . . and to a certain extent, causing trouble because up until now there has been a lot of apathy and complacency.[28]

The GGEP2 paid attention to conceptual and institutional issues more than either previous group. Yet discussions concerning them did not always lead to coherent Group positions on policies. For instance, discussions concerning economic and monetary union and the Common and Foreign and Security Policy (CFSP) uncovered major schisms in the Group concerning the desirability of a federal Europe. A clear divide emerged between those who desired closer European union (led by the Italians and some Germans) and those who opposed further European integration (led by the Swedish).[29] The second Group included members firmly opposed to the EU and ambivalent about European integration. Within the GRAEL this position was shared by certain German members and manifest in opposition to the single market.

After 1994, the opposition stance was shared by some of the newer entrants, especially the Swedish and Irish. Often these MEPs' attitude towards the EU echoed with remarkable similarity the views expressed by the GRAEL. For example, Swedish MEP Per Gharton led the Swedish Greens' campaign against accession to the EU. He wrote a series of articles warning against the creation of a 'Fortress Europe'. Most threatening to Gharton was the EU's desire to become one political entity/unity, a kind of West European superpower. They want to become a superpower in competition with the US and Japan. Earlier of course, [the EU] was very much against the Soviet Union, but that has changed now. It is not said so openly, but it is also against Africa and Asia and not least against the Muslims, the closest neighbor of Europe. . . . I think this is one of the most threatening and unsympathetic aspects of the EC.[30]

Such an oppositionist stance, though shared by the GRAEL, was significantly muted during the GGEP1 era. In the second Group, division on these issues usually resulted in an 'agreement to disagree' rather than a concerted effort to reconcile opposing views. One long-serving Green MEP mused that 'some new members today are totally against European integration. . . . but they will learn. Europe is not what they think it is.'[31]

In addition to national, strategic and conceptual differences, the second Group was characterised by individual, personal differences that seemed certain to have a considerable impact on the Group's operations. Each member had his or her own 'pet' projects or policy areas. This individualism had positive consequences: with limited resources it made sense for a small group to concentrate on specific issues. Moreover, MEPs enjoyed considerable freedom. Said one new member: 'In bigger groups, you lose your individuality; here you can act as an individual, not get swallowed up by the group.'[32]

But this individualism limited the GGEP's ability to act as a coherent whole. GGEP MEPs were described by one long-serving member as 'a bunch of loose cannons, shooting off in different directions'.[33] Comparing the second Group to the first, a staff member noted that 'before we had a lot more common meetings. Now each MEP is off on their own crusade. We here in the office don't know what's going on.'[34] Moreover, MEPs often argued over and competed for 'owner-ship' of policy issues. For example, two German MEPs competed fiercely for energy policy. Whilst the two did not differ fundamentally on policy content, they did differ as to who should follow it on behalf of the Group. The conflict was described by a member of the administrative staff as 'a contest not of position but of possession'.[35] An experienced parliamentarian within the Group summed up the problem:

a weakness of our Group is that we let disagreements lie, and don't try to form common positions. . . . There's not enough common policy-making. This is an internal problem but it also effects our presentation to the outside world. There's no composite view, nothing for the public to hold on to.[36]

V DILEMMAS OF A GREEN MANDATE: THE GRAEL AND THE GGEP

In fairness, Green MEPs from both the GRAEL and the GGEP worked under a difficult green 'mandate'. Green MEPs were expected to represent the wishes of both their green party and the wider green movement. The Green MEPs' task thus involved reconciling apparently incongruous structures (parliamentary, centralised) and principles (grassroots, decentralised). This section focuses specifically on how the Greens' mandate evolved over time.

The GRAEL

The movement-party dilemma was particularly acute for the first group of Greens to enter the EP. During the Greens' first term, the desire to achieve more grassroots participation within the GRAEL often clashed with the party's wish to act effectively in parliament. When asked what the ecology movement expected of the GRAEL, MEP Schwalba-Hoth responded that the movements expected disruption: 'They expected us to . . . behave as "ecological Rambos" in representing movement interests' (Schwalba-Hoth 1989: 204). Yet while movement proponents opposed constructive parliamentary work, party proponents expected concrete results. GRAEL co-deputy Edeltraud Ennich (1986: 29) complained that 'we were under tremendous pressure to be "effective" in the EP. It's as though we were being accused: "We voted for you so that you'd go in there and change things and get things done!"'

But being 'effective' carried its own consequences for representatives of a movement-party. The Green MEPs sent to represent the Greens in the EP operated in an institution whose structures and procedures often conflicted with core green principles of decentralisation and grassroots democracy. The MEPs could thus be accused of collaborating with the 'bureaucratised, conservative' structures of the EU.

For example, one GRAEL MEP felt that she was finally 'getting her green views across' to MEPs from other parties when attacks of 'collaborator' came from her own Group.[37] Several other Green MEPs felt overwhelmed by the parliamentary process and feared losing sight of their movement-party mandate. One frustrated MEP described the movement-party dilemma this way: 'to be effective in the institutions, to exploit them, essentially means to serve the institutions, to feed them' (Ennich 1986: 30).

Perhaps, above all, Green MEPs in the GRAEL received little or no support or direction from their parties or movements back home. National green parties generally demonstrated little interest in the MEPs or their activities. A German GRAEL member complained that 'The [national] executive committee doesn't follow our activities regularly; its members pop up every now and then, but usually only when there's been some sort of row' (Nostitz 1986: 4). A member of the German Greens' national executive agreed: 'Yes, well Europe is ignored by the national level.' But, he quickly added, 'you have to remember that the Euro-MPs are just as fixated on their own work – and themselves – as we are here in Bonn'.[38]

The GGEP

The movement-party or radical-reformist conflict was not as acute for the GGEP. Most members had accepted the Group's clear shift towards parliamentarisation. Some German members felt that the movement-party dilemma had been more or less reconciled. 'It's easier for us than for GRAEL. . . . The question of whether the German Greens want to work as a party or movement is part of history.'[39] Yet despite such reassurances, the green strategic dilemma was not 'solved'; it continued to effect the GGEP's organisation and practice.

First, unlike other party groups, the GGEP was still under enormous pressure to retain its 'greenness' and individuality. To some extent, the group's internal conflicts were a product of the need to practise grassroots accountability and democracy on the European level. But compared to the GRAEL, GGEP Greens came under even greater pressure to perform because of their larger size and because they were publicly committed to more coherent, effective political action than that practised by the GRAEL. One MEP complained that the GGEP could not afford to be alternative or obstructionist all the time, because their expected role in the EP is 'not only to push our own green goals' but to act effectively. 'We're told by the voters in concrete terms that where we've a chance to reform something, we must do so with all our strength.'[40]

The problem of neglect of Green MEPs and the EU by national green parties afflicted the GGEP as it had afflicted the GRAEL. In the case of Les Verts, one MEP expressed similar frustration:

No [French] MEP is a member of executive committee or national council [in France]. We can attend executive meetings but very little attention is given to European affairs. . . . Informal links do exist. Some MEPs are former MPs. We tried to institutionalise links. For example we put out a bulletin or newsletter twice a month. But it's not given much attention on the national level.[41]

Nor was this an isolated complaint. Most MEPs complain of the lack of support and direction from back home. A member of staff described the plight of one Italian MEP: 'He's a great guy, but he gets no support from home; 98 per cent of them probably don't know what he's doing.'[42] From a German MEP came a similar assessment:

While it remains a fundamental green principle (*grüne Anspruch*) that what we do here is carried back to the national and even grassroots level, it remains very difficult for us. EC work is much more exhausting than most realise. Lots of travel and time away means we can't be directly influential and involved in government and issues back home.[43]

The MEP continued that the lack of knowledge by parties and members back home was a fundamental part of the problem:

The EC is still something that's quite unknown. One of our functions is explanatory work, to bring debate to the public and grassroots. But this isn't always appreciated . . . there's still an awful lot of work to do on both sides.[44]

In the case of the UK's representation in the GGEP, the lack of 'home base' support was more acute. Although the UK's representative, Jean Lambert, was paid travel and daily expenses by the GGEP, her part-time salary was paid by the UK Greens. But by early 1993 this funding had dried up and the party chose not to continue financial support. One party executive member closely involved with the decision explained why the position lapsed: 'First, the money wasn't there to pay it. Nor was there much political will from the party to see that the position . . . did remain funded.'[45]

Thus, green parties at home appeared largely unwilling or unable to support or prioritise the political goals to be pursued at the European level. Green MEPs were given no definition of what key points to work for and implement through the EU. In particular, MEPs received no guidance on how to turn the 'Europe of the Regions' conception into reality.

Consequently, Green MEPs were forced to conceptualise, theorise and organise Green European policy for themselves. This emphasis on individual effort encouraged internal competition and conflict. An inside observer noted that the GGEP was not really able to systematise their priorities, in large part 'because the group remained above all a collection of national parties and individuals. Defining priorities is difficult when everybody likes to do their own thing.'[46] Without a 'team goal', in this case a Euro-political conception, 'we don't exploit the EP, it exploits us' (Nostitz 1986: 5). In short, the MEPs from both the GRAEL and the GGEP suffered from a lack of party and grassroots interest and support. Their work in the EP was either not acknowledged, or deemed a waste of time. MEPs felt that, despite their 'international worth and reputation', they were often 'treated as second-class representatives at home' (die Grünen 1989a: 1).

VI   CONCLUSION

Despite their reservations, Green MEPs have become well-established bearers of the European green mandate. Throughout their terms, Green MEPs have suffered under pressure of conflicts relating to national, personal and strategic differences. Above all, Green MEPs have been faced with the unique green dilemma of attempting to represent alternative, decentralised politics within a bureaucratised, hierarchical structure. Yet the unique green mandate has brought advantages as well as disadvantages. Working from the 'inside' clearly has had benefits deemed worthwhile by most Green MEPs.

One advantage has been the liberty to pursue individual policies. Whereas members of most national parliaments are expected to vote with their party, MEPs are under no comparable pressure. In seeking to encourage party unity within the EP, no sanctions can be invoked against those who did not 'toe the line'. Consequently, the practicality of working with MEPs from other parties is much greater in the EP than in many national parliaments. In their work within EP parliamentary committees, several Euro-Greens worked closely with members of the Socialist Group and European Peoples' Party (Christian Democrat) Group. One long-serving German MEP recalled that:

> It wasn't like in Bonn where we [Greens and CDU members] never spoke to one another. Within the EP there was an understanding that you needed to work together. . . . I wish the Bonn MPs could have come here and seen how parliamentarians can interact with one another. Parliament doesn't have to be a war zone.[47]

This advantage was echoed by another German MEP in the GGEP who noted that 'the fact that the EP doesn't have a strict division between government and opposition allows for more discussion between groups and certain successes [in the form of] compromise solutions'.[48] Others saw membership in the EP as an advantage precisely because the EP's policy-making role was comparatively weak. GRAEL MEP Wolfgang von Nostitz claimed that the relatively ineffective role of the EP opened up new opportunities for the Greens. Free from the responsibilities of real power, 'the Greens could use the EP as a sort of think tank, a forum to theorise on European visions unfettered by restrictions of everyday politics' (Nostitz quoted in Scheuer 1989: 191). Put another way, the Green's flexibility to act in the EP was greater than on the national level precisely because 'in the EP, the decisions aren't decisive' (Uexküll 1986: 25).

This particular advantage has not been as apparent to GGEP members. First, treaty revisions and practice have rendered the EP a more powerful body than it was when populated by the GRAEL. Second, unlike the GRAEL, the GGEP has taken seriously the EP's potential role as an important player in the formulation of EU policies. The growing role of the EP (and EU more generally) has heightened its appeal for green activists. For the GGEP, the EP is a 'particularly suitable forum for Greens, essentially "crossborder" in their concerns and convictions. The importance of environmental issues on the agenda of EC business also makes election of Green MEPS . . . highly appropriate and urgent' (GGEP 1994: 6).

Yet to exploit these advantages requires some shared interest in developing a coherent conception of green goals in Europe. For a green party, moreover, such a strategy would also require interest and engagement from the grassroots. The MEPs receive neither coherence from the party nor support from the grassroots. As members of a distant parliament, they enjoy freedom but no guidance, independence but little respect. For the Green MEPs, the possibilities and freedom provided by the unique green mandate are ultimately outweighed by its paradoxical consequences.

6 The Greens' policy influence in the European Union

INTRODUCTION

This chapter assesses the Greens' attempts to influence EU policy-making. It begins by outlining the key features of agenda-setting and policy-making in the EU (Section I). It then explores green actors' attempts to lobby the European Commission (Section II) and raise public awareness more generally of green issues (Section III). The next sections focus on the growing importance of the EP as a channel of green influence in agenda-setting (Section VI) and in EU policy formulation (Section V). The conclusion asseses the Greens' impact. It suggests that individual Greens occasionally have had a significant impact on the EU's environmental policy-making process. However, as a group working together, the success of the Greens has been strictly limited.

I POLICY IMPACT IN THE EU: CONCEPTS AND CONTEXT

The EU is an extraordinarily complex policy-making system. It legislates for 370 million people and thus incites a vast multitude of interests to seek to influence EU policy. The impact of any one group or set of actors on EU policy is usually impossible to assess or measure precisely.

Traditionally, public policy analysts have gauged the impact of interest groups in terms of policy change; groups are deemed successful if their actions result in the adoption, alteration or cancellation of a particular policy. But studies that focus exclusively on policy outcome may underestimate or neglect the impact of seemingly marginal or oppositional groups, such as social movements or protest parties. Instead, it is worthwhile to focus on the impact of actors on the policy *process*, not just on outcomes. Rochon and Mazmanian (1993: 76) suggest that this approach involves 'taking a longer term view of the impact of social movements and appreciating the potential influence resulting from incorporation into the ongoing mechanisms of governance'.

To become incorporated into the policy process, interest groups must first establish themselves in the eyes of policy-makers as the legitimate representatives of valid interests and concerns (Gamson 1990). Groups must represent their constituents effectively to show that they deserve a seat at the policy-making table. Greens thus have the potential to alter the policy process by expanding the range of interests that are consulted as policy is formulated.

The relationship between pressure groups and social interests is two-way. By raising public awareness, groups such as the Greens may help themselves to become more effective political agents by changing broader social values, and thus expanding the size of their green constituency. Such action also may help 'movements expand the range of ideas about what is possible' and help redefine the political agenda and shape the policy process (Rochon and Mazmanian 1993: 77). At least in theory, Greens have considerable potential to act as the mouthpiece of an expanding grassroots movement, and as the agent for promoting new ideas for actual policy.

The EU's policy process is striking in its receptiveness to new ideas that may abet the process of European integration or enhance the Union's image or legitimacy. As such, it is fertile soil for 'policy entrepreneurs': proponents of a policy willing to invest resources such as time, energy and reputation in the advocacy of an idea (Kingdon 1984). By 'bringing to life' ideas, policy entrepreneurs can serve as the catalysts and facilitators of change. As is shown below, several green NGOs and Green MEPs – much as they may loathe the market label – have worked as effective 'policy entrepreneurs' in the EU's policy-making process.

The relative success of policy entrepreneurs depends primarily on the structure of the policy-making system in which they operate and the resources they command. Initially – at the agenda-setting stage – the EU's policy-making structure is relatively open to oppositional interests and entrepreneurs such as the Greens. Peters (1994: 21) goes so far as to describe the EU as a 'prospective agenda setter's paradise':

> the existence of a number of points of access, of a large number of influential policy advocates, and of a wide range of policy options that have been legitimated in one or more of the constituent countries makes agenda setting substantially easier than in most other settings.

(Peters 1994: 11)

This open character is especially apparent in the environmental policy realm. As described in Chapter 2, environmental policy-making takes place within relatively loose 'issue networks' populated by a wide range of actors with different conceptions of the problems and solutions. As there are few entrenched methods of policy-making in environmental policy, the access for outside groups such as environmental NGOs and parties is greater than in more established areas, such as agriculture (Bomberg 1998). Indeed, in a number of cases, NGOs have been able to secure the enactment of environmental regulatory policies stricter than those achieved at the national level (Vig 1990: 272–3; McCormick 1991: 131).

Clearly, however, EU environmental policy-making should not be taken as some sort of 'pluralist paradise'. Imbalances in ease of access still exist. Green lobbyists continually complain of limited access to the environmental policy process, but are even more dismayed by their exclusion from policy-making on related issues such as transport, agriculture or the single market. As one environmental lobbyist noted: 'We're not always welcomed with open arms by the Commission and we definitely face a struggle to get our voices heard compared to [other] lobbies.'[1]

Green actors are clearly outnumbered as EU lobbyists. Producer interests account for almost 75 per cent of the interest groups in Brussels (Euro-groups). Only 5 per cent of the Euro-groups represent trade union, consumer and environmental interests (Mazey and Richardson 1993: 7).

Green actors are out-resourced, as well as outnumbered. Compared to larger and better-funded parties and interests, green actors tend to have relatively few resources – funds, staff, etc. – with which to influence policy-making. For instance, whilst Green MEPs enjoy the resources that accrue to a political group in the European Parliament, they receive only a fraction of what larger groups such as the Socialists and Christian Democrats receive (Corbett *et al.* 1995: 86–8).

The Greens thus have to utilise carefully what limited resources they do have: persistence, information, representational legitimacy and a reputation as the public's environmental watchdog. Their influence on agenda-setting and policy-making is exercised primarily through three channels: lobbying the Commission; 'consciousness raising'; and participation in the activities of the EP.

II   LOBBYING THE EUROPEAN COMMISSION

In the EU, perhaps more than other systems of government, the most effective lobbying is done early, while drafts are being written and evidence gathered. Interest groups and parties can gain access to officials drafting legislation while they are drafting it. In the latter stages of EU policy-making, which occur behind closed doors in Council meetings, the chance to influence decisions is remote.

Because the Commission has the sole right to initiate legislation, securing access to the Commission is a key step in setting the EU agenda. Despite common assumptions to the contrary, the Commission is generally receptive to interest group lobbying and advice. As representative of the 'European interest', the Commission welcomes overtures from any interest group that might identify areas of policy that merit European attention. In policy development, 'the Commission relies upon assembling and using external sources of expertise and specialist advice either from, or independent of, the administrations of the member states' (Metcalf 1992: 124). Moreover, contact with a wide array of public groups may encourage these groups to become more closely involved in the EU policy-making process. Metcalf (1992: 125) argues that 'the crucial factor in determining the character of the Commission as an organisation and the key to its effectiveness is its ability to develop networks of cooperation and collaboration across organisation and national boundaries'.

This networking, in turn, makes the Commission appear more democratic and accessible. In his classic study of the Commission, Coombes (1970) argues that the Commission attempts a process of *engrenage*, that is, a 'meshing' or 'interlocking' of various actors concerned with EU policies. In essence, this means the Commission engages a wide network of national ministers, civil servants and interest group representatives in the EU decision-making process. Interest activity broadens the participatory base of the EU and ensures that policy- and decision-making are not completely controlled by officials.

A balder motivation for the Commission's apparent openness lies within the dynamics of EU inter-institutional rivalry. The Commission is enmeshed in its own power struggle with the Council and welcomes support in the way of attention and access to outside groups. The Commission's negotiating hand with the Council is strengthened if it can demonstrate that its proposals are supported by outside interests. Kirchner and Schwaiger (1981: 38) note that the Commission seeks such contact 'in order to underpin its own position of some weakness within the Community'.

Finally, the Commission needs the information provided by lobbyists. Despite its 'technocratic' reputation, the Commission bureaucracy is comparatively small (18,000 full-time staff) and often lacks detailed technical knowledge, especially across 15 nations. Interest groups often have access to specialised information that the Commission requires if it is to exercise its own responsibilities efficiently.

Green actors can exploit the Commission's needs. A British official involved with EU environmental policy underscored the role of environmental groups as a source of information for the Commission:

> Green lobbies are extremely influential. You have to remember that the Commission has no formal system of compiling information. . . . It listens to [green groups] because they are a source of advice and they provide a foretaste of the sort of debate the Commission should expect when the proposal goes to the European Parliament. . . . The Commission does well to keep green organisations on its side.[2]

While a proposal for legislation is being drafted within the Commission's Directorates-General, interested parties can lobby the Commission directly by sending memoranda and nurturing informal contacts. For many public interest groups, lobbying the Commission is the first step towards making their 'pet' issues known. The relationship is one of reciprocal dependency. The groups provide the necessary information and political 'intelligence': the Commission the necessary access.

NGOs

Greenpeace International, the World Wide Fund for Nature (WWF) and the European Coordination of Friends of the Earth (CEAT)[3] are all active lobbyists of the Commission and have operated Brussels offices since the late 1980s. In the case of British NGOs, EU environmental legislation has often been viewed as a progressive force when compared to domestic regulation. Under the post-1979 Conservative governments, these groups increasingly came to see Brussels as a court of redress and a means of out-manoeuvring the British government (McCormick 1991: 132–3).

In addition to specific NGOs working on their own, one of the most visible and active green lobbyists is the European Environmental Bureau (EEB), an umbrella environmental organisation whose creation was supported by the Commission.[4] Because of its expertise in environmental affairs, the EEB is often given access to relevant Commission bodies. It exerts constant and continual pressure on the Commission, lobbying on issues that eventually make their way into

EU legislation. These issues have included the introduction of environmental assessment reports, directives on the protection of songbirds, and the integration of environmental considerations into other areas of EU policy (see Klatte 1988: 220). EEB ✗

NGOs also enjoy access to the Commission through their participation in consultative forums and advisory groups. The Environmental Consultative Forum, for instance, includes representatives from green NGOs as well as from industry, consumers, professional organisations, and local and regional authorities. A DG XI official closely involved in the Forum notes how it has helped build consensus at an early stage and thus helps avoid drawn-out disagreements later on.[5]

Traditionally, NGOs have focused most of their efforts on the Environment Directorate DG XI, neglecting other areas of Commission activity related to the environment. One DG XI official remarked that 'What NGOs have failed to do is recognise that they have to go around to other DGs. It's no use just hammering away at us ... we've already taken on board their views.'[6] In the 1990s, however, NGOs – especially the WWF and EEB – began to make a more concerted effort to lobby other DGs, especially DG XVI, which is responsible for regional policy (see Long 1995).

In addition, green NGOs began to cooperate with one another in order to enjoy the advantages of pooled resources, as well as to maximise their impact within the Commission. To illustrate the point, seven green NGOs, including the EEB, Greenpeace and the WWF[7] held regular monthly meetings throughout the mid-1990s to discuss priority issues and share knowledge. They also published joint policy papers that carried more weight with policy-makers than pamphlets from a single organisation. In short, green NGOs have become more sophisticated EU lobbyists over time.

Green MEPs

As a group, Green MEPs generally have not managed to combine their efforts as effectively as green NGOs. From the beginning of their term in 1984, a few GRAEL members lobbied different sections of the Commission, including the Directorate for Agriculture (DG VI) and Energy (DG XVII). These MEPs sought contact with the Commission in order to push diverse interests ranging from subsidies for sustainable farming to modernising Belgian slaughterhouses (Buck 1989: 171). One German MEP boldly claimed that the GRAEL's success in stopping the construction of an aluminium factory in Greece was due almost entirely to its persistent lobbying of the Commission

(Schwalba-Hoth 1988: ix). Regardless of its veracity, the comment reveals the importance attached to lobbying the Commission. Generally, however, if the GRAEL had any influence within the Commission, it was the result of isolated initiatives of individual MEPs. The majority of GRAEL members avoided Commission officials.

Similarly, most GGEP members chose to work more closely with their fellow parliamentarians, as opposed to the Commission. A member of the Group's secretariat explained that 'given their elected position, MEPs mainly influence DG XI only through the Environment Committee of the EP'.[8] Whilst a few individual GGEP members made concerted efforts to lobby DG XI, very few formed personal or sustained contacts with officials in DG XI or elsewhere. Indeed, several MEPs claimed that they had never spoken directly with anyone in the Commission. And one DG XI official could not think of any particular area where Green MEPs had lobbied him personally or sought to intervene directly in Commission deliberations.[9]

Green MEPs on the whole remain sceptical about this avenue of agenda-setting. They believe the Commission favours legislation that, for example, tends to benefit producers more than consumers and environmentalists. Green MEPs have criticised the close links maintained by the Commission with some major interest groups, such as the Committee of Professional Agricultural Producers (COPA), the Liaison Committee of European Community Automobile Constructors (CLCA) and the Union of Industrial and Employers' Confederations of Europe (UNICE) which represents the interests of industrial employers from over 20 countries (see Mazey and Richardson 1993: 6). German Greens campaigning for the EP in 1984 complained that the Commission's policies 'favour the unbridled pursuit of profits by big business, and are directed against the interest of both human society – especially workers and consumers – and of Nature' (die Grünen 1984a: 6). As representatives of 'non-conformist' parties, several Greens have thus instead preferred to maintain their oppositional character. Not wanting to be part of the problem, and fearful of accusations of collusion, they have opted out of close contact with the Commission.

This same ambivalence is illustrated in the parliamentary Greens' relationship with the EEB and other NGOs. Although the GGEP shares many of the EEB's aims, it usually chooses to stay aloof from the EEB's lobbying activities. Green MEPs have expressed concern over the EEB's close contact with both the Commission and, to a lesser extent, the Council. In particular, they voiced doubts about the 'radicalism' of EEB: 'In terms of political content, the EEB is moderate. It was set up with help from the Commission and is therefore still a useful organization [to the Commission] without posing much of a risk' (GRAEL 1987: 5).

The second Green Group tried to improve relations with NGOs such as the EEB, Greenpeace and the WWF. But the Greens' reluctance remained. The European director of a major green NGO argued that Green MEPs continued to 'adopt an attitude that some of the NGOS ... are less wholesome and pure than they should be and that they are too willing to compromise'.[10] Environmental policy analyst David Baldock suggested that the EEB's style did not suit green actors who 'prefer writing radical pamphlets, and not dirtying their hands dealing with official bureaucracies' (quoted in McCormick 1991: 133). To maintain their more radical, unconventional image, the Greens restricted their dealings with both the Commission and major NGOs lobbying the Commission.

In terms of agenda-setting impact, the Green MEPs' reluctance to work more closely with NGOs and the Commission is a 'purist' strategy that carries strategic costs. Obviously, larger, better-established interests enjoy closer access to Commission officials. Yet smaller groups and environmental organisations have made their presence heard within the Commission, especially within the corridors of Directorate-General XI. The Green MEPs' decision to keep an arm's length from their NGO allies, and their dismissive attitudes towards the Commission, have diminished their success in shaping EU policy agenda at a critical stage.

III PUBLIC CONSCIOUSNESS-RAISING AND ISSUE AWARENESS

An obvious strategy for any policy entrepreneur hoping to influence agenda-setting is to publicise environmental concerns and attract media attention. Usually, the Commission's draft on a particular proposal becomes available while still in an early and rough form. At this point it is often still possible for policy entrepreneurs to add concerns and issues not already included in the draft legislation, or even to change the legislative agenda entirely. Various interests thus vie for media coverage and public support of their views on proposed EU legislation.

NGOs

On the local and national level, NGOs have been active public lobbyists for decades, and are widely viewed as 'guardians of the environment' (see Dalton 1994). Beginning in the 1980s, several NGOs began focusing on cross-national issues and cross-national campaigns to raise public awareness of European environmental issues. For example, in 1995, Greenpeace demonstrated its lobbying skill in its campaign against Shell's plan to sink the oil platform *Brent Spar* into the North Sea. The campaign led to widespread protest and Shell's decision to abandon their plan (see Dickson and McCulloch 1996).

[margin note: Greenpeace and Shell]

Other NGOs such as the EEB and WWF have used the rotation of the EU Council Presidency as an opportunity to publicise environmental concerns and raise awareness. Typically these groups issue a memorandum to both the outgoing and incoming Presidencies, calling for certain measures to be taken or certain issues to be addressed. These memoranda are invariably issued to the press as part of the NGOs' strategy not only to inform Member State officials of environmental concerns, but to alert the public as well. To reach a broad public with limited lobbying resources, Brussels-based green NGOs have agreed to pool information but to specialise in different areas. For instance, WWF has become the lead NGO in matters relating to the structural funds, whilst the EEB concentrates on pollution issues.

Finally, NGOs, such as Friends of the Earth, have used appeals to the European Court of Justice to publicise infringements of environmental legislation (for instance in the areas of water quality) and ensure issues reach or remain on the political agenda. A good example concerned the UK's alleged failure to implement the EU's directive on environmental impact assessments in the building of a motorway across Twyford Down (Young 1993: 26). Such actions by NGOs have brought media attention and sharpened their role as watchdogs.

Green NGOs have enjoyed noticeable success in publicising their concerns. An official in the *cabinet* of an Environment Commissioner claimed that the NGOs were 'neither small nor powerless' when it came to agenda-setting. For instance, in the nuclear energy sector:

> the NGOs have captured the hearts and minds of the vast majority of people. . . . They make the agenda in the nuclear area. . . . They might not have the money that the nuclear industry has, or the other resources. But if it's got the public, however irrationally . . . that's very important. Because the politicians have to realise that the opinion of their electors are being formed in the area by the NGOs. Now clearly they will have in the long term some input on the formulation of our policy.[11]

Green MEPs

Whilst not as adept at lobbying the Commission as their NGO counterparts, Green MEPs are able to use their position in and resources of the EP to raise issue awareness and lobby the public. GRAEL members staged several demonstrations or 'happenings' in the lobby of the plenary hall in Strasbourg, protesting Commission and Council actions or inactions. The group also led actions unrelated to any specific Commission proposal, such as a demonstration to commemorate the death of Salvador Allende (GRAEL 1988a: 56–8). These demonstrations and gatherings were used to publicise a variety of wider themes important to the Greens, such as peace, human rights and civil liberties (see Schwalba-Hoth 1988: ix).

During the 1984–9 term, the GRAEL also provided space and translation services for 'The Alternative Economic Summit', a 'Congress on Women and Genetic Engineering', and even hosted the '2nd World Congress of Prostitutes'. These conferences were part of the Greens' efforts to set the agenda 'from below'. But the media soon grew bored with GRAEL 'happenings' in Brussels and Strasbourg, and media coverage fell off after the first few years of the GRAEL's tenure (Buck 1989: 170). GRAEL members complained that the decrease in exposure was indicative of the scant media attention given the EP in general, and the EP Greens in particular. One MEP revealed: 'It got to the point where I began to feel sorry for the journalists stationed in Strasbourg. They prepared endless Telex reports, none of which appeared in the daily press, not even in the "miscellaneous" columns.'[12]

Following the dramatic electoral success of green parties in the 1989 EP election, the new Green Group was in a strong position to sustain media attention and public awareness of green issues. The group sought to raise public awareness through protests, demonstrations, guest visits and seminars. Throughout the GGEP's first year in the EP, the MEPs adopted protest tactics similar to the GRAEL's. A Green-led demonstration in 1990 protested the building policy of the EU. The demonstration involved unfurling a huge banner from the roof of the Belliard restaurant and lowering an ironic 'I Love Brussels' board from another abandoned building. While the resulting publicity may have helped to create a group identity, the reaction from other MEPs was mixed and the charge was made that 'The Greens were not behaving themselves' (Lambert 1991: 8). Other symbolic measures taken early in the GGEP's terms received a disparaging reaction from other MEPs. One socialist MEP recalled:

When they [GGEP MEPs] first came to Brussels they wanted to buy bicycles and get around that way. To try to use a bicycle to travel around here you'd be out of your mind. . . . And it's that kind of loopy thinking that from time to time distinguishes them.[13]

Indeed, by mid-term the frequency of such gestures or demonstrations had diminished considerably. A French Green MEP explained that the group had become far less flamboyant: 'GRAEL used to organise demonstrations or happenings regularly. We do it only on very specific necessary matters.'[14] For the GRAEL, the EP was seen primarily (if not exclusively) as a forum for protest. Demonstrations, rallies and boycotts of EP sessions were common. By contrast, both the GGEP1 and the GGEP2 employed a wider range of parliamentary means – conventional and unconventional – to publicise their concerns.

One strategy designed to raise awareness of green issues was the Group's decision to host visits of people with a particular case to make to the EP. For instance, in autumn 1995 the GGEP invited to Brussels the founder of the Pugwash movement against nuclear weapons and winner of the 1995 Nobel Peace Prize, Joseph Rotblat. In addition to hosting visitors, Green MEPs themselves also travelled extensively to spread their green message. To deflect charges of 'political tourism', Lambert (1991: 15) explained that travel by Greens was crucial to the Group's efforts to 'express solidarity' and 'to learn and to use that knowledge to move things within the Community and outside it'.

The GGEP use their position as MEPS to organise and fund a wide variety of conferences and seminars. Initially these seminars were designed primarily for the Group and invited experts. But the GGEP soon began to exploit as fully as possible the EP's rather generous provisions of funds, rooms, halls and translations services. A sample of topics covered in the GGEP's first term suggests the wide agenda of the GGEP (see Table 6.1).

Although designed in part to widen the Group's profile, many of these seminars and wider publicity tactics reached only a small audience. By the early 1990s, the GGEP was complaining of the serious lack of media and public attention, despite their lobbying efforts. Expressing the frustration of several members of the Group, one Belgium MEP complained: 'I work myself dead in and out of the EP but my work is not even acknowledged by my own national media'.[15] The GGEP press spokesperson lamented: 'How many press releases can you press in the hands of unwilling journalists?'[16]

By its second term, the GGEP had improved their conference strategy, narrowing the number of topics covered, but widening the scope and range of participants beyond a select 'green fringe'. For

Table 6.1 Green Group in the European Parliament seminars

Year	Topic(s)
1990	Eco-taxes Policing in Europe
1991	The Plutonium Connection Human Pro-creation as Bio-industry Sustainable Development and Regions The Situation of Women Immigrants
1992	Young People in Cities Pesticides in Europe Alternative Economy for Solidarity
1993	Towards a Sustainable Energy Policy in Europe Democracy and Development in Africa Conversion of the Arms Industry in Europe
1994	Middle East – Beyond Peace The Use of Newsprint Obtained from Forests of British Columbia The Social and Environmental Impact of Growing Flowers in the Third World for Export to Europe

Note: For a more complete list of conferences and seminars held by the Green Group, see GGEP (1994: 215–21).

instance, in 1995 the GGEP hosted a conference on eco-taxes – an issue at the forefront of EU policy debates – that included not only prominent Greens but also representatives of industry, academia, trades unions and national governments.

Moreover, according to a senior Commission official, elected Green MEPs wielded a sort of democratic legitimacy that gave them policy influence: 'We [in the Commission] automatically have to pay greater attention to the elected representatives of the environmental movement – the elected Greens.'[17] But whilst Green MEPs may enjoy advantages over NGOs, their policy influence remains limited by two key factors.

First, most of the GGEP's publicity work has been done in isolation, unconnected to the work of NGOs. The GGEP occasionally joined in protest events hosted by other organisations. For instance, the GGEP cooperated with a group of NGOs opposing the weakening of the EU packaging waste directive. But these events represented primarily individual, *ad hoc* collaboration rather than systematic cooperation. Whilst individual MEPs maintained close links with particular groups, the GGEP as a whole had very little systematic or organised co-ordination with green NGOs. The limits to NGO–MEP cooperation were echoed by the head of the EEB, who admitted to:

no special relationship with Green MEPs. We work with environmentally minded MEPs from all different parties. We have contact
with the GGEP but it's irregular, informal, *ad hoc.* Nothing is
formalised, there is no 'GGEP hotline' on my desk.[18]

A director of another major green NGO suggested reasons for the
lack of contact:

It would not be difficult for us to make links with [the GGEP] on
particular issues. One reason we don't is that they are quite a
fractured bunch. They tend to fight with one another on principles
and on personality . . . and they tend to fight with outsiders as well.[19]

A second explanation for the muted impact of Green MEPs is their
tenuous roots to their national parties or constituencies. MEPs'
projects and work have tended to remain unpublicised and generally
unnoticed back home. A British representative to the GGEP explained
the difficulty in coordinating European and national party work:

We haven't found a useful way of doing that. . . . It became
very difficult to see what you could present to the public or party in
concrete terms about what you've done. And the British media has
tremendous problems covering European issues anyway, let alone
[covering] the Parliament. I mean its coverage of the EP you could
put on a postage stamp.[20]

In short, the impact of Green MEPs' public lobbying is weakened by
its isolation from both the lobbying activities of environmental
NGOs, and the wider campaigns sponsored by national green parties
back home.

IV   USING THE PARLIAMENT ITSELF

The Greens' most direct means for influencing the EU's policy agenda
are parliamentary. Powers granted to the EP through the Single
European Act (SEA) and Treaty on European Union (TEU) have
made the EP a more weighty institution in the EU's policy process.
Although MEPs themselves seldom set the policy agenda, they now
have better access to those setting or operationalising the agenda
because of the EP's power to amend. A range of parliamentary devices
exist to help the EP generally and the Greens specifically to maximise
their policy influence.

An important device is the use of *oral and written Questions.* Questions can be used to solicit information on topical issues of general

interest or specific policy matters. MEPs also use the parliamentary Question system to communicate the concerns of their constituents to the Commission and Council. Moreover, members of the Commission are expected to attend committee meetings of Parliament and may have to respond to questions advanced there. The subject of the environment makes up over a tenth of questions asked (Arp 1992: 12).

Green NGOs and MEPs view the Questions process as a way to promote 'agenda-setting from below'. Working through sympathetic MEPs, outside organisations and grassroots movements have suggested motions or directed questions to the Commission. A high-ranking Commission official involved in environmental policy noted that parliamentary contact with the Greens could not be avoided: 'Well obviously we hear the most from the Greens in the EP in that we are down there and in front of them every week. . . . They're a small group but an important small group in the EP.'[21]

Second, MEPs can table *urgency resolutions*. These are mostly on broad issues such as human rights or nuclear safety. Given their urgent subject matter, the resolutions receive priority in plenary sessions of the EP. More often than not, these are issues over which the EP has no direct influence. Yet in terms of agenda-setting they are quite effective because they require immediate attention from parliamentary committees and are directed promptly to the Commission, Council, appropriate Member State or international body.

Green members are well known within the EP for introducing provocative urgency resolutions on issues ranging from nuclear waste to protection of the North Sea to protection of the rights of immigrants. For example, the Greens have filed a motion on the Sellafield nuclear reprocessing plant; on the action to be taken on the pollution of the Rhine; on the accident at the French nuclear power plant at Cattenom; and on the fate of Chernobyl.

Whilst accepting the limited European media impact of these resolutions, Greens argue that the urgent resolutions 'gain resonance with distance: in Bogota or Kuala Lumpur, the fact that the faraway European Parliament has passed an urgent resolution protesting against a local violation of human rights attracts notice' (GGEP 1994: 15). Former British representative to the group Jean Lambert (1991: 17) reports that on average about a quarter of the GGEP's urgency resolutions are accepted by the EP, and that '[e]ven if such resolutions are not always debated in Parliament they provide a means of educating other Parliamentarians, and [are] a tangible demonstration of support for the peoples themselves to use'.

Yet the utility of these resolutions is not universally accepted within the Green Group. Swedish Greens, in particular, complain of the EP's tendency to spend a large part of its time on issues over which it can have little or no formal impact. To make their point, the Swedes point out that during the EP's June 1996 plenary session, only 11 of the 22 reports on the agenda were in policy areas where MEPs have formal powers.[22]

Another channel of expression is *plenary speeches*, but they remain a fairly unimportant channel for the Greens. First, the amount of speaking time in the EP's plenary is allotted to each political Group based on its size. A smaller Group like the Green averages only around six or seven minutes of speaking time in any given plenary session. In a discussion dominated by MEPs from the larger Socialist and Christian Democrat Groups, Green MEPs must 'learn to say it all in 90 seconds' (GGEP 1994: 14). A further difficulty for the Greens is that it is often not possible for them to agree a snappy position that represents the inevitably varying positions of the Group.

Perhaps the most important tools of agenda-setting in the EP are wielded by standing *parliamentary committees*. The EP's 20 committees each cover different issue areas ranging from agriculture to youth. These committees may take the initiative in studying any matter within the aims and scope of the Communities as defined by Treaties. Working through these committees, MEPs may set the agenda by use of 'own initiative reports'. These reports are designed to raise a new issue on the policy agenda, or to give a view on a Commission Communication on which Parliament had not been formally consulted (Corbett *et al.* 1995: 125). Whereas generally the EP can act only on matters presented to it by the Commission, own initiative reports allow the EP to stretch its role to policy initiator. For instance, the Environment Committee, on which Green MEPs were over-represented, initiated its own report on waste management to guide the Commission as the latter was formulating proposals on the issue (see Judge and Earnshaw 1994: 264–5). The Environment Committee is especially active in producing these reports. Although its legislative burden is amongst the heaviest of any committee, it draws up more own initiative reports than almost any other committee (Corbett *et al.* 1995: 126).

A final parliamentary tool for raising issue awareness is the establishment of special *committees of inquiry*. At the request of a quarter of its current members, the EP may set up committees to investigate 'incidents of maladministration with respect to Community responsibilities'. Freestone notes (1991: 141) that the committee is especially apt at raising important environmental issues not yet receiving attention, such as the cross-border handling of waste and the consequences of a rapid rise in the sea level along Europe's coasts.

Several Green MEPs are active members on these committees. Bloch von Blottnitz headed the committee of inquiry into the storage and transport of nuclear materials which received attention within the EU and Member States. In summer 1995, the Greens led an effort to establish a committee of inquiry to investigate French nuclear testing in the South Pacific. By October 1995, the Greens had obtained enough signatures to request the creation of a committee. The call was part of a much broader campaign against the testing spearheaded by the Greens.[23] At the height of the protest, key leaders in the EP (including leading Socialists) verbally supported green threats to sanction the Commission for not proceeding against France with adequate rigour. But in the end the EP's other groups backed down and the Greens could not muster enough support for either the action of sanction or the committee of inquiry. The Greens were thus, in the words of one member, 'left all alone in our lonely protest'.[24]

The failure of the Green Group to maintain plenary support for a committee or sanctions against the Commission on the nuclear testing issue is indicative of more general difficulties that the Green Group faces within the Parliament. To get other groups on board, a compromise is usually needed. Many Greens loathe such compromise because of the dilution of green principles it implies. Moreover, going along with the larger Groups often means that the Greens' ideas are swallowed up and become indistinguishable from those of the 'mainstream' parties. Yet to hold out often leaves the Greens isolated, marginalised, and no nearer to achieving their goals. One Green MEP closely involved in the nuclear protest underlined the dilemma:

> It's a tough choice. You have to ask yourself: is it more important to stay independent on an issue – and get credit for something – or just accept the fact that the Socialists are the biggest Group in the Parliament and if you want to do anything you have to get them on your side?[25]

V   THE GREENS AND POLICY FORMULATION

Agenda-setting aside, the traditional role of the EP is as scrutiniser of measures already on the EU's agenda. The Council of Ministers must submit all Commission draft resolutions to the Parliament for an Opinion. In this sense, the agenda has already been 'set'. However, the Parliament can exert important influence in shaping policy options through the weight of its opinion and formal powers to amend (see Lodge 1989b: 64–77; Dinan 1994: 273–80).

The cooperation procedure introduced under the SEA significantly increased the EP's power. The procedure granted the EP the right to a second reading of Community legislation in a range of policy sectors related to the internal market. Whereas under the consultation procedure the Council's first draft was final, the EP in cooperation cases had a second chance to table amendments. Generally these amendments have been taken seriously. For instance, of nearly 4,000 first reading amendments adopted by the Parliament by the end of February 1993, the Commission accepted 56 per cent, and the Council of Ministers retained 43 per cent. At second reading, the EP proposed 904 amendments of which 46 per cent were accepted by the Commission and 24 per cent by the Council (Judge and Earnshaw 1994: 267–8). The figures indicate that both the Commission and the Council have been forced to take EP views seriously and engage in considerable inter-institutional bargaining.

The EP's ability to shape policy increased further after enactment of the Maastricht Treaty (TEU). The 'co-decision procedure' introduced by the TEU further extended the formal legislative power of the EP and applies to most areas covered by the cooperation procedure. Essentially, the new procedure gives the EP the formal right to veto Council decisions under certain conditions. Yet, the real potential of the procedure lies in the Parliament's increased informal influence. In particular, co-decision requires much greater sensitivity on the part of the Commission to the policy aspirations of the EP (Judge and Earnshaw 1994: 269). One senior member of a Commissioner's *cabinet* argued that the co-decision has made an 'absolute difference. The Commission just can't ignore Parliament anymore. It's much more of an interchange now.'[26]

Green issues and actors have benefited from general moves by the Parliament to strengthen its own positions within the EU's policy-making process. Both the GRAEL and the GGEP groups sought to shape policy within the Parliament, but with different means and to different degrees. The main difference between the two groups is seen in their key parliamentary priorities, their level of cooperation with other Groups, and their approach to committee work.

The GRAEL

The GRAEL was not a terribly active player within the parliamentary committees. Because of its small size, the GRAEL was represented on only 13 of the 18 (at the time) committees of the EP. The lack of representation on the Budget, Legal Affairs, Transportation, Monetary Affairs, and Social Issues committees limited its ability to influence a wide range of policies.

The most important committee positions are chair, vice-chair and *rapporteur*. Whilst no GRAEL members held positions of Committee chair, a few served as vice-chairs or *rapporteurs*. The role of *rapporteur* can be key in shaping a committee's position on an issue put before it: 'he is permitted to express an opinion first and as often as liked'[27] (Fitzmaurice 1978: 18–19; see also Corbett *et al.* 1995: 128–32). Usually, the *rapporteur* has close contact with the Commission's research services and with other experts. For GRAEL members the more frequent contact was with movement leaders and activities, and other organisations involved in the issue area concerned. This is another way is which Greens hoped to encourage policy influence from the bottom up.[28]

During the 1984–9 term, several parliamentary reports were filed by individual GRAEL members on environmental issues. These included concrete proposals relating to agriculture, nuclear safety and toxic waste as well as more symbolic initiatives.[29] Yet, overall, the GRAEL's record of policy influence in Parliament was uneven. Those Greens willing to compromise on the content of their reports usually had more success in receiving parliamentary acceptance. A few MEPs chose to retain authorship of reports despite changes made to their text in plenary sittings. For example, Green agricultural specialist Grafe zu Baringdorf drafted a report on the effects of the use of biotechnology on the European farming industry. The EP adopted the report in 1986, but only after considerable changes in the language and prognosis were made (GRAEL 1988b).

Many GRAEL parliamentary reports, however, were filed by Green MEPs who later withdrew their authorship on the grounds that their original report had been completely altered (or 'adulterated') by amendments in committee or in plenary sittings. For example, in February 1987, GRAEL MEP Dorothee Piermont withdrew her name from a report dealing with chemical and biological weapons after the report was significantly changed by amendments in the Political Affairs Committee. Thus, despite the active cooperation of a few individual GRAEL MEPs, the group as a whole was viewed as a source of unreliable or inconsistent committee members.

The GGEP 1 and 2

The GGEP sought to change the GRAEL's image by mapping out a clearer set of political priorities to be pursued in Parliament, and adopting strategies that would allow them to be more cooperative and effective parliamentary actors. Unlike the GRAEL, the GGEP sought to formulate and follow a coherent set of Group priorities for each year. This goal met with limited success. For instance, the Group's 1991 theme was sustainable development and regions. According to the GGEP (1994: 20), the idea was to undertake a thorough study of four contrasting regions across the EU and to help develop regional programmes 'for ecologically balanced and sustainable development'. But this project was never completed as it became clear that 'its goals in retrospect appeared too ambitious for the Group's resources, especially the scarce resource of time' (GGEP 1994: 20).

In 1992, the UN Conference on Environment and Development (the Earth or Rio Summit) provided a new theme for Green parliamentarians. The Group produced its own 'Green Agenda' to take to the NGO meeting in Rio. However, both the Green Agenda and the earlier sustainable development initiative were difficult to translate into concrete parliamentary tasks.

By the mid-1990s, the Group decided to forgo the practice of designating one Group theme per year. Instead, the GGEP sought to attack a wide array of 'priority' issues within the EP. These included:

> the demand for democratization of European institutions, pursuit of the goals of eco-development and ecological conversion of industry, starting with energy, armaments and transport industries, support for organic farming, the critique of GATT, the combat against social exclusion on economic or ideological grounds, protection of animal species and their habitat.
>
> (GGEP 1994: 21–2)

This list is indicative of the GGEP's ambitious agenda. The Group's Record (GGEP 1994: 22) claimed that 'all these things are mutually linked by a powerful internal logic', but this logic was not explicated. Nor was it always clear to all of its members. One MEP conceded that the Group's priorities were simply a collection of individual priorities: 'These are Group decisions but they seldom bring us good results; maybe a study or a colloquium, but nothing concrete.'[30] Put simply, whilst the GGEP's priorities were more targeted than those of the GRAEL, the GGEP has had great difficulty in agreeing on one single overarching theme or set of priorities to guide their activities within the EP.

The GGEP also adopted parliamentary strategies significantly different from those of their predecessors. Compared to the GRAEL, which used the EP almost exclusively as a tribune for social movement protest, the GGEP has become an adept user of a wide variety of insitutional and informal policy-making channels. Noted a DG XI official:

A lot of Green MEPs have learned to use the machinery as it exists. They've learned to recognise the realities of the situation – that they're much better off making use of the system to achieve their ends rather than trying to be seen to be outside the system, trying to fight it.[31]

The GGEP's efforts to be accepted as serious parliamentary players was evident in their active committee work and cooperative strategies. Unlike the GRAEL, the GGEP had at least one member sitting on every EP committee by the mid-1990s. The GGEP was able to secure as many as five full positions on those committees deemed more important to the Group (such as Environment, Energy and Institutional). This number was clearly out of proportion to the GGEP's small size.[32]

The GGEP's first few months of committee service were made difficult by the GRAEL's legacy of non-cooperation. For instance, one French MEP serving on the Fisheries Committee, Renee Cona, reported that 'nothing had been done by the old Group [GRAEL]' and that other MEPs on the committee 'expected only speeches along the lines of "Save the Whales"'. In contrast, Cona was willing to compromise and work closely with other MEPs in drawing up several reports (Lambert 1991: 11).

Scepticism towards Green MEPs was strongest on the Political Affairs (now Foreign Affairs) Committee which, according to one Italian GGEP member, held 'an extremely negative attitude towards the Greens who were seen as stupid idealists, out of touch with reality, and incapable of holding sound views on the "important" subjects'. By September 1990, however, GGEP members claimed that Committee views towards the Green MEPs were more favourable: 'fortunately the atmosphere is now changing and members are often pleasantly surprised to find Greens making points regarded as intelligent' (Ratti 1990). Over time, the Greens became accepted and usually cooperative players on most committees.

The shift resulted in part from the leadership of Paul Lannoye, co-president from 1990–4.[33] Lannoye believed that the Group's parliamentary strategies needed to reflect a knowledge of the EP's powers and limits. He felt that too much energy was wasted on proposals that came under the consultation procedure because 'Even if [these] measures might seem interesting at first sight, the role of the rapporteur is very limited, as is the weight of the Parliament.' Lannoye (1990: 2) did concede, however, that 'We should most probably make an exception for some interesting reports that can be politically exploited.'

Second, in contrast to the more leftist GRAEL, Lannoye sought to steer the Group towards developing issue-related rather than ideological alliances. He argued that to form automatic alliances with leftist majorities in the EP would be 'non-credible and politically wrong'. Instead the GGEP needed to remain open to the possibility of alliances with a wide range of political Groups represented in the EP. He reminded his colleagues that these groups

> are not monoliths. We can break them up around themes for which we can act as a leading force and so bring about if not majorities, then strong minorities around these themes. I'm thinking about genetic engineering or the arms trade for instance.
>
> (Lannoye 1990: 2)

Four years later, Lannoye reinforced the need to work with other groups of all political hues: 'We must work with others. When the big Groups are in opposition to one another, the Green Group is able to tilt the balance. [We can] push new ideas and new proposals and we are able to sway others. . . .'[34] In short, Lannoye recognised and exploited the Greens' unique opportunity to play a pivotal strategic role as part of an EP coalition on centre-left or cross-cutting issues.

A final indicator of the Group's attempt to play a more traditional parliamentary role was seen in the way in which the Group distanced itself from extra-parliamentary groups and social movements. The GGEP's 1994 record (GGEP 1994: 18) concluded that:

> In 'the last analysis, the Green Group's political priorities were defined in the course of events less according to any enumeration of traditional green commitments to social movements than by developing coherent responses of political ecology to the demands of the EP and of contemporary problems.

Taken together, these strategies effectively shifted the Greens towards the mainstream of EP politics. Observers inside and outside of the Group agreed that, compared to the GRAEL, the GGEP was willing to play a more serious and constructive role in Parliament. One staff member of the GGEP noted that:

the GRAEL was a purely technical group formed against the EC. They acted out of principle and would often reject policies flat out because they weren't considered 'green'. But they didn't offer real constructive alternatives. They were more clearly the mouthpieces of the movement. GGEP is clearly more professional. It offers concrete proposals. It takes a particular problem and decides which parliamentary tool to use. . . . GRAEL did not use these tools.[35]

Outside observers as well recognised the Group's shift to a more pragmatic stance: a long-serving member of the EP's Environment Committee noted that the Green MEPs 'are a bit more realistic now than they were, that is certainly true. Between 1984 and 1989 you would have found it impossible to work with them. . . . They were pure but impotent.'[36]

But the Group's shift in strategy went too far for some, and not far enough for others. First, many Green MEPs overestimated the impact the new professionalism brought them. According to one MEP:

You know, some members get very excited because they've become rapporteur on some issue. . . . After a battle of a year the committee comes to a decision and maybe the EP even votes in favour of their report. I've seen people dancing on the table when this happens. But in the end it doesn't make any difference: the Commission or Council reject the report and that's that.[37]

Other MEPs felt that the new pragmatism had gone too far: 'It's difficult to speak of any green success here because our successes are all compromises and our defeats many.'[38] Moreover, some outside observers of the Group insisted that little had changed. An EP official working with the Budget Committee complained that the Greens serving on this Committee offered the same

clichéd reply; the same old lines. They don't seem aware of the constraints or limits of power of the Budget Committee or Parliament more generally. . . . [Their representative] would never stand up and say, 'OK my group can go along with that'. They're always outsiders in that sense. And I think that's true generally; its very difficult to get them to accept the rules of the game. And the rules of the game are all about trying to reach consensus.[39]

In short, despite a clear shift towards cooperative, reformist strategies, the Greens are not willing to abandon totally their unconventional principled stance within the EP.

VI   CONCLUSION: ASSESSING GREEN IMPACT

It is difficult to isolate the Greens' impact on specific policies. In assessing their influence, a DG XI official noted that, 'they are there as a part of a much wider range of pressures coming in. . . . They push issues which are later taken up by other actors and parties.'[40]

If Greens have had some agenda-setting influence, they have had little success in shaping policies once they have left the Parliament, and almost no measurable influence over policy outcomes. Even when successfully gaining the support of the EP, green reports and demands have often been subsequently ignored by the Commission, Council of Ministers or Member States.

Still, this chapter has highlighted ways in which Greens have become increasingly accepted players in the EU's policy-making *process*. Comparing the strategies and policy role of green actors since the early 1980s, this chapter has shown ways in which green actors have gradually become accepted as valid representatives for a public interest. Green NGOs and MEPs are now widely viewed by the public and other EU actors as legitimate representatives of environmental concerns. They have become established as the 'environmental watchdogs' of the EU.

Green Euro-NGOs as well as Green MEPs have insinuated themselves into the EU's policy-making process and made themselves more relevant by providing needed information, support or legitimacy. Most Euro-NGOs have been quick to adopt a more cooperative stance on EU matters (see Dalton 1994). Whilst Green MEPs remain more reluctant 'team players' in the EU policy-making game, they too have become much more integrated into the process since 1989.

Many Greens are not yet full players in this process: they covet and retain their 'outsider' image. Divided between 'outsiders' and aspiring 'insiders', the Greens, as a group working together to further green goals, have enjoyed only limited success. In particular, three related deficiencies – ambivalence towards the policy process, limited strategic coordination, and insufficient conceptualisation – help explain the Greens' tenuous policy impact.

The Greens' first difficulty springs from their continuing unease with the EU's policy-making structures and conventional cooperative methods of policy influence. The normal methods necessary to influence EU policy – such as the effective lobbying of officials or enacting parliamentary manœuvres – depend on coalition building, cooperation and compromise. Compared to their activities in the early and mid-1980s, Greens have undoubtedly become more willing to play by these rules. This shift towards a new pragmatism was especially apparent among individual Greens working on particular projects within the EP committees. But many Greens continued to project the image of 'outsider'. More generally, the Group as a whole tended to shun or ignore possible non-green or 'grey' allies in the Commission, other parties and other interest groups lobbying the EU.

The inability and/or unwillingness of Green MEPs to cooperate and compromise with other established actors is a prime feature of the green strategic conundrum. The original notion that the Greens should preserve their fundamental oppositional character and remain close to extra-parliamentary movements does not mesh with the compromise and cooperation required of sustained work in the EP. As representatives of non-traditional parties, the Green MEPs are loathe to compromise or 'sell out' to the established powers as represented by the Commission, Council, or more conservative NGOs. An EP official familiar with the Group noted that

> The Greens don't really fit into this Parliament because they're a very difficult group to negotiate with. . . . Their dilemma is: what's in it for them if they do go along with big groups and accept consensus? It looks as if they've sold out.[41]

The fear of cooptation makes many Greens wary of embracing fully the bargaining and compromise inherent in EU policy-making.

The second explanation for the Green's limited success refers more specifically to Green MEPs and is rooted in their lack of coordination with their parties and supporters back home. Lacking resources enjoyed by larger groups (such as political weight, or access to national decision-makers), the Greens rely heavily on genuine representational claims. It is, in other words, essential that the Greens maintain close links with the voters and grassroots they were mandated to represent. This is the link that enables 'agenda-setting from below' to function.

Yet communication between the MEPs and their grassroots constituencies remains spotty. Green MEPs remain relatively isolated from their national parties and grassroots who demonstrate only scant interest in the European level. Despite attempts to foster contact with and among various movements, it is generally admitted that these contacts and activities do not create the expected 'web relationship' among movements and between the grassroots and MEPs (Buck 1989: 171).

The final cause of the Green's limited success is related to the first two. The Greens lack a coherent European policy, i.e. a shared set of goals and strategies to pursue within the EU. Greens' policy actions are often unconnected to any long term, collective green goal. Most lobbying activity results from individual initiatives by green policy entrepreneurs. For instance, one inside observer noted that the Group's priorities are not clear because the Group 'remains above all a collection of national parties and individuals. . . . Defining priorities is difficult when everyone likes to do their own thing.'[42] Another MEP admitted that his own projects were by far the most important aspect of his work within the GGEP:

> I've taken on a lot of fact finding reports [and am] working on a lot of dossiers outside the Group. I want to stress my own priorities. Otherwise, I'm afraid I'd get to the end and ask did I really work on the things I wanted to, the things that are important.[43]

The Group's incoherence and individualism was even more evident to outside observers. An EP official noted that

> within the Group there are too many tensions between different components of the Green Group for them to be able to nominate someone to represent them inside committees. . . . That tension exists in every Group but [other Groups] nevertheless are able to establish a system of more or less coordinated response throughout the Committees. . . . But because of the internal culture of the Green Group, this doesn't seem possible.[44]

A long-serving member of the Environment Committee made a similar point less sympathetically. Whilst he could think of effective individual Green MEPs, he described the Group's efforts as a 'collective tragedy': 'Their problem is that they . . . don't deliver a common position and find it diffilcut to stay together.'[45]

7 The Greens' policy-making role: three case studies

INTRODUCTION

Specific policy initiatives reveal the varying strategies and influence of green actors, in the context of opportunities available to them, in EU policy-making. The case studies presented here – on vehicle emissions, biotechnology and packaging waste – underline the fundamental dilemma faced by green actors: policy influence within the EU depends on cooperation and conciliation, but Greens are under fierce pressure to hold out for 'greener' or 'purer' strategies and positions. Greens thus play a difficult game, seeking to balance their role as radical, moral watchdog with their desire to become an effective, cooperative partner in EU policy-making.

I VEHICLE EMISSIONS

The Greens have longed bemoaned the increase in private transportation and its pollution costs within the EU. Green MEPs claim that increased private and commercial transport are 'not merely a by-product but a deliberate aim' of the single market (GGEP 1994: 32). They have approached stricter emission standards as part of their campaign to overhaul the EU's transport policy and practices. The case of the 1989 directive on vehicle emissions standards for small cars (OJ L 226 3.8.89) reflects the Greens' early attempts to shape EU pollution control policy. Above all it demonstrates the importance of the EP as a vehicle of green influence in EU policy-making.

The origins of the directive date back to earlier legislation regulating emissions for large and medium sized cars (see Bomberg 1998). Although this legislation aimed to promote environmental protection, its primary purpose was the removal of non-tariff barriers to trade in cars. Using earlier legislation as a guide, the Commission issued in 1987 a draft directive setting emission limits for small cars. The emission standards initially specified in the draft directive were significantly weaker than those standards enforced in the United States, and much weaker than standards advocated by Greens, the EP and Member States such as Denmark and The Netherlands. In its first opinion in September 1988, the EP proposed far stricter ceilings and advocated the mandatory introduction of catalytic converters. The Council of Ministers ignored the first opinion of the EP. Voting by qualified majority (QMV) in November 1988, the Council adopted the weaker standards in its common position. The Netherlands, Denmark and Greece opposed the position but were outvoted.

Because the directive was proposed under Article 100a, the EP was granted a second reading of the common position as well as the right to reject the common position by majority vote. Greens took the opportunity to mount an awareness campaign directed at the public and other potential allies within the EP. Greenpeace, the EEB and GRAEL members lobbied hard for drastic amendments to or complete rejection of the Council's position. For instance, the EEB, speaking on behalf of over 110 (at that time) environmental NGOs, held press conferences and issued reports calling on the EP to 'make use of its powers under the SEA to amend the common position'. However, according to a Commission official (Hull 1993: 89), real pressure came from within the Parliament where the strength of green feeling was especially strong.

Responding to green concerns, the EP amended the common position, insisting that norms be obligatory from 1993 that were 'at least as strict' as US standards to be obligatory from 1 January 1993.[1] The EP threatened that if its amendments were not accepted, it would reject outright the EU norms proposed by the Commission and agreed by the Council. Had the Parliament done so, the Council of Ministers would have had to act by unanimity (an unlikely prospect) to overturn the position.

The Commission and Council were forced to reassess their positions. The Commissioner for Environment, Carlo Ripa di Meana,[2] was able to convince the Commission to recognise the EP's preference for stricter US standards and to revise the common position on the draft directive. In return, the EP's Environment Committee compromised by dropping two amendments unacceptable to the Commission (Judge 1993b: 202). On 5 April 1989, one week before the EP's threatened vote, the Commission announced that it was set to propose stricter small car emission standards in the near future. The Council either had to approve this revised position by a qualified majority; amend it by unanimity; or see it fail. The latter option effectively was no option: it would have divided the internal market and caused chaos in the car industry.

In June 1989, the Council adopted by QMV the stricter legislation. The resulting EU directive introduced mandatory standards for exhaust emissions. It also required three-way vehicle catalysts on all new cars from 1993 and all new models from July 1992.

The directive was a political triumph for the EP because it signalled its growing influence *vis à vis* other EU actors. David Grant Lawrence, a member of Carlo Ripa di Meana's cabinet, conceded: 'This was a turning point for the Commission. It came just before the European elections. It was becoming clear that the Greens would do well everywhere. No minister could afford to be seen to sabotage a good decision.'[3]

The outcome was also a triumph for green actors. Many Greens within and outside of the EP hailed the agreement as a case of environmental interests winning over the vested interest of car firms. Mazey and Richardson (1991: 15) asserted that the Danish and German governments 'acting in concert with the small, but active parliamentary grouping of Green MEPs ... successfully forced the pace and content of EC environmental legislation on exhaust emissions'. Even a spokesman for the car lobby conceded the growing importance of green actors. John Phelps, technical manager of the International Organization of Motor Vehicles Manufacturers, observed, 'The situation has changed dramatically as the Green movement has gained force.'[4]

Although GRAEL members accepted credit for the victory, its MEPs did not play a leadership role in this case. Not all GRAEL members were actively involved, and many within the Group regretted the compromise made by the EP. But the case nonetheless illustrated to the GRAEL the opportunities for influence available to Greens acting within the EP. Working in concert with other EP Groups (especially the Socialists) as well as NGOs, Green MEPs could share victory on concrete pieces of EU policy. The case also demonstrated the importance of a supportive public and the effect of public lobbying. The upcoming EP elections, which predicted a strong showing for Greens across the EU, provided an important added resource for the Greens.

The Greens' more recent experience in influencing vehicle emissions has not yielded similar success. For example, the *auto oil programme* began in 1992 as a series of consultations between Commission officials and representatives of the oil and motor vehicle sectors. The idea was to get industry 'on board' from the start. An official in DG XI described it as a

> structured dialogue, a shared responsibility approach: agreeing what the problem is, what the solution is, and then trying to agree in policy terms how best to deal with it. It's not enough just to look at the legislative approach. For instance reducing vehicle emissions has partly to do with setting standards but also looking to see if there are other things we can do . . . such as helping to develop alternative technologies.[5]

Green lobbies were not invited to participate in these consultations and thus became suspicious about the entire process. A high-ranking Commission official in DG XI indicated the difficulty of including the Greens: 'The radical [green] groups find it very hard to accept that we should be consulting industry because they say "you don't consult the polluter about pollution, you consult us"'.[6] Yet, for many Greens, the exclusion cut deep. According to a lobbyist from one major green NGO: 'We were willing to sit down and talk with the polluters but were not invited.'[7]

The Commission presented an early draft of its auto oil proposals in December 1995 and another draft proposal in June 1996. The latter proposal outlined two broad aims of the programme. First, it sought to reduce the level of vehicle emissions over the next 10 years by requiring vehicle manufacturers to introduce 'cleaner' technology. From the year 2000, the Commission would require the proportion of carbon monoxide, nitrogen dioxide, diesel particulates and other pollutants to be reduced by between 20 and 40 per cent from their present levels. After 2005, emissions would be reduced by a further 30 per cent. Second, the proposal required the oil refining industry to reduce levels of sulphur in diesel and petrol, and to phase out leaded petrol by the year 2000. (Poorer Member States would be exempt from this stipulation until 2003.)

Whilst these standards represented a significant tightening of current emission limits of some pollutants, they did not, in the view of most Greens, represent a serious effort to curb emissions.[8] First, Greens claimed that the stricter standards included in the Commission's December 1995 draft had been watered down in face of intense lobbying from industry. Suggesting that the directive reflected pressure from leading oil companies, Finnish Green MEP Heidi Hautala noted that: 'There is good reason to ask what pressure made the Commission set standards at such a low level.'[9] Second, the standards fell far short of standards in the United States and Nordic countries. Moreover, according to the director of the European Federation of Transport and Environment, Gijs Kuneman, the proposed measures did not represent a tightening of current emissions of some substances, such as olefins or so-called 'aromatics', some of which are carcinogenic. The EEB was most concerned about relaxed standards of emission limits for nitrous oxides (NOx) which are one of the main causes of ozone. Finally, even the plan to phase out leaded petrol was described by one Greenpeace lobbyist as a mere tactic 'to keep the European Parliament happy'.[10]

Compared to the 1989 vehicle emmissions directive, the auto oil programme was developed in the absence of much input or influence by the Greens. Several factors explain this diminished influence. First, whereas vehicle emissions continued to be a priority issue for several NGOs, it was not a key priority for the Green Group in the EP, and was left largely to one or two MEPs to work on emissions as well as a wide range of other issues. Undine Bloch von Blottnitz gave constant attention to emission legislation throughout her multiple terms in the EP. She was later joined by Heidi Hautala, who also made emissions legislation a priority. Yet neither worked closely with NGOs in this area, choosing instead to concentrate on the parliamentary arena.

Second, the cooperation between Green MEPs and NGOs, which proved decisive in the 1989 vehicle emmissions case, was lacking. Green MEPs and NGOs shared many of the same concerns about the auto oil programme, but they did not mount any joint lobbying efforts or campaigning. Lobbyists from the major NGOs were not aware of who in the Green Group was working on this issue.

For their part, Green MEPs chose to concentrate on parliamentary avenues of influence. This strategy was partly due to a lack of resources within the Green parliamentary Group and the decision to focus on other priorities. But it also suggested the continuing unwillingness of MEPs and NGOs to work together on common issues.

A third and broader set of problems for the Greens arose due to a change in the character of EU environmental policy. A shift away from specific legislation and towards broader framework packages made it more difficult for Green MEPs to target specific pieces of legislation, particularly given their limited resources. Moreover, in an effort to improve relations with industry, DG XI placed a new emphasis on 'voluntary negotiations' and 'cooperative corporatism', which often mandated governments to set targets, but allowed industry to decide how to meet those targets. The auto oil programme embodied this methodology. Greens feared that such agreements merely allowed industry to duck responsibility. EEB secretary general Raymond van

Ermen argued that 'there are a number of problems with these agreements. The provisions are too weak, the companies are seldom monitored and bad behaviour is never punished. That is why they are, on the whole, ineffective.'[11]

Finally, the role of the Greens in the auto oil programme revealed an irony: at a time when the Green MEPs and NGOs had proved themselves more willing to compromise, they were prevented from playing a full role in the early consultations. Their exclusion was due in part to their legacy as a radical actor unwilling to compromise.

II BIOTECHNOLOGY

The increasing focus of EP Greens on biotechnology and bioethics since the late 1980s reflects both the explosion of biotechnology as a 'sunrise' industry and the EU's significant policy role in regulating the sector. Biotechnology refers to a loosely grouped set of techniques for applying novel biological organisms, systems and processes to industrial production. Most of these techniques result in new methods of making products, rather than new products *per se* (see Sharp 1985). While the biotechnology industry is still in its infancy, biotechnology as a science is on the upward slope of a 'take-off' phase.

Biotechnology is of concern to European Greens for four essential reasons. First, and most generally, biotechnology involves genetic engineering: manipulation in the laboratory of the 'blueprints' that determine variations between life forms of the same species. A range of crops is now produced using cloning techniques, including self-pollinating varieties of wheat and disease-resistant types of legumes. Greens may take different views of the desirability of such techniques, but nearly all oppose more controversial experiments in gene therapy to develop 'transgenic animals' that yield 'healthier' meat. By its very nature, biotechnology involves highly sophisticated techniques by experts to alter the natural state of life on earth. It is little wonder that Greens instinctively oppose it. In the words of one former Green MEP: 'It is industry which is setting the scientific agenda in this young and technical field of genetic engineering, which lacks the tradition of responsibility for its innovations' (Härlin 1990: 255).

Second, the maturity of biotechnology cannot help but have profound environmental impacts. A significant amount of research is underway into the development of biological substitutes for chemical pesticides and herbicides. The aim is to add genes to seeds that give resultant plants the anti-pest or anti-disease properties of pesticides and herbicides. While this branch of biotechnological research may have attractions for Greens,[12] the behaviour of large multinationals such as Shell and Monsanto has provoked green ire. Both firms, which have significant interests in chemical pesticides, started buying up small, innovative firms working on chemical substitutes, beginning in the mid-1980s (Daly 1985). Large petrochemical firms have clear incentives to obstruct technological innovation in the research and development of seeds that require fewer agro-inputs (see Viehoff 1986). However, a significant amount of the European effort in this area of biotechnology is underway in university laboratories. Green MEPs have pushed the Commission to 'let 1000 flowers bloom' by ensuring that more EU research funding for biotechnology is spent on environmentally promising techniques, if biotechnology must be funded at all.

Third, biotechnology promises to have enormous impacts for the agricultural sector (see Peterson 1989). Many biotechnological techniques seek to increase yields – meat or milk – from livestock. For example, the controversial cattle growth hormone, bovine somatotropin (BST), boosts milk production in dairy cattle by as much as 30 per cent and, more generally, enhances the growth and feed efficiency of beef cattle. Green concerns about this aspect of biotechnology stem from, first, the likelihood that biotechnology will increase the problem of agricultural surpluses in the EU and, second, that expensive new techniques will widen the already yawning income gap between rich and poor farmers. For the Greens, the case of BST illustrates the typical approach of the EU to technology. First, the Union embraces a narrow-minded concept of competitiveness. 'Companies appeal to the patriotic short sightedness of the EC, expressed as "If we don't do it, others will do it before us"' (Härlin 1990: 258). Moreover, it demonstrates the remoteness of the European Commission in Brussels from public opinion: 'The only real pressure on the Commission, apart from governmental, is from the well organised industrial pressure groups' (Härlin 1990: 259).

Similar concerns were voiced during the 1996 'beef crisis' sparked by official British acknowledgement of the probable connection between Bovine Spongiform Encephalopathy (BSE) in cattle and the deadly Creutzfeld-Jakob Disease in humans. The EP's March 1996 plenary session was dominated by the debate. Green MEP Friedrich Wilhelm Graefe zu Baringdorf, vice president of the Parliament's Agriculture Committee, told the plenary that responsibility for the 'mad cow' disaster lay squarely with the 'unholy alliance between industrial agriculture and politicians'. He called for legal action against the British Government for criminal negligence in failing to adopt any action play to eradicate BSE during the 10 years since the disease came to light. The Parliament rejected a Green amendment calling on its President to look into such a possibility. But five of eight Green amendments were adopted, including a recommendation to the Commission to adopt preventive strategies that reduce risk of epidemics by putting an end to mass assembly line feeding, and encouraging appropriate humane methods of animal husbandry. Greens insist that the heart of the problem is the promotion of export-driven industrial farming methods with unforeseeable consequences. 'BSE and growth hormones are part of the same process that is undermining food safety and quality, with potentially devastating effects on coming generations.'[13]

Finally, Greens are concerned with the question of accountability. As the time taken to convert basic research into technological innovation shortens, so too does the time available to engage in 'technology assessment' of these innovations. Greens insist that a short-term assessment is useless because the consequences, for example, of releasing genetically engineered organisms into the environment, have to be considered on a time scale which is potentially infinite:

> No technology can be regarded as sustainable whose environmental consequences are impossible to predict. At present there is far too little knowledge of their eventual impact for genetically modified organisms to be regarded as solutions to problems of environment or development.
>
> (GGEP 1992c: 19)

Despite the clear rationale for action by Green MEPs on biotechnology, the efforts of the GRAEL were limited to a rather lonely battle fought by one MEP, Benedict Härlin. The highly specialised nature of biotechnology, as well as lack of interest from fellow GRAEL members, precluded a more unified strategy. However, Härlin did work closely with wider movements such as the Genetic Resources Action International (GRAIN).

In February 1989, the GRAEL and the GRAIN organised an international conference at the Parliament. The conference was designed to 'offer a platform for European citizens to voice their opinions and concerns about the proposed patenting of life forms and to initiate a broad consultation process among groups most affected by the directive' (GGEP 1991f: 2). Moreover, in the area of biotechnology related to agriculture, Härlin was aided by another MEP, Friedrich Wilhelm Grafe zu Baringdorf. Whilst limited in its effect, the work of individual GRAEL MEPs and their aides was an important precursor to the emergence of biotechnology as a priority issue for the Greens.

The efforts of the GGEP were more substantial and effective. Green activity on biotechnological issues was spearheaded by MEPs Graefe zu Baringdorf and Hiltrud Breyer, working closely with expert staff Hannes Lorenzen and Linda Bullard. The more concerted position of the Group was seen in the Greens' sustained involvement in the Commission's '*Proposal for a Council Directive on the Legal Protection of Biotechnological Inventions*' of 17 October 1988, better known as the Patenting Directive (COM 88 496). The aim of the directive was to harmonise legislation providing legal protection for biological inventions and thus provide the European pharmaceuticals industry with uniform protection for its inventions throughout the EU.

The legislation was first introduced in October 1988. Its implications for the Greens were monumental. Whilst Greens differed over the potential benefits of biotechnology generally, they remained fundamentally opposed to patenting forms of animal and plant life. Their key objection was moral:

> the psychological, social and ethical implications of extending commercial property rights to the very heart of living matter are enormous. The value system implicit in the reduction of segments of plant and animal life, and even human life ... to pieces of patented property is scarcely compatible with the exalted view of human rights and individual freedom still commonly expressed by some of the same political leaders favouring such measures.
>
> (GGEP 1991f: 4)

Following introduction of the draft legislation, Greens in the EP and a network of NGOs immediately sought to raise public awareness in Member States 'in order to build counter pressure to the powerful influence of biotech industries' (GGEP 1991f: 2). In addition to conferences and consultations, a leaflet (*12 Reasons for 12 Member States to say No Patent on Life*) was made available in all EU languages and distributed widely.

The Greens were able to express their critique of the Commission's directive through the 1991 draft Opinion written for the Agricultural Committee by Green MEP Graefe zu Baringdorf.[14] On 25 September 1991, the Agricultural Committee adopted the conclusion of Baringdorf's Opinion and rejected the Commission's initial proposal on scientific, ethical and economic grounds. Incorporating elements of the Agricultural Committee's decision, the EP put forward several significant amendments in its first reading in October 1992.[15] One amendment put forward by the Greens advocated the total rejection of the Commission proposal. It failed to pass, but only by 12 votes. Several less radical amendments were accepted by the Commission, which revised its proposed legislation in December 1992 by adding safeguards guaranteeing that only genetic manipulation carried out for therapeutic purposes may be patented, and stipulating that processes intended to modify the genetic identity of the human body were not patentable as they were contrary to the dignity of man.

The Commission presented its amended proposal to the Council in November 1993 and it went before the Parliament for its second reading in May 1994. The EP pushed for the adoption of further amendments, several of which the Commission accepted.[16] However, the directive fell under the co-decision procedure that obliges the Council of Ministers to negotiate with the EP. In three sessions in three months the Council and Parliamentary delegations (led by German Socialist Willi Rothley) met for difficult negotiations. Several rounds ended in deadlock, but in the end the delegations hammered out a deal. The joint text prohibited the patenting of inventions 'where publication or exploitation would be contrary to public policy or morality'. The joint text did not go so far as to prohibit the patenting of life. The Parliament was expected to approve the deal reached by their delegation. But on 1 March 1995, the directive was defeated in the EP by 240 to 188 votes (and 23 abstentions). The Greens and many Socialists voted against it.[17]

The Parliament's rejection of the directive was historic because it was the first time that MEPs had ever used the ultimate sanction available under co-decision to reject draft legislation. Although most observers were surprised by the obstructionist vote, several factors explained the outcome. Six years of compromise between the EP, Commission, Council, industry, Greens, scientists and farmers had produced an extremely vague document open to varying interpretation. Biotechnological firms themselves were divided on the vote.

Second, campaigning by the Greens was instrumental. The Greens within and outside the EP had mounted a fierce campaign leading up to the plenary vote. For instance, in the run-up to the vote, Greenpeace employed a series of dramatic tactics, such as climbing a bridge connecting two EP buildings and dangling over five lanes of traffic. French Socialist MEP Jean-Pierre Cot explained that the 'anti-directive lobbies were quite efficient and I don't think the pros realised the danger'.[18]

The patenting case also revealed the growing role of the EP and the Greens within it. *The Economist* (15 April 1995) noted that '[A]s the only directly elected element of the EU's power structure [MEPs] see themselves as tribunes of the people, never to be taken for granted. Upsetting a deal crafted in ministerial and bureaucratic chambers is just the sort of thing they like to do.' The case also indicated the moralistic tone taken by Greens, and the resonance such a stance can have among wider parliament and public.

However, the Greens' moral victory carried costs. Industry responded with fury, attacking MEPs for being irresponsible and accusing Greens of peddling misleading information. Nor did the Greens' victory win them allies within the EU institutions. Council representatives charged the EP with incompetence and inconsistency. The vote raised the questions about the extent to which Council ministers could trust the EP's conciliation delegation to deliver 'the goods' (i.e. the support of its colleagues in plenary). A frustrated EP official wondered if 'any Parliament that could be held captive by Greens and incompetence deserved respect'.[19]

Yet the Greens worried little about the 'credibility smashing' effect of their campaign. Green MEP Graefe zu Baringdorf noted that 'This had been a long process and very positive decision against the appropriation of human life.'[20] Another Green campaigner noted that 'people think we are being unnecessarily radical, but we think we are simply sending our message in the clearest possible way'.[21] More potentially damaging to the Greens' campaign was a new proposal introduced by the Commission in December 1995 which had a smoother ride through the institutions and received parliamentary approval in 1997. The Greens' battle over biotechnology clearly is set to continue.

III PACKAGING WASTE

Packaging waste is a visible sign of what Greens consider a mounting waste crisis in Europe. Greens object to the extraction and processing of raw packaging materials which can cause environmental damage by consuming energy and generating pollution in the production process. Therefore they emphasise first the need to avoid unnecessary packaging; second the need to reuse packaging; and third the need to recycle packaging materials. Lowest on the Greens' hierarchy of desired treatment are valorisation (incineration) and disposal of waste. Greens concede that some packaging will always be needed to protect and preserve products. But they argue that packaging has a significant environmental impact that should be substantially reduced. 'Only that packaging which is necessary to protect the product from the environment, and the consumers from the product, should be used' (Southworth 1993: 8).

In this context, Greens have long lobbied the public and officials about the increasing amounts of resources used and waste generated by current packaging practices within the EU. For instance, one of FoE's first 'agenda-setting' demonstrations in the UK was to dump 1,500 bottles on the doorway of Schweppes headquarters in protest against the decision to abandon returnable bottles (see Southworth 1993). The Greens' efforts paid off in the early 1990s when the European Commission introduced legislation to address the growing problem of resource depletion and waste disposal (see Table 7.1). The impetus for the directive came not only from growing public concern over mounting piles of waste, but also from the desire to harmonise waste management policies across the (then) 12 Member States (Bomberg 1998).[22] The Commission's directive introduced an EU-wide waste management policy designed to reduce the impact of packaging waste on the environment. Formal discussion within the Commission began in earnest in 1990, but a final agreement was not reached until December 1994 (EP and Council Directive 94/62/EC).

Table 7.1 Time line of Packaging Waste Directive

1990	Informal discussion within Commission
1991	SPAN established
1992 (Oct)	Commission's formal proposal published
1993 (March)	Greens launch alternative proposal
1993 (June)	EP's first reading
1993 (Sept)	Revised Commission proposal
1993 (Dec)	Council of Ministers adopt common position
1994 (May)	EP's second reading
1994 (Sept)	Conciliation talks commence
1994 (Dec)	EP and Council agree Directive

The Greens were one of many diverse interests involved in the formulation of this legislation. Porter and Butt Philip (1993: 17) note that even within the Commission itself, 16 different DGs were involved in the progress of the proposal at different stages of its formulation. Moreover, over 50 Euro-level interest groups were active at different times during its development. Several dozen environmental NGOs from EU and Eastern European countries lobbied separately or under the auspices of SPAN (Sustainable Packaging Action Network), which was set up by Friends of the Earth in 1991. Umbrella groups such as SPAN, the European Environmental Bureau and the German Federation for Environment and Nature (BUND) were especially active early on in the process (i.e. throughout 1991). They were joined by key GGEP members including long-serving collaborateur Alexander de Roo. Green NGOs and MEPs enjoyed frequent access to DG XI during this period. One involved GGEP member noted that the Commission was 'in the beginning fairly open to us; it listened to us in 1991–92'.[23]

Green demands were reflected in informal targets proposed by the Commission in 1991 and early 1992. Later, more formal proposals were also environmentally ambitious. Following over a year of consultation, negotiation and re-drafting, the Commission published in October 1992 a formal proposal for a Council Directive on Packaging and Packing Waste (OJ 12.10.92: 92/C263/01). The proposed directive established quantified targets for recovering waste and minimising its final disposal for all packaging waste.[24] It stipulated that within 10 years of coming into force, 90 per cent of packaging had to be recovered, 60 per cent of which was to be recycled. The October proposal represented a first attempt to regulate disposal of all types of packaging within the EU, and to do so with recycling targets that were well above the EU average.

However, this formal draft was softer than drafts produced earlier in 1991 and 1992. One source revealed that 'the lengthy consultations organised during the preparation of the proposal have induced the Commission to tone down its initial ambitions'.[25] Indeed, after their early activity, Greens became far outnumbered and out-resourced by business and professional groups. A plethora of trade and industry groups (such as INCPEN, ERRA and EUROPEN)[26] lobbied on the issue. They sought to prevent unfavourable new packaging legislation on the national level while pushing for quicker harmonised EU action. Manufacturing and processing industry interests had more sophisticated lobbying techniques, more lobbyists, and more extensive command of scientific and technical data. One Socialist MEP aide who followed the directive underscored the resource advantage of actors representing the packaging industry: 'They had consultants, scientists and lobbyists in every corridor . . . and that is where decisions are made.'[27]

Greens found the Commission's October proposal uneven and disappointing. Speaking for the Greens, MEP Paul Lannoye complained that 'the packaging industry has been making its presence increasingly felt and the objective of the text has deteriorated' as a result.[28] Greens vowed to work through the EP (and especially the

Environment Committee) to toughen up the proposal. This tactic necessarily involved cooperation with the Socialist Group. Although there was initial agreement between the parliamentary Greens and Socialists on the fundamental need for and shape of the directive, conflict soon developed. By spring 1993, well before the EP's first reading, the Greens were expressing disappointment at the extent to which Socialists were willing to accept a modified, watered-down document. During a parliamentary debate in April 1993, rapporteur for the packaging directive, Luigi Vertemati (Socialist), expressed his willingness to accept a 'toned down' directive rather than see it fail:

> Some of the attitudes that have been adopted could well put the Directive at risk, and I would prefer to have a low-key Directive, rather than an extremely tough one that cannot be applied. There is a need to set realistic and therefore attainable objectives.[29]

Vertemati's opinion was shared with other Socialists on the Environment Committee including Ken Collins and David Bowe. The Greens eschewed the 'realistic' or 'low key' approach and Green MEP Jean Pierre Raffin reminded fellow parliamentarians that 'the utopists [sic] of today are the realists of tomorrow'. Major green NGOs, including the FoE, EEB and SPAN, criticised the Vertemati report as a 'hotch potch ... fit for the dustbin' that 'responds more to industrial concerns than to the need for environmental protection'.[30]

The GGEP went further in its criticism. Insisting that the Commission's proposal was now so flawed as to be 'non-amendable', the GGEP instead floated an 'Alternative Proposal for Council Directive on Packaging and Packaging Waste' on 30 March 1993. The proposal was presented to MEPs, the Commission, and EU Environment ministers. The alternative proposal called for a stricter hierarchy emphasising prevention and reuse above recycling or incineration; the introduction of three different eco-taxes (for packaging, incineration and landfill sites); a ban on PVCs; and a ban on exports to non-EU countries of packaging not allowed on the EU level (GGEP 1993).

Whilst well received by green NGOs and the press (over 100 journalists were present at its launch), this tactic risked alienating potential allies in the Socialist Group and on the Environment Committee. Greens claimed: 'Our text is not being issued on a take or leave it basis. ... We are not trying to compete with the Vertemati report'.[31] But clearly the move was interpreted as such by some. An aide to Vertemati said the move was indicative of the 'Greens' need to make a symbolic point, to show resistance at any cost'.[32]

A few of the Greens' alternative demands made their way into the EP's official amendments. At its first reading in June 1993, the EP adopted the Vertemati Report and several amendments that sought to strengthen the draft directive by, *inter alia*, introducing a hierarchy of treatment (prevention, reuse, recycling, incineration, landfill disposal), and measures to prevent production of unnecessary packaging. Despite the inclusion of several green amendments, most Greens still judged the Vertemati Report to be too weak, and abstained. In the event, the Commission's amended proposal, presented in September 1993, rejected many of the EP's tougher amendments (including those pushed by the Greens and listed above) as inappropriate or incompatible with the aims of the single market.

Months later, and following further negotiations within COREPER and the Council, the Environment ministers adopted in December 1993 a common position on the Packaging Waste Directive (OJ C 285 15.12.93) that was considerably weaker in content and tone than any previous drafts. The Council agreed that within five years of the directive's implementation, not less than 50 per cent, nor more than 65 per cent of packaging waste should be recovered rather than dumped. Minimum recycling targets were dropped to 25 per cent from 40 per cent. Within 10 years the Council would have to agree a 'substantial increase' in these percentages. Several concessions were made to poorer countries because of their peripheral status and comparatively low consumption of packaging. A final significant change in Article One stated that the purpose of the directive was not only to *contribute* to the functioning of the internal market, but to *ensure* its functioning, thus placing enhanced emphasis on the internal market as opposed to the environmental goals of the directive.

Although the Council's decision received cautious welcome from packaging organisations, it was harshly criticised as regressive by Green MEPs, several NGOs and three Member States (Germany, Belgium and The Netherlands). Indeed, Dutch Environment Minister Hans Alders complained that the directive had been so weakened that it had 'nothing to do with the environment'.[33] Greens were equally dismayed, but because this directive fell under the co-decision procedure, the Council's decision was not final. Under co-decision, the directive was subject to a second reading by the EP in May 1994.

Whilst it was widely believed that the EP would insist on its earlier, tougher amendments, including the imposition of a hierarchy and prevention of unnecessary packaging, Greens within the EP failed to 're-secure' the parliamentary majority (260 votes) needed to pass the more stringent amendments passed in the first reading. By the time of the second reading, several other actors (especially professional and industry representatives) had stepped up considerably their lobbying of MEPs.

The increased intensity by industry lobbyists of the EP before its second reading became legendary. The directive is now widely considered 'the most heavily lobbied dossier in the history of the European institutions' (Golub 1996: 314). Whilst representatives from packaging organisations describe the Parliament's second reading as a 'victory of common sense over emotion',[34] green organisations charged industry lobbyists with 'brainwashing, and a campaign of misinformation and deception'.[35] The GGEP's press release (5 May 1994, Brussels) immediately following the second reading expressed their dismay at the Parliament's decision:

> At the very least the Parliament should have stuck to its earlier amendments. . . . The Greens deplore this sell-out which allows the trash mountains to keep growing, and which threatens the efforts of Denmark, Germany and The Netherlands to make a start toward dealing with the problem.

Greens had another chance to push for tougher conditions when the decision went to conciliation in September 1994.[36] Bargaining within the conciliation committee was mostly informal, and centred on trialogues between representatives from the Commission, the Council Presidency and the parliamentary delegation. The EP delegation, which included Green MEP Paul Lannoye, wanted to widen the discussion to include the Parliament's 'tougher' amendments, but the Council refused, knowing the EP probably could not muster the necessary majority to veto the common position. Greens within the EP and NGOs were effectively 'shut out' at this stage. Following several subsequent meetings of the conciliation committee, the EP and Council gave their final approval to the directive in December 1994. The agreed directive, which differed only slightly from the common position of December 1993, maintained the loose targets stipulated in the Council's common position. One amendment (number 31) was reworded to allow Member States with 'appropriate capacities for recycling and recovery' to set higher targets, provided they did not distort competition or the operation of the single market. Yet even this change did not significantly alter the spirit or content of the common position previously passed by the Council.

When the joint text arrived in Parliament for final approval, Greens voted against it. They objected to the agreed directive for several reasons: it included no hierarchy for waste processing; the recycling target of 15 per cent was 'absurdly low'; and the introduction of a maximum objective of 45 per cent for recycling of all packaging waste was a 'negative and unnecessary' addition to the body of European legislation. Moreover, Greens maintained that the directive violated the polluter pays principle by not making packaging manufacturers themselves responsible for packaging.[37] Green objections aside, the joint position was approved by the EP plenary in December 1994.

The outcome illustrated the constraints on EP influence, and the Greens within it. After the early stages of policy formulation, the Greens were soon overshadowed by the other actors. In addition to being out-resourced by industry groups, green impact was hampered by internal problems as well. Internal splits among Greens, and between Greens and their non-Green allies, reduced their overall impact on the directive. First, GGEP cooperation with NGOs was double-edged. On the one hand green NGO and MEP efforts on the packaging directive were better coordinated than in other cases such as vehicle emissions. At the outset, MEPs indicated a willingness to work with the more radical NGOs such as FoE.[38] But internal rifts remained. SPAN – itself made up of over 50 environmental groups from Western and Eastern Europe – was harmed by internal disagreements related to geography and nationality. Even more apparent were differences between MEPs and NGOs that revolved around questions of tactics: should parliamentary manoeuvres be given prominence, or should outside protest and campaigns receive the most attention?

Second, the GGEP itself was divided on certain issues. Green MEPs from different Member States brought with them different priorities and views on packaging waste. For example, Danish and Dutch members were more comfortable with valorisation options (the Danes use this at home), whereas German members were fervently opposed to incineration. These disagreements highlighted the ticklish nature of many environmental issues like recycling. Greens agree that recycling is a step in the right direction and is preferable to landfill disposal. But disagreement exists concerning its intrinsic value. Some more pragmatic or 'shallow' Greens view recycling as a worthy goal and willingly embrace legislation requiring high recycling targets. Others see recycling only as a 'delaying tactic' (Southworth 1993) that will not solve the fundamental problem of profligate consumption. Indeed, recycling itself can be problematic because of its cost and its use of further resources. Moreover, the focus on recycling may divert attention from the real problem of over-consumption and alternative solutions such as the introduction of a price mechanism for waste disposal.

Yet the most damaging disagreements for the parliamentary Greens occurred between them and the Socialist Group. The earlier loose alliance between Greens and the Socialists crumbled as Green MEPs refused to vote for the Vertemati report, complaining that it provided inadequate protection of the environment. Socialists charged Greens with irrational opposition; Greens charged Socialists with selling out to packaging industries. One GGEP member conceded: 'We fell out with Socialists for good reason, but we Greens really need Socialist support to get items through EP committees or plenary.'[39]

This disagreement illustrates the continuing strategic dilemma faced by Greens. By holding out for the 'greenest' of solutions, the opportunity to influence a compromise solution may be lost. Yet the alternative is often that Greens are forced to support legislation with which they are profoundly unhappy. In the case of the packaging waste directive, the Greens were caught on the horns of the dilemma. They were unhappy with the directive yet wanted to see some sort of progress made in this area. In this instance, they opted for the 'purer' stance, preferring no directive at all rather than the watered-down version. Yet their moral watchdog role had strategic costs as well as benefits. In this case, their stance reinforced their image as green protectors, but it brought them few friends within the EP, and threatened to harm their ability to participate in future compromises.

IV   CONCLUSION

The three case studies examined here highlight several themes. First, the Greens have permeated the EU policy-making process and become established players on a wide range of issues. But their influence is not consistent throughout the policy-making process or across policy areas. In most cases, their influence is most pronounced at the early agenda-setting stages of the EU's policy-making process. For instance, in the packaging waste directive, the Greens' input was instrumental in the early formulation, but later diminished considerably. The vehicle emissions and biotechnology cases demonstrated how the Greens' role can be extended to the later 'policy-shaping' stages of policy-making. In the 1989 vehicle emission standards case, the Greens were able to shape the final directive by working through a newly empowered Parliament. Similarly, the Greens' role in the patenting directive illustrated their potential to shape the later stages of EU decisions. In these instances, the Greens' role was not as agenda-setter but as moral guardian. In the Patenting Directive particularly, the Greens acted as a mouthpiece for widespread public concerns over the ethical and moral implications of a complex industry and science. It is likely that the Greens' role as moral guardians in the area of biotechnology will continue to expand.

A related theme illustrated by the above case studies is that green activity and impact within the EU policy-making process is contingent on both their internal and external resources. The Greens are dependent on the 'external' resource of wide public support for green goals. The 1989 vehicle emissions case occurred at the height of the 'green tide'; later emissions legislation, as well as the packaging waste directive, were formulated and decided in an atmosphere of waning ecological and rising economic concerns. The Greens' ability to shape these decisions was in part determined by the extent to which Greens could draw on the resources of public support and legitimacy.

The Greens' impact was also shaped by internal resources such as finances, staff, cohesiveness and determination. Clearly, the Greens could not compete financially with larger industrial lobbies. The intensity of industry lobbying in the later stages of the packaging waste directive suggested the extent to which packaging organisations could muster vast numbers of staff, lobbyists and data to make their case. A DG XI official responsible for waste management noted that the Greens'

> main difficulty is that they do not have enough staff and financial resources. . . . They simply don't have the resources to follow what is being done here. . . . If you have time and money and economic resources on your side than you can specialise and tell one person that in the next two years he/she has to prevent this directive from occurring. No NGO can afford to do this kind of thing.[40]

Financial resources aside, the extent to which the Greens can put forward a cohesive and coherent case also determines their role in the policy-making process. Conflicts and contradictions within the GGEP and between the GGEP and green NGOs have diminished the Greens' impact.[41] The case studies revealed successful outcomes when co-operation and mutual support were high (as in the 1989 vehicle emissions case) and failure when Greens proved unable to put forward a strong 'united green front' (auto oil programme). More generally, failure was also evident when Greens were unable to rally support from allies within the EP or back at home. Finally, for the GGEP in particular, the cases reveal the extent to which their sporadic success is a result of the priorities and tireless efforts of individual members, rather than the result of broad strategic goals of the Group as a whole. The Greens' role in the EU thus remains limited not only by their comparatively small size and financial resources, but by their inability to form and pursue common, coherent positions on European issues.

A final theme illustrated by the case studies is the persistence of the Greens' continuing strategic dilemma. The EP has proven to be a key channel of green influence. In several cases, the Greens have used their resources of public support, legitimacy and innovation to try to shape the legislation. But their influence has been decidedly limited. First, the Greens working alone can accomplish little. They must rely above all on allies in the other larger groups, usually the Socialists. But such cooperation often threatens the Greens' fundamental principles and forces unpalatable compromises. Support from home and the wider green movement usually suffers. The result is often a devil's choice between support for sub-optimal outcomes, or, as seen in the packaging waste directive, complete marginalisation.

The dilemma is not always as stark as that: partial compromise and moral victories count for something. Moreover, all parties are forced to decide when to compromise and when (and how rigorously) to stand by their principles. But for the Greens, whose *raison d'être* remains radical, principled behaviour, the strategic dilemma is especially sharp and will continue to define their activities and impact in EU policy-making.

8 Conclusion

INTRODUCTION

This chapter provides a concluding assessment of green activity and prospects in the European Union. Section I reviews the central strategic dilemma facing green actors in the EU, and the effect this dilemma has had on green activity thus far. Section II suggests the possible direction of green activity, highlighting the Greens' move towards transnational activity that extends beyond the EU. The concluding section evaluates the continuing relevance of green goals and demands for EU politics and policies.

I GREENS IN THE EU: AN ASSESSMENT

The Greens' achievements in Europe are not insignificant. First, the Greens have forced onto the EU's agenda issues neglected by major political parties and actors in Europe. Working both within parliamentary chambers and 'on the streets', Greens have highlighted the costs of economic growth and technological advancement by emphasising the ways in which uncontrolled industrial growth threatens Europe's quality of life. In this sense, one accomplishment of the Greens has been their ability to raise new issues and thereby alter the policy orientation of major political actors within the EU and EU Member States (see Collier and Golub 1997: 234).

The Greens' second achievement is related to the first. Chapter 3 presented the Greens' critique of current structures of the EU and their alternative visions of a 'Europe of the Regions'. The Greens' critique constitutes an intellectual as well as political challenge and addresses wider concerns of centralisation, bureaucratisation and degradation of the natural environment.

Finally, the last two chapters illustrated the Greens' attempts to influence the EU's policy-making process. Whilst their direct policy impact remains marginal, the Greens' role as environmental 'policy entrepreneurs' and 'moral watchdogs' is widely acknowledged by a range of EU actors. In short, Greens have infiltrated the EU's policy-making structures and become accepted players in its policy process.

The Greens' ability to influence the policy process is all the more striking when one considers the disadvantages they face. Chapters 6 and 7 highlighted the formidable logistical impediments confronting green actors. Relatively small and poorly financed, Greens must rely on less tangible resources such as public support and moral legitimacy.

Yet the Greens' core strategic dilemma remains: how can they achieve 'green' goals through structures that are deeply implicated in the status quo they seek to shift? This strategic quandary is further complicated by the transnational nature of the Greens' European policy. In particular, four 'European' complications exacerbate the Greens' strategic conflict (Bomberg 1998).

First, whilst the growing role of the EU provides Greens with enhanced strategic opportunities, it also poses risks. EU policy-making procedures remain centralised and largely dominated by bureaucracies and technical experts. Thus Green MEPs, more than MEPs from traditional parties, struggle with the dilemma of pushing for decentralised politics within the centralised structures of the EU.

Second, the MEPs have entered a Parliament with relatively little policy-making power and limited influence on EU legislation. For the first three years of Green participation in the EP (prior to the 1987 enactment of the SEA), the policy-making role of the EP was strictly advisory. Whilst subsequent Treaty revisions significantly expanded the EP's power and influence, it remains the weakest link in the policy-making triad of Commission, Council and Parliament. In the Greens' view, the subordinate position of the EP undermines the democratic legitimacy of the entire EU structure. Concern over this 'democratic deficit' is not unique to the Greens. But lack of democratic legitimacy is made more urgent by the Greens' characteristic emphasis on open democratic structures and grassroots participation.

Third, Green MEPs face the difficulty of drumming up grassroots support and interest in a distant arena. MEPs operate primarily in Brussels and Strasbourg, well removed from the grassroots base they are sent to represent. Whilst this difficulty is faced by all MEPs, it is particularly troublesome for the Green MEPs whose movement-party tradition is based on grassroots participation and control. Sustaining open communication with grassroots movements across a vast distance and array of issues is a formidable task for any party. Even on the national level, this style of operation requires 'inordinate patience for parliamentarians and assumes a wide range of knowledge on the part of the citizenry' (Schoonmaker 1988: 63).

At the supranational level, the difficulties are compounded. Green MEPs cover a staggering variety of subjects in the EP, not just those directly related to citizen movements or initiatives. Geographically, the distance between the MEPs is made greater by the multiple locations of EP operation. Maintaining links with the grassroots is extraordinarily difficult for MEPs, whose routine travel schedule (shuffling between Strasbourg and Brussels) may be described as a 'travelling circus' (Hrbek and Schweitzer 1989: 6).

Finally, Green MEPs face difficulties synchronising their European activities and goals with those on the national level. To pursue party politics effectively in a supranational structure like the EU requires constant communication and coordination with the national party executive and members. But several MEPs have complained of the nearly non-existent coordination of national and supranational policies. The Greens' loose organisational style – designed to discourage formation of a bureaucratic oligarchy – precludes an institutionalisation of national–supranational coordination.

In matters relating to the EU, the quantity and quality of publicity at the domestic level thus remains dependent almost exclusively on the efforts of individual MEPs. Again, this lack of communication and coordination is a problem shared by other, non-green parties. But it is exacerbated by the Greens' loose organisational style and made more serious because of the their grassroots-democratic principles. The challenge facing the Greens is how to tackle these persistent structural hurdles, whilst remaining true to their radical, grassroots tradition. This, in essence, is the green strategic conundrum on a supranational scale.

The way out of such a conundrum is a firm and decisive stance on the proper balance of radical-reformist (or movement-party) strategies. More importantly, a coherent concept is needed of the goals these strategies are designed to achieve. An important prerequisite is internal discussion and consensus. Yet this study has shown the strategic and conceptual limits of green coordination on the EU level.

In terms of strategy, green movements initially harboured feelings of mistrust towards parties and party organisations. Ultimately, however, many Greens chose to campaign for parliamentary seats and to join other parties and actors trying to enact change through the established institutions and processes of the EU. Yet whilst the Greens adopted parliamentary tactics, they did not succumb entirely to the cooptive forces of parliamentarisation. Greens have not agreed how far to integrate themselves into the parliamentary structures. Despite their more professional disposition, Greens continue to rely on unconventional as well as conventional tactics, and they remain eager to pursue a movement-inspired 'agenda-setting from below'.

In short, the Greens have not sold out entirely to parliamentary structures and methods. Nor have they remained inextricably tied to their grassroots members. Most Green MEPs have only limited contact with their supporters back home. The Green Group thus cannot exploit fully its potential as a transnational representative of green movements. More specifically, it cannot use the resources potentially available to it: the knowledge, expertise, contacts and support of its overall membership. Greens thus hover between the grassroots and Parliament, answerable to both, but loyal to neither.

This study has also shown that while the strategic paradox is formidable, the Greens' European policy suffers equally from a lack of basic consensus among its members about the goals to be pursued in Europe. The Greens' debate on strategy has been ultimately divorced from the goals of a green European policy. For instance, the Greens share conceptual 'building blocks' that comprise their altern-ative visions of Europe. But they also fail to agree on the importance or priority of these principles.

The point is that objectives should guide strategies. For the Greens, strategies have defined objectives. The Greens have ignored the fact that the relative effectiveness of different operating strategies depends on a coherent set of goals. A choice of tactics must be informed by a clear understanding – or at least discussion – of objectives. Put more bluntly, the Greens agonise between conventional or unconventional strategies: but to what purpose?

II   GREEN PARTIES BEYOND THE EU

Due in part to the limitations of green involvement in the EU; Greens have sought to extend their European policy and activities beyond the EU and its Member States. For instance, during the UNCED's Earth Summit in 1992, Green MEPs were key players in the 'First Planetary Green Meeting', an alternative summit attended by hundreds of NGOs and green activists. Closer to home, the GGEP has supported fledging green parties and movements across Europe. To illustrate the point, in 1990 it organised (and financed) a 'Green Parliament of Europe' – a three-day debating extravaganza that brought together over 100 elected members of East European national or regional parliaments.

More ambitiously, green parties have sought to develop a pan-European coordination or federation whose activities and membership are not exclusive to the EU. After several false starts (see Chapter 3), efforts were consolidated in the creation of the *European Federation of Green Parties* with its seat in Vienna.[1] The Federation imposes strict membership criteria,[2] and has agreed a joint policy programme designed to change the EU into a 'democratically controlled federation that is open to all European countries'.[3] By 1997, the Federation consisted of 29 parties from 25 countries.

The Federation has received logistical and financial support from the GGEP since 1989. The GGEP has helped fund a Brussels information office as well as two administrative posts. Aided by the GGEP, the European Federation has grown into an active network of green parties from EU and non-EU countries alike. It has issued a series of common statements on a wide range of policies including the fate of Chernobyl, democratic self-determination in Eastern Europe, and the 1996–7 reform of the Maastricht Treaty. It is particularly active on the issues of EU enlargement and coordination of East–West environmental projects.

Contact between the Federation and the GGEP is close. All GGEP members are invited to all Federation meetings, and the Federation's secretary general is invited to all GGEP Bureau meetings. The two groups also hold joint seminars and conferences on issues, especially those related to East–West cooperation. However, cooperation is still limited by different strategies and priorities. The Federation's secretary general contends that the Federation can choose to focus on the issues it feels most relevant to green politics in Europe, whereas 'the GGEP needs to work on specific issues. . . . They often become absorbed in issues defined by others. We don't want to be bound by the EU's agenda.'[4]

More generally, the Federation's remit allows its members to sidestep the dilemma of working within (EU) structures that are incompatible with green aims. The Federation is unfettered by the constraints of parliamentary structures, or the need for conventional forms of political behaviour and compromise. On the other hand, it remains relatively ineffectual in terms of influencing European policies or structures. In short, it is pure but powerless.

The GGEP's involvement in the Federation suggests the extent to which EU Greens are increasingly interested in issues that extend beyond the immediate geographic expanse of the EU. For instance, the prospect for political and ecological reform of Eastern Europe has long been a priority issue for Western Greens – not least because of the potential role played by Eastern green actors in this process. Consequently, Greens began to focus on Eastern enlargement of the EU long before most other EU actors.

From the early 1990s, Greens highlighted the enormous political, economic and environmental implications of Eastern enlargement through workshops, seminars and emergency resolutions. In particular, Nordic Greens were instrumental in prompting GGEP/Federation-sponsored projects on sewage, nuclear safety and conservation as part of a wider effort to encourage the environmental transformation of the Baltic area. Integral to this effort was intensified cooperation amongst Baltic green parties (EFGP 1996).

The Greens' focus on Eastern Europe and Eastern enlargement illustrates a broader point about green activities in Europe. Above all, Greens remain determined to address issues neglected by most major actors. Environmental sustainability, eco-taxes, subsidiarity and a 'Europe of the Regions' were buzzwords of the Greens long before they entered EU parlance. In the case of Eastern enlargement, it became clear by the mid-1990s that – contrary to earlier expectations and applicant aspirations – the Union would not enlarge until well after the year 2000, and almost certainly after the Eastern enlargement of NATO. Eastern and central European governments and citizens thus remained stuck in limbo: keen to be part of the European project but neglected by decision-makers in Brussels, very few of whom worked on enlargement issues on a day-to-day basis. Meanwhile, Greens have shown the foresight to seize on an issue that clearly will have far-reaching implications for Europe and which the EU cannot ignore forever.

III THE GREENING OF THE EU?

This book has underlined the link between a growth in EU powers and green activism. As the EU's competence has increased, Greens have raised concerns about characteristics of the EU that they criticise as undemocratic or 'un-green'. This section highlights the wider relevance of these green concerns and the extent to which national and EU policy-makers have addressed them.

In the area of environmental legislation, the EU has gone some way towards addressing problems of environmental degradation caused by industrial growth. For instance, the reduction of sulphur dioxide emissions in Europe is due in no small part to EU legislation introduced to clean up emissions from power plants and other large combustion plants (Osborn 1996). Even Greens acknowledge the role of the EU in combating key environmental problems (see Real World Coalition 1996: 112).

Nonetheless, the priority placed by the EU on economic growth means that it will continue to be a target for green critique. Greens highlight the environmental costs of production, transport and consumption encouraged by the single market. These concerns extend beyond the Greens. The wider political appeal of the environment theme has not been lost on EU and national officials. One of the issues given priority at the 1996–7 Intergovernmental Conference was the 'citizen and the environment'. The Irish Presidency's draft EU Treaty underlined the emerging consensus for strengthening the environmental protection. Whilst the extension of majority voting (QMV) on environmental issues was not forthcoming, the IGC's agenda suggested that public support for a stronger EU environmental policy is widespread and not limited to a few green 'doom sayers'.

The Greens' critique refers not only to the substantive policy outcome, but also to the processes by which the rules of the policy game are formulated and developed. Greens highlight what they see as an undemocratic or 'un-green' policy process in which the concentration of power rests with unelected bodies, and policy decisions ultimately are taken after horse-trading behind closed doors. This mode of operation contradicts at least three key green notions: grassroots democracy, accountability and openness (or 'transparency').

The notion of grassroots democracy is central to green politics, but it has wider relevance as well. Shorn of its green imagery, the term highlights the need for politicians and elected officials to listen to the 'grassroots' – the voters and citizens they were elected to represent. EU and government leaders have often ignored this lesson when formulating policies of the EU, or agreeing on fundamental constitutional change.

The difficulties surrounding ratification of the Maastricht Treaty illustrate the consequence of such neglect. Signed by government ministers after extensive internal debate, the Maastricht Treaty paved the way for ambitious pseudo-constitutional changes towards closer European integration.[5] Yet public debate was generally muted across the EU. Limited public discussion centred on a complicated, murky debate surrounding a single currency and closer economic union. The problem with the Treaty was thus 'never the goal, always the immoderate manner of its pursuit. . . . Above all there was the whiff of coercion in the air, of governments frog-marching public opinion along.'[6] In short, governments neglected the grassroots.

The consequences of neglect were felt on 2 June 1992 when, to the surprise of national and EU leaders, Danish voters rejected the Maastricht Treaty. Regardless of the particular reasons for the 'no' vote, the defeat signalled to EU and government leaders the dangers of taking for granted the consent of the grassroots. The vote unleashed doubts and grassroots protests elsewhere in the Union. The lesson from the Danes was that popular consent matters and could not be assumed.

Since the 'ratification crisis', the EU has gone some way towards addressing popular concerns about a lack of democracy, accountability and transparency within the EU's institutions. Ironically, many of the tools needed to fortify its democratic legitimacy were embodied in the Maastricht Treaty itself. First, in addition to strengthening the EP's powers, the Maastricht Treaty invoked the notion of 'subsidiarity' as a means to strengthen the Union's accountability and legitimacy. The EU's democratic deficit exists in part because Member States have pooled sovereignty at the EU level without pooling accountability. 'Policy-making is thus "delinked" from democratic controls' (Scott *et al.* 1994: 55). Subsidiarity promises to strengthen political accountability by devolving power downwards to the regional, local or community level. As invoked in Article A of the TEU, the principle suggests that political decisions should be taken 'as closely as possible to the citizens'. Yet the notion is vague and ambiguous. Elsewhere in the Treaty the principle is less a tool for democratic control so much as a 'procedural criterion' to determine when the EU – rather than Member States – should take action (see Scott *et al.* 1994: 48). Member States have chosen to focus primarily on this latter interpretation, sidestepping the wider problem of political accountability.

The TEU also sought to offset grassroots concerns by creating the office of an ombudsman to which citizens could complain if they felt badly treated by an EU institution. However, the ombudsman's remit is sorely limited: he can deal only with cases arising from 'maladministration on the part of Community institutions or bodies'. He cannot address grievances concerning the manner in which EU legislation is applied in Member States. The result is that by 1997 approximately 80 per cent of the complaints sent to him were outside his jurisdiction and ruled inadmissible.[7]

Finally, EU and national officials have also made moves towards more openness or 'transparency'. The Commission was quick to join in the 'transparency game' (Peterson 1995c). In July 1993, it announced a new policy of openness, promising to present information to the public and the media 'on demand, speedily and without techno-babble'.[8] The promise has been at least partly fulfilled. A Commission review issued in spring 1996 found that only 15 per cent of requests for access to internal Commission papers were rejected.[9]

At the Birmingham Summit in October 1992, Member States, too, committed themselves to a 'more open Community' by providing more information on the role of the Council of Ministers and its decisions, and simplification of (and easier access to) EU legislation. But the Council has been slow to deliver on such promises. It has yet to make up its mind on how to increase public access to Council documents, or on the possibility of some sort of freedom of information rule as operates in the United States. National ministers on the Council cling to the notion that EU law is essentially the product of negotiations between sovereign governments and that this sort of decision-making requires governments to make trade-offs that would be impossible to conduct under public scrutiny. The result is that the 'European public feels itself to be in the grip of something covert and uncontrolled.'[10]

The EP also has some way to go towards achieving more openness or transparency. Despite multiple proposals for reform, MEPs have failed to establish guidelines for the disclosure of outside professional interests, or receipt of gifts from lobbyists. For example, in summer 1996 new rules were proposed (the Nordmann report) that stipulated that members declare in a register all contributions received (in money or kind) and disclose the name of the contributor.[11] Green MEPs felt that the Nordmann proposal did not go far enough. They pressed instead for the requirement that MEPs state how much they earn from their outside activities. They also wanted a complete ban on gifts, and the introduction of uniform parliamentary rules on the declaration by members of their assets. Yet not only were the Greens unsuccessful in tightening the requirements: the Nordmann proposal for a register of lobbyists failed to win parliamentary approval.

Grassroots democracy, accountability and openness are not just green slogans. If the EU is to uphold its claim as a legitimate supranational body made up of democratic Member States, it must make its institutions more transparent, demonstrate accountability for its actions, and secure wider grassroots support for its policies. Greens have the potential to play an important role in this process of reform. Whatever their shortcomings as political actors, Greens offer an undeniably refreshing critique of the EU. Any debate about the future of Europe is invariably enriched by their participation.

Appendix 1
Green parties in the European Union: profiles

This appendix provides a brief 'profile' of green parties within the EU. It highlights the origins, programme and recent electoral fortunes of green parties, and suggests selected references for further reading.

AUSTRIA

The Austrian Green Party (die Grünen Österriech) emerged from a collection of disparate environmental and alternative social movements active in the 1970s and 1980s. Several rival green parties arose in the 1980s, including the moderate United Greens of Austria (VGÖ) and the more radical Alternative List of Austria (ALÖ). In 1986, members of both parties merged to form the Grüne Alternative (GA), which later became known as die Grünen Österreich. Campaigning on issues of ecology, decentralisation, neutrality and social equality, the Greens slowly built up electoral support on both the Länder (state) and national levels throughout the 1980s. A decisive electoral success occurred in the October 1994 general election when, under more professional (and media-friendly) leadership, the party secured over 7 per cent of the vote and 13 seats. Internal disunity contributed to a resounding defeat in the 1995 general election (in which they lost four seats). However, the Greens rebounded in the special EP election in October 1996, winning 6.7 per cent of the vote and one MEP.

The Greens initially opposed Austria's 1995 accession to the EU. However, following the 1994 referendum in which two-thirds of the population approved membership, the Greens reversed their position and vowed to reform the EU 'from within'. They have had one MEP to represent them in the Green Group in the European Parliament (GGEP) since 1995. For further reading see Parkin (1989); Lauber (1995).

BELGIUM

Belgium has two green parties, Agalev and Ecolo, which represent the Flemish (Agalev) and Wallonian (Ecolo) populations. Agalev ('Live differently') grew out of various grassroots movements concerned with peace, ecology and Christian ideals. Forming a political party in 1982, Agalev's programme centred on three principles: a holistic approach to ecology, grassroots democracy and non-violence. It later added to its platform a firm commitment to combat the rise of the far right in Belgium. Agalev steadily increased its share of the vote in elections on the regional, national and European level throughout the 1980s. Whilst initially intent on keeping its distance from other parties, it has since formed several parliamentary alliances. Agalev has been represented in the EP since 1984. In the 1994 EP election it secured over 10 per cent of the vote and sent one MEP to the GGEP for the 1994–9 term.

In Wallonia, Ecolo emerged out of several ecological and regionalist movements. Ecolo's programme reflects its roots: direct democracy, radical federalism and environmental concerns are central to Ecolo's ideology. In 1980 it launched itself as a 'new kind of party' beholden to neither the left nor the right. Under this banner, Ecolo won two parliamentary seats in 1981. Its vote increased steadily throughout the 1980s and early 1990s, as did its willingness to form coalitions under certain conditions. Internal conflicts and the emergence of other 'protest parties' resulted in an electoral setback (and loss of half its seats) in the 1995 parliamentary elections. On the European level, Ecolo has been represented in the EP since 1984. In the 1994 EP election, it won 13 per cent of the vote and one seat. For further reading see Kitschelt (1989); Rihoux (1995).

FEDERAL REPUBLIC OF GERMANY

See Chapter 1 for a profile of the German Greens (Bündnis 90/die Grünen).

FINLAND

The Finnish Green Party (Vihreä Liitto, or the 'Green League of Finland') grew out of an eclectic range of alternative movements in the late 1970s and 1980s. Conflict between 'purer' ecological movements and 'rainbow' or leftist groups precluded the formation of a broad based green party until the late 1980s. Vihreä Liitto was formed in 1988 and soon began capturing seats at the local and national level. In 1992, they won 6.8 per cent of the vote and 10 seats. Although their vote share fell slightly in the 1995 parliamentary election (to 6.5 per cent), the Greens were rewarded with the appointment of one of their members, Pekka Haavisto, as Finnish Minister of the Environment and Development.

During their campaigns, Vihreä Liitto has exhibited both 'purist' and leftist green tendencies. Among its key objectives are social and gender equality (many of its leading members are women), and a shift of the tax burden towards environmentally damaging practices. Upon Finland's accession to the EU in 1995, Vihreä Liitto secured one MEP based on its national representation. In Finland's EP election held in October 1996, Vihreä Liitto campaigned on the need to promote greater openness and democracy within the EU. They secured 7.6 of the vote and retained their MEP within the GGEP. Suggested readings include Paastela (1989); Parkin (1989).

FRANCE

The main green party in France is Les Verts (the Greens), which was formed in 1984 out of several green lists and movements. Les Verts has been notable for its 'pure' green ideology. Standing on principles of 'autonomy, ecology and solidarity', it traditionally has kept its distance from other parties, whether on the left or the right. Les Verts' electoral fortunes have been uneven and hampered by the emergence of numerous rival green lists and parties. For instance, one main competitor – Generation Ecologie – was formed in 1990 as a 'pragmatic' umbrella party under the leadership of Brice LaLonde.

Les Verts' defeats in the early 1990s (it failed to win any seats in the 1993 general election, and it lost its previous seven EP seats in the 1994 EP elections) provided the impetus for a more pragmatic electoral strategy. In 1997, the party endorsed an electoral alliance with the Socialists for the first round of national assembly elections in May/June 1997. The alliance paid off: Les Verts captured seven seats (out of 577) in the second round of voting and entered, for the first time, the French national assembly. For further reading see Prendville (1994); Faucher and Doherty (1996).

IRELAND

Originally know as the Ecology Party, the Irish Greens (Comhaontas Glas or 'Green Union') operated primarily as a grassroots movement before participating in elections. In its first national election in 1989, it won one seat in the Dail. Promoting itself as a broad based movement, Comhaontas Glas emphasises sustainable development, local democracy, decentralisation, individual freedom and a fairer distribution of wealth.

In the 1992 national elections, the party won 1.4 per cent of the vote and one seat. Another breakthrough occurred in 1994, when Dublin elected its first Green Lord Mayor. In the 1997 general election, the Greens increased their seat in the Dail to two. Campaigning on an anti-nuclear and a Euro-sceptical platform in the 1994 EP election, Comhaontas Glas polled 7.8 per cent and won two (out of 15) seats. Its two members joined the Green Group in the EP. For further reading see Baker (1990); Holmes and Kenny (1994).

ITALY

Despite serious environmental problems, a green movement was slow to emerge in Italy. Until the 1980s, Greens relied on the Radical Party to make its case. In the 1980s, a disparate range of leftist and ecological movements began contesting municipal elections. Coordination of various ecological groups led to the creation of Liste Verdi, or 'Green Lists', which contested a 1985 regional election on a 'pure' or 'green-green' platform. A competing 'red-green' or rainbow coalition (Verdi Arcobaleno or Rainbow Greens) also formed in the late 1980s. In 1990, the two merged to form Federazione Verdi (Green Federation), a federation comprising close to 100 different lists and groups. On the national level, the Greens have never secured more than a few per cent of the vote. Their appeal as a protest party has been diminished by the existence of several more effective protest or reform parties.

On the European level, the Greens have fared better. Although Liste Verdi and Verdi Arcobaleno ran separate lists in the 1989 European election, both were able to secure EP seats (three and two, respectively). In the 1994 EP election, the Federation won 3.2 per cent of the vote and two seats. An additional MEP, representing the reform party La Rete, also joined the GGEP. For further reading see Diani (1990); Rhodes (1995).

LUXEMBOURG

The emergence of the Luxembourg Green Party (Dei Greng or 'the Greens') was preceded by the efforts of numerous citizen initiatives to form electoral lists. In 1979, a list of activists contested elections (national and European) under the label of 'Alternative List–Resist' (AL–WI), but they won no seats. Elections on the national and European level in 1984 served as an impetus for the transformation of the AL–WI list into the Green Alternative Party (GAP) made up of many AL–WI members as well as members from environmental, peace and women's groups.

Despite moderate electoral success on the national level, the GAP was beset by internal conflicts that resulted in the creation of a rival splinter group, the Green Left Ecological Initiative (GLEI), which adopted a purer ecological stance than did the GAP. The two parties competed with one another during the 1989 national and European elections. However, in the run-up to the 1994 EP election, the two parties put aside their differences (temporarily) and joined together on a single list. They were rewarded with one MEP who joined the GGEP before leaving for the Radical Alliance in October 1995. For further reading see Koelble (1989); Frankland and Schoonmaker (1992, ch. 9).

THE NETHERLANDS

In The Netherlands, new social movements (NSMs) did not coalesce into a green party as occurred in many other countries. Instead, several other small radical parties such as the Radicals (PPR), Pacifist Socialists (PSP) and the Communists (CPN) represented NSM members and concerns. These small parties merged to form the Green Progressive Accord (GPA) in the run-up to the 1984 EP election, in which they won 5.6 per cent of the vote and two seats. In 1989, the GPA's constituent parts formed 'Groen Links' (Green Left) to contest elections on all levels. Adopting a red-green programme, Groen Links won 4 per cent of the vote (and six seats) in the 1989 national, and 7 per cent (and two seats) in the EP election of the same year.

Meanwhile, a 'purer' green party, De Groenen, was created in 1982. Despite The Netherlands' generous proportionality electoral system, De Groenen have failed to win national or EP seats. Competition between rival green parties has caused a drop in the number of green EP seats. In the 1994 EP election, Groen Links won only one seat; De Groenen won none. For further reading see Parkin (1989); Voerman (1995).

SWEDEN

The Swedish Green Party (Miljöparteit de Gröna) was founded in 1981 following a referendum in which the public supported the eventual phasing out of nuclear power. Spearheaded by anti-nuclear protesters, the new party also attracted members of women's, ecological and peace movements. Adopting a platform of ecological sustainability, decentralisation, small-scale production and local self-rule, the Greens have sought to distance themselves from the various other parties that have adopted green issues. On the national level, the Greens' electoral fortunes have vacillated from a high of 5.5 per cent of the vote and 20 seats in the 1988 parliamentary election, to a humiliating defeat in 1991 and the loss of its Riksdag seats. In the 1994 election, the Greens bounced back with over 5 per cent of the vote and 18 seats.

Campaigning on a platform highly critical of the EU and opposing Swedish membership, the Greens fared well in Sweden's 1995 EP election in which it won over 17 per cent of the vote and four seats in the EP. Green MEPs retained their highly Euro-sceptical stance within the GGEP, where they comprised the second largest national contingent in the 1994–9 term. For further reading see Bennulf (1995); Burchell (1996).

THE UNITED KINGDOM

Founded in 1973 as 'People', the British Green Party is amongst the oldest in Europe. (It also has undergone the most name changes: in 1975 it changed its name to the 'Ecology Party', and changed it again to the 'Green Party' in 1986. In 1989, the Scots broke away, forming their own independent 'Scottish Green Party'.)

Despite a small leftist-anarchist component within their ranks, the British Greens more closely resemble a 'purist' green party. Its programme emphasises ecological sustainability and sets out an alternative agenda for economic management, including work sharing and a reorientation of investment away from military and industrial enterprises. It also is a strong proponent of decentralisation and greater powers for sub-national authorities.

Although the Greens have contested elections at all levels, they have enjoyed only limited success. On the national level, the Greens have never averaged more than 2 per cent. They have fared better on the local level (where they hold a few hundred council seats). On the European level, the Greens received a spectacular 14.9 per cent in the 1989 EP election, but were still unable to secure any seats. Their share of the vote plummeted to 3.2 per cent in the 1994 EP election. Clearly the UK's plurality (first past the post) electoral system (used in both domestic and EP elections) makes it difficult for a small party without a geographic stronghold to win seats. Contesting elections in the UK is also expensive: British electoral law requires constituency deposits and offers no public funding for party campaign expenses. Feeling the financial strain, the Party adopted a 'targeting strategy' in the 1997 general election whereby only a few strategically selected seats were contested.

Yet the Greens' poor electoral performance has deeper roots. Unlike green parties elsewhere, the British Greens did not emerge from a widespread grassroots base of protest movements. They thus have never been able to draw on wider movements for electoral or logistical support. Moreover, the Green Party does not necessarily represent the most obvious political channel for the expression of green sentiment amongst the British public. Some voters view other parties as offering a suitable vehicle for their goals; many more prefer to express their 'green consciousness' through membership of green pressure groups. Finally, like many green parties, the British Greens' image and electoral prospects have suffered because of internal squabbling and poor organisation. For more reading see Young (1993); Rootes (1994).

OTHERS

Green parties in Denmark, Greece, Portugal and Spain either have failed to contest a European seat or have done so only in combination with other parties. Despite relatively high environmental awareness in *Denmark*, the small Danish Green Party (De Grönne) has failed to win seats at either the national or European level. Several other Danish parties successfully have adopted green themes into their electoral platform. For instance, Denmark's Socialists People's Party has strong elements of green ideology; one of its MEPs joined the GGEP from 1992–4. In the 1994 EP election, De Grönne stood on an anti-EU list that won over 18 per cent of the Danish vote.

Green party politics in *Greece* is complex. No national green party exists. Instead, several disparate green or ecological lists have competed with one another. No green list won national seats until 1989, when a loose 'Federation of Organisations of Alternative Ecologists' won one seat (with less than 1 per cent of the vote). However, this coalition was short-lived and had dissolved by the time of the next parliamentary election in 1993. On the European level, no Greek green party has contested EP seats, although several disparate green movements have stood alone or with other lists. No such list gained over 1.2 per cent of the vote or any EP seats. For further reading see

Demertzis (1995); Pridham *et al.* (1995).

In *Portugal,* a green party (Os Verdes) emerged in 1981. They have won national parliamentary seats, but only by standing on lists sponsored by Portugal's Communist Party. The same strategy has been adopted on the European level, where one Green MEP was elected for the 1989–94 parliamentary term. See Parkin (1989) for further reading.

In *Spain,* a green party (Los Verdes) was founded in 1984 by grouping together several hundred ecological, regionalist and leftist movements. However, ideological and personality clashes have plagued Los Verdes. The result has been a fluid creation and dissolution of various lists and parties, and a multiplicity of competing 'green' lists for national and European elections. For instance, in the 1989 EP campaign, Los Verdes joined a small left wing party (Izquierda de los Pueblos) to contest the EP election. This strategy enabled Los Verdes to send one MEP to the GGEP for the 1989–94 term. However, in the 1994 election, Los Verdes' list won only 1 per cent and no seats. For further reading see Aguilar-Fernandez (1994).

Appendix 2
Key policy-making institutions of the EU

EUROPEAN COMMISSION

The Commission is the main initiator of EU policy. Legally, it is the only body with the authority to table legislative proposals. It is headed by 20 Commissioners who are appointed by national governments for five years. In theory, Commissioners must renounce any loyalties to their own countries and henceforth serve only the 'general European interest'. In practice, Commissioners bring national orientations and political links to their posts that are never entirely abandoned.

The Commission acts as 'Guardian of the Treaties' and proposes to the Council measures for the development of EU policies. It is divided according to policy areas into 24 compartments or Directorates-General (DGs). For example, DG XI is responsible for Environment, Nuclear Safety and Consumer Protection. These Directorates are themselves tightly compartmentalised into units that often tend to pursue their own bureaucratic mission in isolation from whatever the rest of the Commission is doing. Very rarely is there a single 'Commission' view on any environmental issue. For instance, DG III, which is responsible for the single market, is keen to ensure that the setting of high environmental standards by 'greener' countries does not create new non-tariff barriers to trade. By contrast, DG XI is more concerned that the search for common solutions does not yield 'least common denominator' results or inadequate environmental policy.

COUNCIL OF MINISTERS

The Council of Ministers is composed of national government ministers and is the primary decision-maker. Its principal function is to accept or reject proposals put to it by the Commission, after seeking the advice of the EP and the Economic and Social Committee. The Council is assisted by the Committee of Permanent Representatives (COREPER), which coordinates the groundwork for most Council meetings (there is a special committee for agriculture). COREPER is made up of national delegations from each Member State which each act as a sort of Embassy to the EU. A host of working parties or committees conduct essential preparatory work of the Council and carry out tasks assigned to it by the Council. On less important, routine matters, decisions are adopted without debate if COREPER and Commission's representatives are unanimously agreed.

Council meetings are attended by different ministers according to the subject under discussion. Deliberations from the meetings are kept secret, although results of the votes can be made public. Foreign ministers serve as each Member State's main representative on general Council meetings. But other ministers meet for specialised meetings (i.e. agricultural ministers attend meetings on agricultural policy; environment ministers attend meetings on environmental affairs, etc.). Because the ministers who sit in the Council are leading political figures holding power in their own countries, considerations of national politics clearly motivate their behaviour (see Peters 1992). Although the Commission holds a monopoly on the right to propose policies, the Council of Ministers can request the Commission to undertake any study or initiative of interest to particular governments.

Thus, in contrast to the Commission and EP, both of which are essentially supranational bodies, the Council is an inter-governmental body 'where national officials and ministers, working behind closed doors, seek to secure the best possible deal for their home government' (Mazey and Richardson 1991: 11). Its secretive, cabalistic nature precludes close scrutiny by media, critics, or citizens' groups. In short, the Council is a natural conduit for the interests of national governments, but not for the interests of oppositional groups or public organisations.

EUROPEAN PARLIAMENT (EP)

Like national parliaments, the EP has directly elected members. Every five years its members are chosen to represent the EU's 370 million citizens. The 626 Members of the European Parliament (MEPs) are organised into political groups (nine in the 1994–9 term) that cut across nationalities. The basic organisation is supranational and partisan. For instance, Green MEPs from several Member States joined together to form the Green Group in the European Parliament (GGEP). To conduct their business, MEPs divide their time between different committees and geographic locations. The Parliament has developed an elaborate structure of 20 specialised committees. Committee meetings take place in Brussels, but most EP plenary sessions meet in Strasbourg, while its administration is located in Luxembourg.

Unlike national parliaments, the formal role of the EP is primarily consultative rather than legislative. It examines the Commission's proposals in detail and offers advice and consultation before the proposals are passed to the Council in the form of a formal EP Opinion. The Council may pass no legislative proposal into law until it has been the subject of a parliamentary Opinion. Moreover, subsequent Treaty revisions gradually have increased the EP's powers and it now holds co-legislative status in certain areas. But compared to most national parliaments, the EP's power to legislate is weak.

The EP's influence in policy-making stems also from informal sources. The Parliament derives its authority directly from the people: the Council and Commission do not. The EP has seized upon environmental issues to strengthen its own position within the EU's decision-making process. In particular, it has taken advantage of the rising environmental awareness amongst its electorates. Through direct elections and through its links with environmental groups, the EP has translated public support for environmental protection into institutional influence in the EU policy-making process.

EUROPEAN COURT OF JUSTICE (ECJ)

The European Court of Justice is responsible for interpreting and enforcing Community law which overrides national law. The Court consists of 15 judges and nine advocates-generals appointed on the basis of consensus with agreement of the Member States. Cases can be brought by the EU institutions against one another, by the Commission against Member States and by Member States against the Commission. If EU rules are working unfairly, the ECJ is also open to non-governmental organisations (NGOs), local authorities, companies or individuals to complain and seek redress. The Court has the power to impose fines on companies and governments found guilty of a breach of specific Community laws. The Court can also levy moral pressure on a government if it is found guilty of violating Community law. These moral sanctions have been effective as governments have sought to avoid public embarrassment.

ECONOMIC AND SOCIAL COMMITTEE (ESC)

The ESC is an assembly consisting of 220 members nominated by Member States. It represents a wide array of interests including industry, trade unions, agriculture, consumer and environmental organisations. Although the Council must consult the ESC before adopting legislation, the ESC itself enjoys little policy-making influence.

COMMITTEE OF THE REGIONS AND LOCAL AUTHORITIES (CoR)

Article 198a of the Maastricht Treaty established the CoR as an advisory body. It legally must be consulted on most EU legislation that touches upon the interests of sub-national government, including proposed regional development. The CoR also has the right to issue its own initiative reports on a wide variety of policy matters, including energy use and environmental protection. Thus far its impact has been muted. It is hampered by internal divisions, rivalry with other EU institutions and lack of an electoral base (its members are appointed by Member States, not elected).

EUROPEAN ENVIRONMENT AGENCY (EEA)

The EEA was agreed in 1990 but the Council of Ministers could not agree a site for the institution until 1993. It came into operation in 1994. Based in Copenhagen, the EEA's function is to ensure the supply of objective, reliable and comparable information at the European level on the state of the environment. In the late 1990s, the Council will decide on further tasks for the EEA, such as promoting environmental technologies and (more contentiously) monitoring the implementation of EU environmental legislation.

Notes

INTRODUCTION

1 In this book, 'green' appears in lower case when used as an adjective but in upper case when used as a proper noun (i.e. green politics, green parties but German Greens, European Greens and also Green MEPs).

2 For the sake of consistency, I use the term European Union (EU) to refer to the Union as well as to its constitutional predecessors, the European Community (EC) and the European Economic Community (EEC). However, references to the EC and EEC in verbatim quotations remain unchanged.

3 The reader will not find here a detailed analysis of national green parties or groups. This domestic perspective is covered competently elsewhere. For instance, see Müller-Rommel (1989); (1993); Parkin (1989); Poguntke (1989); and Richardson and Rootes (1995) for comparative analyses of several European green paries. Also, see Appendix 1 for a brief profile of green parties in EU Member States.

4 But see Rüdig (1985); (1995); Buck (1989); Judge (1993a); Long (1995); and Bomberg (1996).

5 For instance, Doherty (1992), Kitschelt (1990) and Poguntke (1990) compare the Greens' paradox with the strategic dilemmas confronting Communists or radical Socialists earlier in the century.

6 See Doherty (1992) for an examination of this conflict on the domestic level.

1 GREEN POLITICS IN EUROPE

1 What follows is a brief and simplified overview of an extremely rich and complex field of political thought. For a more in-depth examination of green political thought and its many nuances, see Dobson (1995); Doherty and de Geus (1996); Eckersley (1992); Goodin (1992); Hayward (1995); Martell (1994); and Pepper (1996).

2 For deep ecologists (see below) this belief leads to the idea of 'bioethics' which stipulates that nature has intrinsic worth, regardless of its usefulness or value to humans. 'Humans are therefore morally obliged to respect

plant, animals and all nature which has a right to existence and humane treatment' (Hayward 1995: 15). Whilst this spiritual aspect is more pronounced amongst deep Greens, it remains an important shared core value amongst all Greens.

3 For a less sympathetic treatment of these contradictions, see Bramwell (1989) and McHallam (1991).

4 Other writers use different terms to describe this ideological split. Dobson (1995) contrasts 'ecologism' and 'environmentalism', while Eckersley (1992) draws a distinction between 'ecocentric' and 'anthrocentric' approaches.

5 But see Kitschelt (1995) for a trenchant criticism of the post-materialist thesis associated primarily with Inglehart.

6 Figures from the *Financial Times*' 'FT Exporter' July 1996, p.3. Greenhouse gases are implicated in the incidence of global warming which can cause climatic disruption and devastating consequences in the form of increased storms, flooding and desertification.

7 For instance, the economic cost of pollution and other forms of environmental degradation cannot be calculated precisely, in part because traditional accounting systems and indicators (such as Gross National Product) take no account of environmental loss. Indeed, certain environmental disasters such as oil spills may actually contribute to the appearance of economic growth because the expense of the clean-up adds to GNP.

8 For instance, opinion polls in the United Kingdom, which usually registered relatively lower levels of environmental awareness compared to other EU Member States, indicated that popular awareness increased significantly from 1990–4. A Mintel survey showed a significant fall during this period in the number of British respondents who said they were either unaware of, or unconcerned about, green issues (*Financial Times* 5 January 1995, p.14).

9 See the *Financial Times* 10 July 1996.

10 Interview, Brussels, November 1995.

11 The UK was one important exception until 1997, when voters approved new legislative bodies in Scotland and Wales

12 Some authors have questioned the use of 'new' in this context (see Marks and McAdams 1995). I use it to refer to those movements connected with 'new' post-materialist issues that emerged in the 1960s and 1970s.

13 But see Koopmans (1996) who argues that NSMs are now just as, if not more, likely to adopt conventional forms of political action.

14 This categorisation represents a rough distinction only. Clearly, overlap will always exist between these three types of green actors. Moreover, not all green groups fit neatly into one of these categories.

15 Conservation or 'moderate' environmental groups such as the Royal Society for the Protection of Birds (RSPB) may share with the Greens certain environmental goals, but they are not 'green actors' in that they do not advocate a fundamental transformation of industrial society and practices. Nor do they subscribe to the broad values and practices outlined in Section 1.

16 The WWF was formerly known as the World Wildlife Fund. It still goes by this name in the United States.

17 The EU lobbying activities and policy impact of these NGOs will be discussed in Chapter 6.
18 Although primarily used to distingish green parties from one another, this ideological distinction is also apparent within green parties.
19 See Appendix 1 for a brief profile of other European green parties.
20 In particular, NATO's 1983 decision to deploy missiles on German soil swelled the ranks of the peace movement and clearly helped the Greens in their 1983 campaign (Breyman 1998).
21 Schily left the Green party for the SPD in the early 1980s; Joschka Fischer became parliamentary leader for Bündnis 90/die Grünen in the mid-1990s.
22 In addition to the broad Fundi-Realo divide, the party suffered under multiple factional splits. Even within the Fundi camp, for example, further divisions emerged between eco-socialists and radical ecologists over a broad range of economic issues. Other factions within the party included autonomous feminists and eco-libertarians. See Raschke (1991: 22); Frankland (1994: 42).

2   GREEN ISSUES AND ENVIRONMENTAL POLICY-MAKING IN THE EUROPEAN UNION

1 An overview of the key EU institutions involved in EU environmental policy is provided in Appendix 2.
2 Under QMV, a total of 87 votes are cast. The number of votes granted each Member State depends on its population. For instance, the four largest Member States – Germany, France, the UK and Italy – each have 10 votes, whereas Luxembourg has two. A qualified majority vote in Council requires 62 votes or 70 per cent of the total, which means that it takes at least three Member States to block a proposal.
3 The Commission's full-time staff is around 18,000. The number of staff involved in policy-making (as opposed to, say, translation services) is considerably smaller (under 12,000).
4 Interview with DG XI official, Brussels, January 1993.
5 Interview, Scotland, February 1993.
6 Interview with official in the UK Department of Environment's Environmental Protection Unit, London, September 1991.
7 The cases of small car emissions and the auto oil programme are discussed in detail in Chapter 7.
8 This directive is explored in more detail in Chapter 7.
9 The Structural Funds include the European Social Fund (ESF), the Guidance Section of the Community Agricultural Fund (EAGGF), the Financial Instruments of Fisheries Guidance (FIFG) and the European Regional Development Fund (ERDF). The ERDF is the largest; it is designed to help disadvantaged regions by supporting economic activity and financing infrastructure improvements.
10 COREPER, or the 'Committee of Permanent Representatives', assists the Council of Ministers by coordinating the groundwork for most Council meetings. See Appendix 2.
11 *European Voice* 17–23 October 1996.
12 See *The Economist* 20 July 1991.

13 See the *Independent* 29 September 1992.
14 Interview with MEP, Brussels, November 1995.

3   GREEN VISIONS OF EUROPE

1 To provide a round comparison, this section relies mainly on literature from green parties in Germany, France and Great Britain. All translations into English are by the author. For the sake of clarity, it should be noted that references to the 'French Greens' refer to Les Verts unless specified otherwise. It also should be noted that the Green Party in Britain has undergone several name changes. It was formed as 'People' in 1973, but changed its name to the 'Ecology Party' in 1975. In 1986 it changed its name again to the Green Party. In 1989 the Scots broke away, forming their own independent 'Scottish Green Party'. All post-1989 references to the British Greens exclude the Scottish Greens unless otherwise noted.

2 'Deep' greens such as Kirkpatrick Sale or Rudolph Bahro would tend to put a greater emphasis on the importance of following such a 'bioregional paradigm' than would more 'shallow' or 'eco-socialist' green thinkers and activists.

3 De Rougemont often cited his native Switzerland as the model for his (con)federal utopia. The relevance of his work to more troublesome regions of Europe is questionable (see Dierker 1987: 12–15).

4 Translated, the title is 'The Greens and Europe. For a Europe of the regions and independent peoples'.

5 Quoted in *Der Spiegel* 29 May 1989, p. 101

6 Examples are numerous: the Sorbs (a Slav language-islet in Saxony), Basque dwellers in Spain and France, Calabrians in Northern Ireland, German-speaking Cimbrians in Trento, or the Romansh peoples of Switzerland. See Ascherson (1992: 31).

7 Academic interest in regionalism is underlined by the explosion of literature and conferences on the topic. In 1988, the journal *West European Politics* devoted an entire issue to the subject. Several new journals dealing with the subject have emerged, such as *Regional and Federal Studies* or *European Urban and Regional Studies*. Key academic surveys and studies in this field include Meny and Wright (1985); Morgan (1986); Sharpe (1989); (1993); Jones and Keating (1995). Regionalism has also inspired models of the EU as a system of 'multi-level governance'. See Marks (1992); Marks, Hooghe and Blank (1996); Hooghe (1996).

8 Quoted in *Die Zeit* 25 September 1987, p. 6.

9 This confusion and neglect was not limited to the German Greens. Rüdig (1995) describes the confusing position of British Greens toward European integration generally, and the desirablity of EU membership more specifically.

10 The multitude of French green party groups is examined in more detail in Chapter 4.

11 For the full text of the Brussels Declaration, see Parkin (1989: 327).

12 Interview, Brussels, May 1991.

13 Interview, Brussels, May 1991.

14 Interview, London, April 1994.

4   GREEN TRANSNATIONAL STRATEGIES AND ELECTORAL PERFORMANCE

1   Green parties confront significantly different electoral rules in different countries. These rules are an important factor in shaping their electoral success. In France, a system of proportional representation is used in EP elections. A party must receive at least 5 per cent of the vote to obtain a seat. Germany's electoral system is effectively proportional, combining simple majority, single member constituencies and straight party lists. A 5 per cent hurdle is also used. In Belgium, a system of proportional representation with sub-national constituencies is used. The British Greens suffer under a simple majority, single member constituency (first past the post) electoral system which greatly limits the chances of small parties to win seats. For an examination of the effects of electoral rules on green parties, see Richardson and Rootes (1995).

2   Unlike German law, British electoral law stipulated that candidates for election to the EP needed to pay a deposit of £750 which was refunded to those obtaining over 5 per cent of the vote.

3   No green candidates were fielded in Denmark, Italy or Greece. In Denmark, a national green party was established in 1983 but did not contest the EP election. No national green parties existed in Italy or Greece. However, local and regional green lists were active in these countries. In all three countries, other parties often took on green issues for the 1984 campaign. For instance, in Italy, the Radical Party, formed in 1955 and led by Marco Pannella, had long played a major role in the campaign against nuclear power. They adopted green issues for their 1984 campaign, but their green integrity was questioned by many who believed they were merely 'trying to exploit the wave of interest stimulated by the success of the German Greens' (Rüdig 1985: 69).

4   For instance, Denmark's small green party, De Grønne, was part of the Danish Popular Movement against the EC, which gained 18.9 per cent of the vote. Denmark's Socialist People's Party has strong elements of green ideology; one of its MEPs later joined the GGEP.

5   Although no Greek green party contested the election, there were several disparate green movements that stood alone or with other lists. No such list gained over 1.2 per cent of the vote.

6   A ninth candidate on Les Verts' list immediately joined the Regionalist Group in the EP.

7   'Green Parties of the European Union. 1994 Election Platform'. This document is discussed in Chapter 3.

8   Quoted in the *Independent* 9 June 1994.

9   As described by Chris Busby, the official Green candiate for Mid and West Wales in the *Independent* 9 June 1994.

10   Quoted in the *Independent* 9 June 1994.

11   *Financial Times* 23 May 1994.

12   Quoted in *Frankfurter Allgemeine Zeitung* 15 Nov 1993.

13   Vlams Blok or the Flemish Bloc is a far right party that campaigned on a platform of Flemish nationalism and anti-immigration.

5 GREENS AND THE EUROPEAN PARLIAMENT: AN INSIDE LOOK

1 Following enlargement of the EP in 1995, the rules stipulated that a political group be made up of at least 29 members from one Member State, 23 from two Member States, 17 from three Member States and 14 members from four or more Member States.
2 One Belgium member from Ecolo left GRAEL in 1987 but stayed within the Rainbow Group.
3 Interview, Brussels, May 1989.
4 Interview, Germany, May 1991.
5 Interview with Dutch member, Brussels, May 1989.
6 Interview, Brussels, May 1989.
7 The British Greens, winning 14.9 per cent of the British vote, represented the hightest share of the *national* vote ever received by a green party. Ecolo's share of the vote was not nationwide, as it was restricted to the French speaking parts of Belgium.
8 Also elected on the French Green ticket was a ninth candidate, Max Simeoni, who immediately joined the regionalist Group.
9 Interviews with three Mediterranean members of the Group, Brussels, May 1991.
10 Interview, Brussels, May 1991.
11 The GGEP's numbers fluctuated throughout the 1989–94 term. In October 1989, German Dorothee Piermont left the GGEP to join the Rainbow Group; in September 1991, Portuguese Maria Santos left for the Socialist Group; and German MEP Karl Partsch switched to the Liberals in December 1991. A Danish MEP, John Iversen of the Danish Socialist People's Party, joined the GGEP in July 1992. The GGEP had 28 elected members at the end of its 1989–94 term.
12 The German MEPs, perhaps because of their unhappy experience in GRAEL, chose not to implement a rotation policy within the GGEP.
13 Interview, Brussels, January 1993.
14 Internal GGEP document authored by E. Falqui and G. Amendola, dated 7 July 1990; see also GGEP (1994: 19).
15 Interview, Brussels, May 1991.
16 Interview, Brussels, May 1991.
17 Interview, Brussels, February 1994.
18 Interview, Brussels, February 1994.
19 Internal memo entitled: 'Memo Regarding the Conflict in the GGEP' by the German members of the GGEP, July 1990.
20 Nel van Dijk quoted in Lambert (1991).
21 In October 1995, the Luxembourg Green Jup Weber left the GGEP for the Radical Alliance.
22 In December 1996, the GGEP gained a French MEP who was previously in the European Radical Alliance Group.
23 Interview, Brussels, December 1995.
24 Interview, Brussels, November 1995.
25 Co-president Alexander Langer died tragically, taking his own life in July 1995, leaving only one acting President for over a year. In 1996, Belgium MEP Magda Aelvoet took on the role as second co-president.

26   Interview, Brussels, December 1995.
27   These activities will be examined in the next chapter.
28   Interview, Brussels, November 1995.
29   The Swedish Greens were formally opposed to Sweden joining the EU in January 1995.
30   Gharton's interview with Mike Feinstein on 15 June 1991; quoted in Feinstein (1992: 41).
31   Interview, Brussels, October 1995.
32   Interview, Brussels, November 1995.
33   Interview, Brussels, November 1995.
34   Interview, Brussels, December 1995.
35   Interview, Brussels, November 1995.
36   Interview, Brussels, November 1995.
37   Interview, Germany, May 1991.
38   Interview, Germany, May 1989.
39   Interview, Brussels, January 1993.
40   Interview, Brussels, November 1993.
41   Interview, Brussels, January 1993.
42   Interview, Brussels, January 1993.
43   Interview, Brussels, January 1993.
44   Interview, Brussels, January 1993.
45   Interview, London, April 1994.
46   Interview, Brussels, January 1993.
47   Interview, Germany, May 1991.
48   Interview, Brussels, January 1993.

6   THE GREENS' POLICY INFLUENCE IN THE EUROPEAN UNION

1   Quoted in *European Voice* 30 May 1996.
2   Interview, London, September 1991.
3   CEAT is the European regional unit of Friends of the Earth International. It uses its French language designation, CEAT (*Co-ordination Europeenne Amis de la Terre*).
4   The EEB groups together around 150 NGOs from across the EU. It receives partial funding from the Commission, but also from national governments, foundations and membership fees (see Dalton 1994: 261).
5   Interview, Brussels, October 1995.
6   Interview, Brussels, January 1993.
7   Informally known as the G7, the other participants include CEAT, Birdlife International, the European Federation for Transport and Environment, and Climate Network Europe.
8   Interview, Brussels, January 1996.
9   Interview, Brussels, January 1993.
10   Interview, Brussels, November 1995.
11   Interview, Brussels, January 1993.
12   Interview, Brussels, May 1989.
13   Interview, Scotland, February 1993.
14   Interview, Brussels, May 1994.

15 Interview, Brussels, January 1993.
16 Interview, Brussels, January 1993.
17 Interview, Brussels, January 1993.
18 Interview, Washington DC, May 1993.
19 Interview, Brussels, November 1995.
20 Interview, London, April 1994.
21 Interview, Brussels, January 1993.
22 These complaints were included in a 23 point programme issued by the four Swedish Green MEPs in June 1996. The programme was designed to stimulate public debate on ways to make the EP more accountable and efficient. See 'Swedish Greens call for internal reform', *European Voice* 27 June – 3 July 1996.
23 The other 'prongs' of the campaign included public demostrations, action in plenary sessions, and travel to Tahiti and Mururoa where Green MEPs took part in direct action campaigns.
24 Interview, Brussels, December 1995.
25 Interview, Brussels, November 1995.
26 Interview, Brussels, November 1995.
27 The *rapporteur* is appointed to draft a report and steer debate both in the Committee and in the plenary session. While they are responsible for all views, and must report the majority opinion, rapporteurs have much room to manoeuvre. The first draft report drawn up by the rapporteur effectively sets the parameters of debate. The rapporteur also has procedural advantages within the committee and on the plenary floor.
28 One of the GRAEL's most active rapporteurs was German Green MEP Bloch von Blottnitz. Her report on the carcinogenic substances released in the vicinity of Windscale Sellafield, a British atomic reprocessing plant, was also adopted by the EP in 1985. This was the first EP report to attack the nuclear industry; its positive reception in the EP contributed to the outburst of publicity that helped convince the Council of Ministers to call a special session on the issue (*The Times* 21 February 1986; Hain 1989: 22).
29 For example, Green member of Petitions Committee, Frank Schwalba-Hoth, found majority acceptance in Parliament for a proclamation of solidarity with environmental activists in Eastern Europe protesting about a planned nuclear plant on the Danube (Schwalba-Hoth 1988: viii).
30 Interview, Brussels, January 1993.
31 Interview, Brussels, January 1993.
32 Committee appointments are decided by the political groups and are based on the overall size of each group within the plenary. However, through inter-group bargaining, a few exceptions to this weighting rule are normally accepted which allows especially keen MEPs to play a larger role as full committee members or substitutes. For instance, in 1994, Green MEP Alexander Langer held more committee posts than most other MEPs. He was a substitute on four committees, and a full member of two other committees (see Corbett *et al.* 1995: 109–11).
33 Given GGEP's internal rules precluding hierarchy, Paul Lannoye was not formally the GGEP's 'leader' but rather one of two rotating co-presidents. Nonetheless, his quiet leadership style during 1990–4 was instrumental in shaping the GGEP's new, more cooperative strategy.
34 Interview, Brussels, February 1994.

35 Interview, Brussels, January 1993.
36 Interview, Scotland, February 1993.
37 Interview, Brussels, January 1993.
38 Interview with German MEP, Brussels, January 1993.
39 Interview, Brussels, February 1994.
40 Interview, Brussels, January 1993.
41 Interview, Brussels, February 1994.
42 Interview, Brussels, January 1993.
43 Interview, Brussels, January 1993.
44 Interview, Brussels, January 1994.
45 Interview, Scotland, February 1993.

7   THE GREENS' POLICY-MAKING ROLE: THREE CASE STUDIES

1 See the *Financial Times* 27 July 1990.
2 Ripa di Meana was particulary sympathetic to the Greens' demands and joined the GGEP as an MEP in 1994.
3 Quoted in the *Independent* 8 May 1990.
4 Quoted in the *New York Times* 2 October 1989.
5 Interview, Brussels, October 1995.
6 Interview, Brussels, December 1995.
7 Interview, Brussels, November 1995.
8 The Greens were not alone in their criticism of the programme. Despite participating in the long negotiations producing the proposals, most vehicle firms and trade organisations were also unhappy with the results, claiming that the proposals were crippingly expensive and would put an unfair burden on their sector while letting the oil industry escape relatively lightly (see the *European Voice* 15 May 1996; the *Financial Times* 16 June 1996).
9 Quoted in the *Financial Times* 11/12 May 1996.
10 Quoted in the *European Voice* 15 May 1996.
11 Quoted in the *European Voice* 30 May 1996.
12 Most Greens would concede some positive biotechnological developments. For example, Härlin (1990: 256) concedes that the

> list of new and beneficial products which genetic engineering promises is long and impressive. It includes herbicide resistant and pesticide resistant plants; biologicial pesticides; pest resistant and disease resistant plants and animals; . . . task tailored microbes for agriculture, environmental control and mineral leaching, and new vaccines.

13 On-line news brief from the GGEP of the 27–8 March 1996 EP plenary 'Mini-Session' in Brussels.
14 Opinion of the Committee on Agriculture, Fisheries and Rural Development (PE 141.183).
15 The Greens tried several parliamentary manoeuvres to delay the first reading and thus allow more time for public debate. For instance, noting that the EU and its Member States had just signed the Convention on Biological Diversity at the UNCED in Rio, the Greens demanded the draft

directive be sent back to committees to ensure it complied with the Convention, especially its provision on intellectual property rights. But they were thwarted in this attempt when the EP's Legal Services claimed that the directive conformed with the Convention.

16 The Commission did not accept the controversial amendment number three which sought to remove the phrase 'as such' from the stipulation that 'the body or elements within the human body as such are not patentable'. The EP believed the phrase 'as such' to be open to abuse.

17 Opposition cut across party lines, however. For instance, some Christian Democrats voted against the directive for religious reasons.

18 Quoted in *The Economist* 15 April 1995.

19 Quoted in *The Economist* 15 April 1995.

20 Quoted in the *Independent* 2 March 1995.

21 Quoted in the *European Voice* 30 May 1995.

22 In particular, the German domestic recycling system was seen as hampering the single market. Germany's national Duales System Deutschalnd (DSD) was established in 1991 and obliged manufacturers and retailers to 're-absorb' packaging material. Problems emerged because the collected material far outstripped Germany's capacity to recycle it. Consequently, large amounts were exported to other Member States and, in the eyes of recepient Member States, were inhibiting development of their own waste managment programmes.

23 Interview with GGEP member, Brussels, September 1995.

24 Previous EU legislation had dealt only with beverage containers.

25 *European Report* 18 July 1992, part IV.

26 The Industry Council for Packaging and the Environment (INCPEN), European Recovery and Recycling Association (ERRA), Association of Plastics Manufacturers in Europe (APME) and the European Organisation for Packaging and the Environment (EUROPEN) were among the most active. In addition to individual lobbying, several packaging and producer groups joined forces under the Packaging Chain Forum (PCF) (see Porter and Butt Philip 1993).

27 Interview, Brussels, March 1994.

28 Quoted in the *European Report* 3 April 1993

29 Quoted in the *European Report* 3 April 1993.

30 Both quoted in the *European Report* 5 May 1993.

31 The Vertemati report was the official parliamentary statement on the directive. Paul Lannoye, quoted in the *European Report* 3 April 1993.

32 Interview, Brussels, March 1994.

33 Quoted in the *Financial Times* 29 December 1993.

34 Interview with EUROPEN representative, Brussels, November 1995.

35 Interview with green NGO lobbyists, Brussels, November 1995.

36 The decision to convene a conciliation committee was due primarily to continued disagreements among national, EP and non-governmental representatives over the wording of one amendment (number 31) concerning the use of national economic instruments.

37 See European Intelligence Unit, *European Trends*, 1st quarter 1995.

38 The Greens' press release in 1994, for instance, was jointly presented by three members of the GGEP as well as a member of the Dutch FoE.

39 Interview, Brussels, September 1995.

40 Interview, Brussels, November 1995.
41 Alternatively, Greens are aided by any lack of cohesion on the part of their opponents. For instance, in the case of the 1989 small car emission directive, the vehicle industry was fragmented along national and product lines (see McLaughlin and Jordan 1993). Similarly, biotechnology firms and larger pharmaceutical firms held diverging views on the value of the patenting directive.

8 CONCLUSION

1 The Federation developed out of the 'Green Coordination' that was set up in 1984. The Federation is sometimes (confusingly) referred to as the 'European Greens'. For an account of its emergence and early years, see Parkin (1989); Bowler and Farrel (1992).
2 Membership is restricted to established green parties agreeing to a broad set of guidelines based on ecological sustainability and democratic reform (see GGEP 1994: 186).
3 See *Agence Europe* 21 June 1993. The move to a federation also implied streamlined internal voting procedures. Whereas the Coordination reached decisions by consensus, the Federation's members agreed decisions by majority vote.
4 Interview with Federation's Secretary General, Brussels, December 1995.
5 Changes included the development of one currency and central bank, the extension of majority voting in the Council, EU-wide citizenship, a fledgling foreign and defence policy, and more EU powers in areas such as social policy, health protection and environmental strategy.
6 *The Economist* 6 June 1992.
7 *European Voice* 26 September–2 October 1996.
8 *Financial Times* 1 July 1993.
9 Reasons for rejection included the need to defend the public interest, or protect the Union's financial affairs. See the *European Voice* 3–9 October 1996, p.2
10 *The Economist* 19 Sept 1992, p.18
11 See the *European Voice* 11–17 July 1996.

Bibliography

Aguilar-Fernandez, S. (1994) 'The greens in the 1993 Spanish general election: a chronicle of a defeat foretold', *Environmental Politics* 3: 153–8.

Alger, C. (1988) 'Perceiving, analyzing, and coping with the local-global nexus', *International Social Science Journal* 117: 321–38.

Anderson, C. (1991) 'EC putting bite in its green bark', *New Scientist* 18 July: 182.

Arp, H. (1992) 'The European Parliament in European Community environmental policy', *EUI Working Paper*, No. 92/13, Florence: European University Institute.

Ascherson, N. (1992) 'The New Europe', *The Independent on Sunday Magazine*, 9 February: 31–4.

Bahro, R. (1986) *Building the Green Movement*, London: Heretic Books.

Baker, S. (1990) 'The evolution of the Irish ecology movement', in W. Rüdig (ed.) *Green Politics One*, Edinburgh: Edinburgh University Press.

Baldock, D. and Wenning, M. (1990) *The EC Structural Funds – Environmental Briefing – 2*, London: World Wide Fund for Nature (WWF).

Barnes, S. and Kaase, M. (1979) *Political Action: Mass Participation in Five Western Democracies*, London: Sage.

Becker, E. (1984) 'Natur als Politik?', in T. Kluge (ed.) *Grüne Politik. Der Stand einer Auseinandersetzung*, Frankfurt: Fischer Taschenbuch Verlag.

Bennulf, M. (1995) 'Sweden. The rise and fall of Milöpartiet de Gröna', in D. Richardson and C. Rootes (eds) *The Green Challenge. The Development of Green Parties in Europe*, London: Routledge.

von Beyme, K. (1982) 'Krise des Parteienstaats – ein internationales Phänomen?', in J. Raschke (ed.) *Bürger und Partein*, Opladen: Westdeutscher Verlag.

Bloch von Blottnitz, U. (1986a.) 'Auch in Brüssel die grünen Nasen überall reinstecken', *Grüner Basisdienst* 10: 36–7.

—— (1986b) 'Alternativer Forschungspolitik: Die EG als "Eisbrecher"?', *Grüner Basisdienst* 10: 38–9.

Bodeman, M. (1985–6) 'The Green Party and the new nationalism in the Federal Republic of Germany', in R. Miliban (ed.) *The Socialist Register 1985/1986*, London: Merlin Press.

Bomberg, E. (1992) 'The German Greens and the European Community: Dilemmas of a movement-party', *Environmental Politics* 1: 160–85.

—— (1994) 'Policy networks on the periphery: European Union environmental policy and Scotland', *Regional Politics and Policy* 4: 45–61.

—— (1996) 'Greens in the European Parliament', *Environmental Politics* 5: 324–31.

—— (1998) 'Issue networks and the environment: explaining EU environmental policy', in D. Marsh (ed.) *Policy Networks in a Comparative Perspective*, Milton Keynes: Open University Press (forthcoming).

Bomberg, E. and Peterson, J. (1993) 'Prevention from above? Preventive policies and the European Community', in M. Mills (ed.) *The Politics of Prevention and Health Care*, Aldershot: Avesbury Press.

—— (1998) 'EU decision-making: The role of sub-national authorities', *Political Studies* (forthcoming).

Bowler, S. and Farrell, D. (1992) 'The Greens at the European level', *Environmental Politics* 1: 132–6.

Bramwell, A. (1989) *Ecology in the 20th Century. A History*, London: Yale University Press.

Braunthal, G. (1996) *Parties and Politics in Modern Germany*, Boulder, CO: Westview Press.

Breyman, S. (1998) *Why Movements Matter: The West German Peace Movement, the SPD and the INF Negotiations*, Boulder, CO: Westview Press.

Brown, M. and May, J. (1989) *The Greenpeace Story*, London: Dorling Kindersley.

Buck, K. (1989) 'Europe: The "Greens" and the "Rainbow Group" in the European Parliament', in F. Müller-Rommel (ed.) *New Politics in Western Europe. The Rise and Success of Green Parties and Alternative Lists*, Boulder, CO: Westview Press.

Budd, S. and Jones, A. (1991) *The European Community. A Guide to the Maze*, 3rd ed., London: Kogan Page.

Bullard, M. (1990). 'Oberwasser für Euro-Grüne', *die Tageszeitung* 12 December: 5.

Burchell, J. (1996) 'No to the European Union: Miljopartiet's success in the 1995 European Parliament elections in Sweden', *Environmental Politics* 5: 332–8.

Butler, A. (1995) 'Unpopular leaders: the British case', *Political Studies* 43: 48–65.

Butler, M. (1986) *Europe: More Than a Continent*, London: Heinemann.

Carter, A. (1995) 'Towards a green political theory?', in A. Dobson and P. Lucardie (eds) *The Politics of Nature*, London: Routledge.

Carter, N. (1994) 'The Greens in the 1994 European Parliament elections', *Environmental Politics* 3: 445–517.

CEC (Commission of the European Communities) (1990) *Environmental Policy in the European Community*, 4th ed., European Documentation Series, Luxembourg: Office for Official Publications of the European Communities.

—— (1992a) *Eurobarometer*, No. 37, June, Luxembourg: Office for Official Publications of the European Communities.

—— (1992b) 'The Principle of Subsidiarity', Communication of the Commission to the Council and the European Parliament, November, Luxembourg: Office for Official Publications of the European Communities.

—— (1992c) 'Protecting Our Environment', European Documentation

Series, Luxembourg: Office for Official Publications of the European Communities.

—— (1992d) *Towards Sustainability: A European Community Programme of Policy and Action in Relation to the Environment and Sustainable Development,* 'Protecting Our Environment', European Documentation Series, Luxembourg: Office for Official Publications of the European Communities.

—— (1993) *Protecting Our Environment,* Europe on the Move Series, July, Luxembourg: Office for Official Publications of the European Communities.

—— (1994) (DG XIII) *The European Report on Science and Technology Indicators 1994,* October, Brussels: CEC.

—— (1996) 'Progress report from the Commission on the implementation of the European Community programme of policy and action in relation to the environment and sustainable development', COM 624, January, Brussels: CEC.

Cecchini, P. (with Catinat, M. and Jacquemin, A.) (1988) *The European Challenge. 1992: The Benefits of a Single Market,* Aldershot: Wildwood House.

Chafer, T. (1984) 'The Greens in France: an emerging social movement', *Journal of Area Studies* 10: 36–43.

Cobb, R. and Elder, C. (1972) *Participation in American Politics. The Dynamics of Agenda Building,* Baltimore: Johns Hopkins University Press.

Collier, U. and Golub, J. (1997) 'Environmental policy and politics', in M. Rhodes, P. Heywood and V. Wright (eds) *Developments in West European Politics,* Basingstoke: Macmillan.

Collins, K. and Earnshaw, D. (1992) 'The implementation and enforcement of European Community environmental legislation', *Environmental Politics* 1: 213–49.

Conradt, D. (1989) *The German Polity,* 3rd ed., London: Longman.

Coombes, D. (1970) *Politics and Bureaucracy in the European Community,* London: George Allen & Unwin.

Corbett, R. (1994) 'Representing the people', in A. Duff, J. Pinder and R. Pryce (eds) *Maastricht and Beyond. Building the European Union,* London: Routledge.

Corbett, R., Jacobs, F. and Shackleton, M. (1995) *The European Parliament,* 3rd ed., London: Catermill.

Court of Auditors (1992) 'Special Report No 3/92 with the Commission's replies', *Official Journal* 92/C245/01, vol. 35.

Curtice, J. (1991) 'The 1989 European Election: protest or green tide?', *Electoral Studies* 8: 217–30.

Dalton, R. (1988) *Citizen Politics in Western Democracies. Public Opinion and Political Parties in the United States, Great Britain, West Germany, and France,* Chatham, NJ: Chatham House.

—— (1989) 'The German voter', in G. Smith, W. Paterson, and P. Merkl (eds) *Developments in West German Politics,* Basingstoke: Macmillan.

—— (1993) 'The environmental movement in Western Europe', in S. Kamieniecki (ed.) *Environmental Politics in the International Arena,* Albany, NY: State University of New York Press.

—— (1994) *The Green Rainbow. Environmental Groups in Western Europe,* New Haven, NJ: Yale University Press.

Daly, P. (1985) *The Biotechnology Business,* London: Pinter.

Demertzis, N. (1995) 'Greece: Greens at the periphery' in D. Richardson and C. Rootes (eds) *The Green Challenge. The Development of Green Parties in Europe*, London: Routledge.

Derschouwer, K. (1989) 'Belgium: the "Ecologists" and "AGALEV"', in F. Müller-Rommel, (ed.) *New Politics in Western Europe. The Rise and Success of Green Parties and Alternative Lists*, Boulder, CO: Westview Press.

Diani, M. (1990) 'The Italian ecology movement: from radicalism to moderation', in W.Rüdig (ed.) *Green Politics One*, Edinburgh: Edinburgh University Press.

Dickson, L. and McCulloch, A. (1996) 'Shell, the Brent Spar and Greenpeace: a doomed tryst?', *Environmental Politics* 5: 122–9.

Dierker, J. (1987) 'Die Grünen und die europäische Integration', unpublished M.Phil. thesis, Westfälische Wilhelms-Universität.

Dinan, D. (1994) *Ever Closer Union? An Introduction to the European Community*, Basingstoke: Macmillan.

Dobson, A. (1995) *Green Political Thought*, 2nd edn., London: Routledge.

—— (ed.) (1991) *The Green Reader*, London: Andre Deutsch.

Dobson, A. and Lucardie, P. (eds) (1995) *The Politics of Nature*, London: Routledge.

Doherty, A. (1992) 'The fundi-realo controversy: an analysis of four European green parties', *Environmental Politics* 1: 95–120.

Doherty, B. and de Geus, M. (1996) *Democracy and Green Political Thought*, London: Routledge.

Eckersley, R. (1992) *Environmentalism and Political Theory. Toward an Ecocentric Approach*, London: UCL Press.

Ecology Party (1984) *Towards a Green Europe. Manifesto of the Ecology Party and Common Programme for Action of the European Green Parties*, London: Ecology Party.

EFGP (European Federation of Green Parties) (1993) *Guiding Principles of the European Greens*, Helsinki: EFGP.

—— (1996) *Update. Newsletter for the European Federation of Green Parties*, No. 9, December.

Ehrlich, E. (1996) 'Success judged on expectations more than performance', *European Voice* Survey on Environment, 30 May: 18.

Ennich, E. (1986) 'Regenbogen oder Wurstmaschine?', *Grüner Basisdienst* 10: 28–31.

Esders, J. (1988) 'Gefangen im Parlamentsbetrieb?', in GRAEL, *Politik im Regenbogen. Grün-alternatives im Europäisches Parlament*, Brussels: GRAEL.

Faucher, F. and Doherty, B. (1996) 'The decline of green politics in France: political ecology since 1992', *Environmental Politics* 5: 108–14.

Feinstein, M. (1992) *Sixteen Weeks with European Greens*, San Pedro, CA: R & E Miles.

Fitzmaurice, J. (1978) *The European Parliament*, Westmead: Saxon House.

—— (1994) 'The European Commission', in A. Duff, J. Pinder and R. Pryce (eds) *Maastricht and Beyond. Building the European Union*, London: Routledge.

Frankel, B. (1987) *Post-Industrial Utopians*, Cambridge: Polity Press.

Franken, M. and Ohler, W. (eds) (1989) *Natürlich Europa. 1992 – Chancen für die Natur?*, Köln: Volksblatt Verlag.

Frankland, G. (1989a) 'Die Grünen', in F. Müller-Rommel (ed.) *New Politics in Western Europe. The Rise and Success of Green Parties and Alternative Lists,* Boulder, CO: Westview Press.

—— (1989b) 'Parliamentary politics and the development of the Green Party in West Germany', *Review of Politics* 51: 386–411.

—— (1995) 'Germany. The rise, fall and recovery of Die Grünen', in D. Richardson and C. Rootes (eds) *The Green Challenge. The Development of Green Parties in Europe,* London: Routledge.

Frankland, G. and Schoonmaker, D. (1992) *Between Protest and Power: The Green Party in Germany,* Boulder, CO: Westview Press.

Franklin, M. and Rüdig, W. (1992) 'The green voter in the 1989 European Election', *Environmental Politics* 1: 129–59.

—— (1995) 'On the durability of green politics. Evidence from the 1989 European election study', *Comparative Political Studies* 28: 409–39.

Freestone, D. (1991) 'European Community environmental policy and law', *Journal of Law and Society* 18: 135–54.

Gamson, W. (1990) *The Strategy of Social Protest,* 2nd ed., Belmont, CA: Wadsworth.

Gatter, P. (1987) *Die Aufsteiger. Ein politisches Porträt der Grünen,* Hamburg: Hoffman und Campe.

Gerdes, D. (1984) 'Europa der Regionen', in W. Woyke (ed.) *Europäische Gemeinschaft. Pipers Wörterbuch zur Politik No.3,* Munich: Piper.

GGEP (Green Group in the European Parliament) (1991a) *Green Leaves. Bulletin of the Greens in the European Parliament* No. 0, March, Brussels: GGEP.

—— (1991b) *Green Leaves. Bulletin of the Greens in the European Parliament* No. 1, April, Brussels: GGEP.

—— (1991c) *Green Leaves. Bulletin of the Greens in the European Parliament* No. 2, May, Brussels: GGEP.

—— (1991d) *Green Leaves. Bulletin of the Greens in the European Parliament* No. 3, June, Brussels: GGEP.

—— (1991e) *Green Leaves. Bulletin of the Greens in the European Parliament* No. 4, Summer, Brussels: GGEP.

—— (1991f) *Green Leaves. Bulletin of the Greens in the European Parliament* No. 5, October, Brussels: GGEP.

—— (1991g) *Green Leaves. Bulletin of the Greens in the European Parliament* No. 6, Winter, Brussels: GGEP.

—— (1992a) *Green Leaves. Bulletin of the Greens in the European Parliament* No. 7, February, Brussels: GGEP.

—— (1992b) *Green Leaves. Bulletin of the Greens in the European Parliament* No. 8, March, Brussels: GGEP.

—— (1992c) *Green Leaves. Bulletin of the Greens in the European Parliament* No. 9, April, Brussels: GGEP.

—— (1992d) *Green Papers: Green Agenda* No. 6, April, Brussels: GGEP.

—— (1992e) *Green Leaves. Bulletin of the Greens in the European Parliament* No. 10, September, Brussels: GGEP.

—— (1993) 'Proposal for a Council Directive on Packaging and Packaging Waste', March, Brussels: GGEP.

—— (1994) *Greens in the European Parliament. A New Sense of Purpose for Europe. Record and Prospects of the first Green Political Group in the European Parliament.* Text by Diana Johnstone, Brussels: GGEP.

Giddens, A. (1994) *Beyond Left and Right. The Future of Radical Politics*, Oxford: Polity Press.

Golub, J. (1996) 'State power and institutional influence in European integration: lessons from the packaging waste directive', *Journal of Common Market Studies* 34: 313–40.

Goodin, R. (1992) *Green Political Thought*, Oxford: Polity Press.

Gordon, J. (1993) 'Letting the genie out: local government and UNCED', *Environmental Politics* 2: 137–55.

GRAEL (Green Alternative European Link) (1984) *Paris Declaration*, Paris and Brussels: GRAEL.

—— (1987) 'Working Group on Energy and Environment', GRAEL Working Paper, Brussels: GRAEL.

—— (1988a) *Politik im Regenbogen. Grün-alternatives im Europäisches Parlament*, Brussels: GRAEL.

—— (1988b) *Rainbow Politics. Green Alternative Politics in the European Parliament*, Brussels: GRAEL.

Gransow, V. (1989) 'Greening of German–German relations?', in E. Kolinsky (ed.) *The Greens in West Germany. Organisation and Policymaking*, Oxford: Berg.

Green Party (England and Wales and Northern Ireland) (1993) *Green Europe? A Green View of European Integration*, London: Green Party.

Green Party (England and Wales) (1994) *European Election Manifesto 1994*, London: Green Party.

Green Party (UK) (1989) *Don't Let Your World Turn Grey. European Election Manifesto*, London: Green Party.

die Grünen (1979) *Das Programm der Grünen. Erklärung der 'Sonstigen Politische Vereinigung,' Die Grünen zur Europawahl*, Bonn: die Grünen.

—— (1980) *Das Bundesprogramm der Grünen*, Bonn: die Grünen.

—— (1984a) *Common Statement of the Greens for the 1984 Election to the European Parliament*, Bonn: die Grünen.

—— (1984b) *Global Denken – vor Ort Handeln: Erklärung der Grünen zur Europawahl 1984*, Bonn: die Grünen.

—— (1986) 'Deutsch–Deutsch. Wider die Mauern auch in den eigenen Köpfen', reproduced as appendix document no.3 in E. Kolinsky (ed.) *The Greens in West Germany. Organisation and Policymaking*, Oxford: Berg.

—— (1989a) *Extra Blatt zur Europawahl*, Bonn: die Grünen.

—— (1989b) *Kurzprogramm der Grünen zur Europawahl '89*, Bonn: die Grünen.

—— (1989c) *Plattform der Grünen zur Europawahl 1989*, Bonn: die Grünen.

die Grünen/Bündnis 90 (1994) *Programm zur Europawahl 1994*, Bonn: die Grünen.

Haaland Matlary, J. (1996) 'Energy policy', in H. Wallace and W. Wallace (eds) *Policy-making in the European Union*, Oxford: Oxford University Press.

Haas, E. (1965) *The Uniting of Europe*, Stanford, CA: Stanford University Press.

Hagland, P. (1991) 'Environmental policy', in L. Hurwitz and C. Lequesne (eds) *The State of the European Community: Policies, Institutions and Debates in the Transition Years*, Boulder, CO: Lynne Rienner.

Haigh, N. (1992) 'The European Community and international environmental policy', in A. Hurrel and B. Kingsbury *International Politics of the Environment: Actors, Interests and Institutions*, Oxford: Clarendon Press.

Haigh, N. and Baldcock, D. (1989) '*Environmental Policy and 1992*, London: British Department of the Environment.

Hain, W. (1989) 'Urnengang furs Abendland. Inteview mit Undine-Uta Bloch von Blottnitz', *Szene Hamburg*, September/October: 20–2.

Hainsworth, P. (1990) 'Breaking the mould: the greens in the French party system', in A. Cole (ed.) *French Political Parties in Transition*, Aldershot: Dartmouth.

Härlin, B. (1990) 'Genetic engineering in Europe', in P. Wheale and R. McNally (eds) *The Bio Revolution. Cornucopia or Pandora's Box?*, London: Pluto Press.

Harvie, C. (1994) *The Rise of Regional Europe*, London: Routledge.

Hayward, T. (1995) *Ecological Thought. An Introduction*, Cambridge: Polity Press.

Heclo, H. (1978) 'Issue networks and the executive establishment', in A. King (ed.) *The New American Political System*, Washington, DC: American Enterprise Institute.

Hegedus, Z. (1987) 'The challenge of the peace movement: civilian security and civilian emancipation', *Alternatives* 12: 197–216.

Heinrich, B. (1986) 'Einiges ist in Bewegung gekommen', *Grüner Basisdienst* 10: 7–8.

Heuglin, T. (1986) 'Regionalism in Western Europe: conceptual problems of a new political perspective', *Comparative Politics* 18: 439–58.

Hey, C. (1989) 'Ecology and the internal market', Paper presented at the International Forum on the European Single Market, April, Cologne, Germany.

Heywood, P. (1996) *The Government and Politics of Spain*, Basingstoke: Macmillan.

Hildebrandt, P. (1992) 'The European Community's environmental policy, 1957–1992: from incidental measures to an international regime?', *Environmental Politics* 1: 13–44.

Holmes, R. and Kenny, M. (1994) 'The electoral breakthrough of the Irish Greens?', *Environmental Politics* 3: 218–25

Hooghe, L. (1995) 'Sub-national mobilisation in the European Union', *West European Politics* 18: 175–89.

—— (ed.) (1996) *Cohesion Policy and European Integration: Building Multi-Level Governance*, Oxford: Oxford University Press.

Horst, H. (1984) 'Für ein anderes, ein grünes Europa', *Grüner Basisdienst* 10: 32–3.

Hrbek, R. and Schweitzer, C. (1989) 'Die deutschen Europa-Parlamentarier', *Aus Politik und Zeitgeschichte. Beilage zur Wochenzeitung Das Parlament* 3/89: 3–18.

Hull, R. (1993) 'Lobbying Brussels: a view from within', in S. Mazey and J. Richardson (eds) *Lobbying in the European Community*, Oxford: Oxford University Press.

Hülsberg, W. (1988) *The German Greens. A Social and Political Profile*, London: Verso.

Inglehart, R. (1971) 'The silent revolution in Europe: inter-generational change in post-industrial societies', *American Political Science Review* 65: 991–1017.

—— (1977) *The Silent Revolution. Changing Values and Political Styles Among Western Publics*, Princeton, NJ: Princeton University Press.

—— (1981) 'Post materialism in an environment of insecurity', *American Political Science Review* 75: 880–900.

Irvine, S. (1989) *Beyond Green Consumerism*, London: Friends of the Earth.

Irvine, S. and Ponton, A. (1988) *A Green Manifesto: Politics for a Green Future*, London: Macdonald Optima.

Jäenicke, M. (1982) 'Parlamentärische Entwarnungseffekte? Zum Ortsbestimmung der Alternativbewegung', in J. Mettke (ed.) *Die Grünen – Regierungspartner von Morgen?*, Reinbek: Rowohlt.

Jahn, D. (1994) 'Unifying the Greens in a united Germany', *Environmental Politics* 3: 312–18.

Jamison, A., Eyerman, R. and Cramer, J. (1990) *Making of the New Environmental Consciousness*, Edinburgh: Edinburgh University Press.

Jesinghausen, M. (1995) 'General election to the German Bundestag on 16 October 1994: Green pragmatists in conservative embrace or a new era for German parliamentary democracy?', *Environmental Politics* 4: 108–13.

Joanny, C. (1990) *Bilan d'activités*, 22 May, Brussels: GGEP.

Johnson, S. and Corcelle, G. (1989) *The Environmental Policy of the European Communities*, London: Graham & Trotman.

Jones, B. and Keating, M. (eds) (1995) *The European Union and the Regions*, Oxford: Clarendon Press.

Judge, D. (ed.) (1993a) *A Green Dimension for the European Community. Political Issues and Processes*, London: Frank Cass.

—— (1993b) '"Predestined to save the earth": the environment committee of the European Parliament', in D. Judge (ed.) *A Green Dimension for the European Community. Political Issues and Processes*, London: Frank Cass.

Judge, D. and Earnshaw, D. (1994) 'Weak European Parliament influence? A study of the environment committee of the European Parliament', *Government and Opposition* 29: 262–76.

Judge, D., Earnshaw, D. and Cowan, N. (1994) 'Ripples or waves: the European Parliament and the European Community policy process', *Journal of European Public Policy* 1: 27–52.

Jünger, E. (1948) *The Peace*, New York: van Loewen Ltd.

Kaldor, M. (1990) *The Imaginary War*, Oxford and New York: Blackwell.

Kelly, P. (1980) 'Die Vierte Partei – Eine wahlbare ökologische, gewaltfreie, soziale und basisdemokratische Anti-Partei', in H. Lüdke (ed.) *Die Grünen. Personen – Projekte – Programme*, Stuttgart: Kröner.

—— (1984a) 'Gedanken zur gegenwärtigen Europadiskussion', internal Grünen memorandum, Bonn.

—— (1984b) 'Skandal Europa', Speech held in the German Bundestag on 28 March, Bonn.

Kemp, P. and Wall, D. (1990) *A Green Manifesto for the 1990s*, London: Penguin Books.

Keohane, R. and Hoffmann, S. (1991) (eds) *The New European Community: Decision-Making and Institutional Change*, Boulder, CO: Westview Press.

Keyes, C. (1991) *The European Community and Environmental Policy: An Introduction for Americans*, Washington, DC: WWF.

Keyserling, C.H. (1928) *Europe*, New York: Hartcourt, Brace & Co.

Kingdon, J. (1984) *Agendas, Alternatives, and Public Policies*, Boston: Little, Brown & Co.

Kirchner, E. and Schwaiger, K. (1981) *The Role of Interest Groups in the European Community*, Aldershot: Gower Press.

Kitschelt, H. (1986) 'Political opportunity structures and political protest: antinuclear movements in four democracies', *British Journal of Political Science* 16: 57–85.

—— (1988) 'Left libertarian parties: explaining innovation in competitive party systems', *World Politics* 40: 194–234.

—— (1989) *The Logic of Party formation: Ecological Politics in Belgium and West Germany*, Ithaca, NY: Cornell University Press

—— (1990) 'The medium is the message: democracy and oligarchy in Belgium ecology parties', in W. Rüdig (ed.) *Green Politics One*, Edinburgh: Edinburgh University Press.

—— (1995) 'A silent revolution in Europe?', in J. Hayward and E. Page (eds) *Governing the New Europe*, Cambridge: Polity Press.

Kivell, P.T. (1989) 'Protecting the Euro-environment', *Geography* 74: 47–52.

Klandermans, B., Kriesi, H. and Tarrow, S. (eds) (1989) *From Structure to Action: Comparing Movement Participation Across Cultures*, Greenwich, Conn.: JAI.

Klatte, E. (1988) 'Vom Statisten zum Aketeur – die Rolle der Umweltverbände', in L. Gundling and B. Weber (eds) *Dicke Luft in Europa. Aufgaben und Probleme der Europäische Umweltpolitik*, Heidelberg: C.F. Muller.

Koelble, T. (1989) 'Luxembourg: the "Greng Alternativ"', in F. Müller-Rommel (ed.) *New Politics in Western Europe. The Rise and Success of Green Parties and Alternative Lists*, Boulder, CO: Westview Press.

Kolinsky, E. (1984) 'Ecology and peace in West Germany: an uneasy alliance', *Journal of Area Studies* 9: 23–8.

—— (ed.) (1987) *Opposition in Western Europe*, New York: St Martins Press.

—— (1990) 'The Federal Republic of Germany', in J. Lodge (ed.) *The 1989 Election of the European Parliament*, New York: St Martins Press.

Koopmans, R. (1996) 'New social movements and changes in political participation in Western Europe', *West European Politics* 19: 28–50.

Lambert, J. (1991) 'The impact of the Green Group in the European Parliament', Paper presented at the European Consortium for Political Research Joint Session of Workshops, University of Essex, Colchester, UK, 22–28 March.

—— (1995) 'Foreword', in D. Richardson an﹏ Rootes (eds) (1994) *The Green Challenge. The Development of Green Parties in Europe*, London: Routledge.

Langguth, G. (1986) *The Green Factor in German Politics. From Protest Movement to Political Party*, Boulder, CO: Westview Press.

Lannoye, P. (1990) 'Contribution to the Debate on the Greens' Political Strategy', internal memo, GGEP.

—— (1991) 'A Green Group in the European Parliament: What For?', in GGEP *Green Leaves. Bulletin of the Greens in the European Parliament* No. 1: 1–2. Brussels: GGEP.

Lauber, V. (1995) 'The Austrian Greens', *Environmental Politics* 4: 313–19.

Lawson, K. and Merkl, P. (eds) (1988) *When Parties Fail. Emerging Alternative Organizations*, Princeton, NJ: Princeton University Press.

Leggewie, C. (1989) 'Natürlich Europa! Vorwort', in M. Franken and W. Ohler (eds) *Natürlich Europa. 1992 – Chancen für die Natur?*, Koln: Volksblatt.

Leonard, D. (1988) 'The Single Act and the Parliament: shifts in the balance of power', *European Trends* 4: 57–63.

Les Verts (1989) *Les Verts et L'Europe*, Paris: Les Verts.

—— (1993) *La Choix de la Vie*, Gentilly: Fèvrier.

—— (1994a) 'Programme Politique des Verts pour les Elections Européennes de juin 1994', *Vert Contact* supplément, no. 333, avril.

—— (1994b) *Vert Contact* supplément, no. 337, 7–13 mai.

Liberatore, A. (1991) 'Problems of transnational policymaking: environmental policy in the European Community', *European Journal of Political Research* 19: 281–305.

Lindberg, L. (1963) *The Political Dynamics of Economic Integration*, Stanford, CA: Stanford University Press.

Lodge, J. (1989a) 'Environment: towards a clean green-blue EC?', in J. Lodge (ed.) *The European Community and the Challenge of the Future*, London: Pinter.

—— (1989b) 'The European Parliament – from 'assembly' to co-legislature: changing the institutional dynamics', in J. Lodge (ed.) *The European Community and the Challenge of the Future*, London: Pinter.

—— (ed.) (1990) *The 1989 Election of the European Parliament*, New York: St Martins Press.

Long, T. (1995) 'Shaping public policy in the European Union: a case study of the structural funds', *Journal of European Public Policy* 2: 672–9.

Loose, G. (1974) *Ernst Jünger*, New York: Twayne.

Lowe, P. and Goyder, J. (1983) *Environmental Groups in Politics*, London: George Allen & Unwin.

Lowe, P. and Rüdig, W. (1986) 'Review article: political ecology and the social sciences – the state of the art', *British Journal of Political Science* 16: 513–50.

McAdams, J. (1989) 'Micro-mobilization contexts and recruitment to activism', in B. Klandermans, H. Kriesi and S. Tarrow (eds) *From Structure to Action: Comparing Movement Participation Across Cultures*, Greenwich, CT: JAI.

McCarthy, J. and Zald, M. (eds) (1977) *Dynamics of Social Movements*, Cambridge, Mass.: Winthrop.

McCormick, J. (1991) *British Politics and the Environment*, London: Earthscan.

—— (1995) *The Global Environmental Movement*, 2nd ed., West Sussex: John Wiley & Sons.

McHallam, A. (1991) *The New Authoritarians*, London: Institute of European and Defence Studies.

MacKenzie, D. (1991) 'Ministers clash over rules for modified organisms', *New Scientist* 3 August: 8.

McLaughlin, A. and Jordon, G. (1993) 'The rationality of lobbying in Europe: why are some Euro-groups so numerous and so weak? Some evidence from the car industry', in S. Mazey and J. Richardson (eds) *Lobbying in the European Community*, Oxford: Oxford University Press.

Maier, J. and Schulz, A. (1988) 'Common statement of the European green parties for the 1989 European Elections. Draft no.3', internal GRAEL memorandum, 18 December, Brussels: GRAEL.

Marks, G. (1992) 'Structural policy in the European Community', in A. Sbragia (ed.) *Euro-Politics. Institutions and Policymaking in the 'New' European Community*, Washington, DC: Brookings Institution.

Marks, G. and McAdams, D. (1996) 'Social movements and the changing structure of political opportunity in the European Union', in G. Marks, F.

Scharpf, P. Schmitter and W. Streeck (eds) *Governance in the European Union*, London: Sage.

Marks, G., Hooghe, L. and Blank, K. (1996) 'European integration in the 1980s', *Journal of Common Market Studies* 34: 341–78.

Marsh, J.S. (1989) 'The common agricultural policy', in J. Lodge (ed.) *The European Community and the Challenge of the Future*, London: Pinter.

Martell, L. (1994) *Ecology and Society*, Oxford: Polity Press.

Mazey, S. and Richardson, J. (1991) 'Lobbying Styles and European Integration', Paper presented at the ECPR Joint Sessions Workshop, 22–28 March, University of Essex, Colchester, UK.

—— (1992) 'British pressure groups in the European Community: the challenge of Brussels', *Parliamentary Affairs* 45: 92–107.

—— (1993) 'Introduction: transference of power, decision rules, and rules of the game', in S. Mazey and J. Richardson (eds) *Lobbying in the European Community*, Oxford: Oxford University Press.

—— (1994) 'Policy co-ordination in Brussels: environmental and regional policy', *Regional Politics and Policy* 4: 22–43.

Meadows, D., Meadows, D. and Randers, J. (1974) *The Limits to Growth*, London: Pan Books.

—— (1992) *Beyond the Limits*, London: Earthscan.

Melucci, A. (1989) *Nomads of the Present. Social Movements and Individual Needs in Contemporary Society*, Philadelphia: Temple University Press.

Meny, Y. (1990) *Government and Politics in Western Europe. Britain, France, Italy, West Germany*, Oxford: Oxford University Press.

Meny, Y. and Wright, V. (eds) (1985) *Centre–Periphery Relations in Western Europe*, London: George Allen & Unwin.

Merkl, P. (1986) 'West German women: a long way from Kinder, Küche, Kirche', in L. Iglitzen and R. Ross (eds) *Women in the World. 1975–1985. The Women's Decade*, 2nd ed., Santa Barbara, CA: ABC Clio.

—— (1987) 'How new the brave new world? New social movements in West Germany', *German Studies Review* 10: 125–47.

Metcalf, L. (1992) 'After 1992: can the Commission manage Europe?', *Australian Journal of Public Administration* 51: 117–30.

Milbrath, L. (1988) 'The significance of the environmental movement for the future of the world', Paper presented at the 14th World Congress of the International Political Science Association, 28 August 28–1 September, Washington DC.

Moravcsik, A. (1991) 'Negotiating the Single European Act: national interests and conventional statecraft in the European Community', *International Organization* 45: 651–88.

Morgan, R. (ed.) (1986) *Regionalism in Politics*, London: Policy Studies Institute.

Müller-Rommel, F. (1985a) 'Das grün-alternative Parteibündnis im Europäischen Parlament. Perspektiven eines neuen Phänomens', *Zeitschrift für Parlamentsfragen* 16: 391–404.

—— (1985b) 'New social movements and smaller parties: a comparative perspective', *West European Politics* 8: 41–54.

—— (1989) 'Green parties and alternative lists under cross-national perspective', in F. Müller-Rommel (ed.) *New Politics in Western Europe. The Rise and Success of Green Parties and Alternative Lists*, Boulder, CO: Westview Press.

—— (1990) 'Political success of green parties in Western Europe', Paper presented at the annual meeting of the American Political Science Association, 30 August–2 September, San Francisco, CA.

—— (1993) *Grüne Parteien in Westeuropa. Entwicklungsphasen und Erfolgsbedingungen*, Opladen: Westdeutscher Verlag.

Myers, N. (1985) *The Gaia Atlas of Planet Management*, London: Good Books.

Naess, A. (1973) 'The shallow and the deep, long range ecology movement: a summary', *Inquiry* 16: 95–100.

Nelkin, D. and Pollack, M. (1981) *The Atom Besieged*, Cambridge, MA: MIT Press.

Newman, M. (1996) *Democracy, Sovereignty and the European Union*, London: Hurst & Company.

Nitsch, E. (1986) 'Wer wildert in welchem Erbhof?', *Grüner Basisdienst* 10: 55–6.

Nostitz, W. von (1984) 'Die Europäischen Gemeinschaften aus der Sicht der Grünen', *Grüner Basisdienst* 4: 18–19.

—— (1986) 'Die Grünen im Europäische Parlament – eine weitere vertane Chance?', *Grüner Basisdienst* 10: 4–7.

Nostiz, W. and Merkel, C. (1986) 'Vorwort. Europagruppe der Grünen/ Regenbogenfraktion', *Grüne Inhalt* (no page numbers).

Nugent, N. (1994) *The Government and Politics of the European Union*, 3rd ed., Basingstoke: Macmillan.

Offe, C. (1985) 'New social movements: challenging the boundaries of institutional politics', *Social Research* 52: 817–68.

O'Riordan, T. (1981) *Environmentalism*, London: Pion.

Osborn, D. (1996) 'Viewpoint: action plan for everyone', *Financial Times* 5 March: 12.

Papadakis, E. (1986) 'The green alternative: interpretations of social protest and political action in West Germany', *Australian Journal of Politics and History* 32: 443–54.

Parkin, S. (1989) *Green Parties. An International Guide*, London: Heretic Books.

Paastela, J. (1989) 'Finland: the "Vihreät"' in F. Müller-Rommel (ed.) *New Politics in Western Europe. The Rise and Success of Green Parties and Alternative Lists*, Boulder, CO: Westview Press.

Pepper, D. (1996) *Modern Environmentalism. An Introduction*, London: Routledge.

Peters, B.G. (1992) 'Bureaucratic politics and the institutions of the European Community', in A. Sbragia (ed.) *Euro-Politics. Institutions and Policymaking in the 'New' European Community*, Washington, DC: Brookings Institution.

—— (1994) 'Agenda-setting in the European Community', *Journal of European Public Policy* 1: 9–26.

Peterson, J. (1989) 'Hormones, heifers and high politics: biotechnology and the common agricultural policy', *Public Administration* 67: 455–71.

—— (1994) 'Subsidiarity: a definition to suit any vision', *Parliamentary Affairs* 47: 116–32.

—— (1995a) 'Decision-making in the European Union: towards a framework for analysis', *Journal of European Public Policy* 2: 69–94.

—— (1995b) 'EU research: the politics of expertise', in S. Mazey and C. Rhodes (eds) *The State of the European Union, Vol. III*, Boulder, CO and Essex: Westview Press and Longman.

—— (1995c) 'Playing the transparency game: consultation and policy-making in the European Commission', *Public Administration* 73: 473–92.

Poguntke, T. (1987). 'New politics and party systems: the emergence of a new type of party', *West European Politics* 10: 76–81.

—— (1989) 'The "new politics dimension" in European green parties', in F. Müller-Rommel (ed.) *New Politics in Western Europe: The Rise and Success of Green Parties and Alternative Lists*, Boulder, CO: Westview Press.

—— (1990) 'Party activists versus voters: are the German Greens losing touch with the electorate?', in W. Rüdig (ed.) *Green Politics One*, Edinburgh: Edinburgh University Press.

—— (1993a) *Alternative Politics. The German Green Party*, Edinburgh: Edinburgh University Press.

—— (1993b) 'Goodbye to movement politics? Organisational adaptation of the German Green Party', *Environmental Politics* 2: 379–404.

Porritt, J. (1985) *Seeing Green. The Politics of Ecology Explained*, London: Basil Blackwell.

Porter, M. and Butt Philip, A. (1993) 'The role of interest groups in EU environmental policy formulation: a case study of the draft packaging directive', *European Environment* 3: 16–20.

Prendville, B. (1989) 'France: Les Verts', in F. Müller-Rommel (ed.) *New Politics in Western Europe. The Rise and Success of Green Parties and Alternative Lists*, Boulder, CO: Westview Press.

—— (1994) *Environmental Politics in France*, Boulder, CO and Oxford: Westview Press.

Pridham, G., Verney, S. and Konstakakopulos, D. (1995) 'Environmental policy in Greece: evolution, structures and process', *Environmental Politics* 4: 244–70.

Raschke, J. (1982) 'Einleitung', in J. Raschke (ed.) *Bürger und Parteien*, Opladen: Westdeutscher Verlag.

—— (1985) *Soziale Bewegungen. Ein historisch-systematischer Grundriß*, Frankfurt: Campus.

—— (1987) 'Die Grünen zwischen Bewegungs- und Parlamentspartei', *Gegenwartskunde* 2: 171–84.

—— (1991) *Krise der Grünen: Bilanz and Neubeginn*, Marburg: Schüren.

Ratti, O. (1990) 'Report on the work of the Political Affairs Committee', Internal GGEP document, Brussels.

Real World Coalition (1996) *The Politics of the Real World*, London: Earthscan.

Rehbinder, E. and Steward, R. (eds) (1985) *Environmental Protection Policy*, Volume 2, Florence: European University Institute.

Reif, K. (1984) 'National electoral cycles and European elections 1979 and 1984', *Electoral Studies* 3: 244–55.

Rhodes, M. (1995) 'The Italian Greens: struggling for survival', *Environmental Politics* 4: 305–12.

Richardson, D. (1995) 'The Green challenge: philosophical, programmatic and electoral considerations', in D. Richardson and C. Rootes (eds) (1994) *The Green Challenge. The Development of Green Parties in Europe*, London: Routledge.

Richardson, D. and Rootes, C. (eds) (1995) *The Green Challenge. The Development of Green Parties in Europe*, London: Routledge.

Ricketts, R. (1986) 'The greening of Europe. An interview with Frank Schwalba-Hoth', *New Zealand International Review* 11: 2–5.

Rieger, E. (1996) 'The common agricultural policy', in H. Wallace and W. Wallace (eds) *Policy-making in the European Union*, Oxford: Oxford University Press.

Rihoux, B. (1995) 'Belgium: greens in a divided society', in D. Richardson and C. Rootes (eds) *The Green Challenge. The Development of Green Parties in Europe*, London: Routledge.

Rochon, T. (1990) 'Political movements and state authority in liberal democracies', *World Politics* 42: 299–313.

Rochon, T. and Mazmanian, D. (1993) 'Social movements and the policy process', *The Annals of the American Academy* 52: 75–87.

Rokkan, S. and Urwin, D. (eds) (1982) *The Politics of Territorial Identity*, London: Sage.

de Roo, A. (1990) 'Towards a green EC-strategy against the greenhouse effect: a tax on non-renewable energy sources', *Green Discussion Paper*, Brussels: GGEP.

Rootes, C. (1995) 'Britain: Greens in a cold climate', in D. Richardson and C. Rootes (eds) *The Green Challenge. The Development of Green Parties in Europe*, London: Routledge.

Roth, R. and Rucht, D. (eds) (1987) *Neue soziale Bewegungen in der Bundesrepublik Deutschland*, Bonn: Bundeszentrale für politische Bildung.

de Rougemont, D. (1965) *The Meaning of Europe*, New York: Stein & Day.

—— (1966) *The Idea of Europe*, New York: Macmillian.

—— (1983) *The Future Is Within Us*, New York: Pergamon Press.

Rucht, D. (1987) 'Zum Verhältnis von sozialen Bewegungen und politischen Parteien', *Journal für Sozialforschung* 27: 297–313.

—— (1989) 'Themes, logics and arenas of social movements: a structural approach', in B. Klandermans, H. Kriesi and S. Tarrow (eds) *From Structure to Action: Comparing Movement Participation Across Cultures*, Greenwich, CT: JAI.

Rüdig, W. (1985) 'The greens in Europe: ecological parties and the European elections of 1984', *Parliamentary Affairs* 38: 56–72.

—— (1990) 'Explaining Green Party development: Reflections on a theoretical framework', *Strathclyde Papers on Government and Politics*, No. 71.

—— (1995) 'Green parties and the EU: Portrait of an uneasy relationship', in J. Gaffney (ed.) *Political Parties and the European Union*, London: Routledge.

Rüdig, W. and Franklin, M. (1992) 'Green prospects: the future of green parties in Britain, France and Germany', in W. Rüdig (ed.) *Green Politics Two*, Edinburgh: Edinburgh University Press.

Sale, K. (1985) *Dwellers in the Land: the Bioregional Vision*, San Francisco: The Sierra Club.

Sarkar, S. (1986) 'The green movement in West Germany', *Alternatives* 11: 19–54.

Saward, M. (1995) 'Green democracy?', in A. Dobson and P. Lucardie (eds) *The Politics of Nature*, London: Routledge.

Sbragia, A. (1996) 'Environmental Policy', in H. Wallace and W. Wallace (eds) *Policy-making in the European Union*, Oxford: Oxford University Press.

Scheuer, T. (1989) 'Tanz auf dem Regenbogen. Der GRAEL im Europaparlament', in M. Franken and W. Ohler (eds) *Natürlich Europa. 1992 – Chancen für die Natur?*, Koln: Volksblatt.

Schoonmaker, D. (1988) 'The challenge of the Greens to the West German party system', in K. Lawson and P. Merkl (eds) *When Parties Fail. Emerging Alternative Organizations*, Princeton, NJ: Princeton University Press.

Schwalba-Hoth, F. (1986) 'Das EP nützen als 'Tribune der Öffentlichkeit', *Grüner Basisdienst* 10: 4–7.

—— (1988) *Rechnenschftsbericht* (April), Brussels: GRAEL.

—— (1989) '1992 droht ein ökologisches und soziales Dumping', in M. Franken and W. Ohler (eds) *Natürlich Europa. 1992 – Chancen für die Natur?*, Koln: Volksblatt.

Schwarzer, A. (1983) *So fing es an! Die neue Frauenbewegung*, Munich: Deutschen Taschenbuch Verlag.

Scott, A. (1990) *Ideology and New Social Movements*, London: Unwin Hyman.

Scott, A., Peterson, J. and Millar, D. (1994) 'Subsidiarity: A "Europe of the Regions" v. the British Constitution?', *Journal of Common Market Studies* 32: 47–68.

Sharp, M. (1985) *The New Biotechnology: European Governments in Search of a Strategy*, Brighton: Sussex Policy Research Unit.

Sharpe, L.J. (1989) 'Fragmentation and territoriality in the European state system', *International Political Science Review* 10: 223–38.

—— (ed.) (1993) *Rise of the Meso Government in Europe*, London: Sage.

Smith, G. (1984) *Politics in Western Europe*, 4th edn, New York: Holmes & Meier.

—— (1987) 'Party and protest: the two faces of opposition in Western Europe', in E. Kolinsky (ed.) *Opposition in Western Europe*, New York: St Martins Press.

Smith, Z. (1992) *The Environmental Policy Paradox*. Englewood Cliffs, NJ: Prentice Hall.

Southworth, B. (1993) 'Packaging and the environment: the challenge', *European Environment* 3: 7–9.

Spretnak, C. and Fritjof, C. (1986) *Green Politics. The Global Promise*, rev. edn, Santa Fe, NM: Bear & Co.

Stöss, R. (1980) *Vom Nationalismus zum Umweltschutz*, Opladen: Westdeutscher Verlag.

Stuth, R. (1984) 'Die Außen-und Deutschlandpolitik der Grünen', in K. Gotto and H. Veen (eds) *Die Grünen – Partei wider Willen*, Mainz: v. Hase & Koehler Verlag.

Tarrow, S. (1988) 'National politics and collective action: recent theory and research in Western Europe and the United States', *Annual Review of Sociology* 14: 421–40.

Telkämper, W. (1986) 'Das vereinnahmende Ungeheuer', *Grüner Basisdienst* 10: 13–16.

Uexküll, J. (1986) 'Was heißt hier Europa?', *Grüner Basisdienst* 10: 24–8.

—— (1989) 'What kind of Europe?', Speech given at the UK Green Party Conference, 31 March, London.

—— (1991) 'Reflections on parliament and government', in S. Parkin (ed.) *Green Light on Europe*, London: Heretic Books.

Urwin, D. (1990) 'The wearing of the green: issues, movements and parties', in D. Urwin and W.E. Paterson (eds) *Politics in Western Europe Today. Perspectives, Policies and Problems Since 1980*, London: Longman.

Vaughan, D. and Mickle, C. (1993) *Environmental Profiles of European Business*, London: Earthscan and RIIA.

Vaughn, J. (1988) 'The Greens' vision of Germany', *Orbis* 32: 83–95.

Viehoff, P. (1986) 'Biotechnology and the role of the European Parliament,' in D. Davies (ed.) *Industrial Biotechnology in Europe – Issues for Public Policy*, London: Pinter.

Verhoeve, B., Bennet, G., and Wilkinson, D. (1992) *Maastricht and the Environment*, London: IEEP.

Vig, N. (1990) 'Environmental policy in Europe and Japan', in N. Vig and M. Kraft (eds) *Environmental Policy in the 1990s. Toward a New Agenda*, Washington, DC: Congressional Quarterly Press.

Voerman, G. (1995) 'The Netherlands: losing colours, turning green', in D. Richardson and C. Rootes (eds) *The Green Challenge. The Development of Green Parties in Europe*, London: Routledge.

Vollmer, A. (1984) 'Für ein Europa der Mütterländer', *Grüner Basisdienst* 4: 3–5.

Weale, A. (1992) *The New Politics of Pollution*, Manchester: Manchester University Press.

——— (1996) 'Environmental rules and rule-making in the European Union', *Journal of European Public Policy* 3: 594–611.

Wistrich, E. (1988) *After 1992: The United States of Europe*, rev. edn, London: Routledge.

Wolf, F. (1986) 'Dossier über die Grünen im Europaparlament', in E. Jurtschitsch, A. Rudnick and F. Wolf (eds) *Grünes und alternatives Jahrbuch 1986/1987*, Berlin: Elefanten Press.

Wurzel, R.K.W. (1996) 'The role of the EU Presidency in the environmental field: does it make a difference which member state runs the Presidency?', *Journal of European Public Policy* 3: 272–91.

Yearley, S. (1992). *The Green Case. A Sociology of Environmental Issues, Arguments and Politics*, London: Routledge.

Young, S. (1993) *The Politics of the Environment*, Manchester: Baseline Books.

Zito, A. (1995) 'Integrating the environment into the European Union: the history of the controversial carbon tax', in S. Mazey and C. Rhodes (eds) *The State of the European Union, Vol. III*, Boulder, CO and Essex: Westview Press and Longman.

Index

QM LIBRARY
(MILE END)

WRITTEN
FROM
WITH
DRAWN